Justice and Welfare in Divorce

AUSTRALIA
The Law Book Company Ltd.
Sydney : Melbourne : Brisbane

CANADA AND U.S.A.
The Carswell Company Ltd.
Agincourt, Ontario

INDIA
N. M. Tripathi Private Ltd.
Bombay
and
Eastern Law House Private Ltd.
Calcutta
M.P.P. House
Bangalore

ISRAEL
Steimatzky's Agency Ltd.
Jerusalem : Tel Aviv : Haifa

MALAYSIA : SINGAPORE : BRUNEI
Malayan Law Journal (Pte.) Ltd.
Singapore

NEW ZEALAND
Sweet & Maxwell (N.Z.) Ltd.
Auckland

PAKISTAN
Pakistan Law House
Karachi

Justice and Welfare in Divorce

by

Mervyn Murch, B.A., D.S.A., C.A.S.S.

London
Sweet & Maxwell
1980

Published in 1980 by
Sweet & Maxwell Limited of
11 New Fetter Lane, London
and printed in Great Britain
by Fakenham Press Limited,
Fakenham, Norfolk

British Library Cataloguing in Publication Data

Murch, Mervyn
Justice and welfare in divorce.
1. Divorce – Great Britain
2. Family social work – Great Britain
I. Title
362.8′2 KD764

ISBN 0–421–27130–2
ISBN 0–421–26400–4 Pbk

Acknowledgements

The research upon which this book is based could not have been done without the help of many people. My first debt is to all those who cannot be named who generously agreed to be interviewed about their experience of divorce. They did so in the hope that it would lead to improvements in divorce procedures which would spare others some of the difficulties they had had to face.

I must also thank the Social Science Research Council who financed the project and those members of the divorce court welfare service in the South-west region who encouraged me to start the research and assisted its progress by approaching divorcing couples on my behalf.

Elizabeth Elston and Jane Fuller, former research associates, played a major role in the main stages of the investigation, helping me plan the fieldwork, interviewing people with sensitivity and processing data carefully. I have greatly appreciated their systematic work when writing up the results. The cheerful endeavours of Grace Yarnell, our first secretary, did much to get the enterprise started. Audrey Morris and Jean Williams of the University of Bristol Department of Public Health kindly provided technical assistance. Others who helped at various times included Ruth Hawkins and Sue Pottle.

Tilda Goldberg, formerly Director of Research at the National Institute of Social Work, Professor Douglas Hooper, Professor Lord McGregor of Durris and Mr. Frank Terry, formerly Chief Probation Officer for Cornwall gave valuable expert advice. Roy Parker, Professor of Social Administration at the University of Bristol and head of my department has given me unwavering support. I have also received much encouragement from other colleagues including Gwynn Davis and Daphne Norbury. I am also most grateful to a number of local practitioners including David Burrows, Lisa Parkinson, Geoffrey Parmiter and John Westcott whose active interest in conciliation has taught me much.

Drafts of the manuscript were typed by Kay Bader, Margaret Borkowski, Lynne Jennings and Ray Sandler, all mastering my almost illegible handwriting. Don Low, Chief Probation Officer for Dorset and Hyacinthe Harford read the typescript and made many useful suggestions. F. E. Mostyn, my severest critic, also spent many hours reading the typescript. I cannot thank him sufficiently for his help and friendship. Whatever deficiencies or errors the book may still contain are my sole responsibility and should not be held against any of my advisers and critics.

My colleague, Margaret Borkowski, has seen the enterprise through many difficult periods while I have been preparing the material for publication. I have made heavy demands on her skill, friendship and tolerance, particularly when through my own shortcomings disaster loomed. I also owe a great deal to my former colleague, Val Walker, who relieved me of many pressures when I was writing the main text. I cannot thank her enough for her kindness, support and forbearance and for the considerable contribution she has made to my understanding.

Finally, I must acknowledge a special debt to Anne Murch and to my three children, Lorna, Julia and Duncan. For some years their lives have been disturbed by my work, and they have accepted it with grace and stoicism. This book, whatever its merits, will be little compensation for them.

Bristol, Mervyn Murch
November 1, 1979

Contents

Introduction

This book examines the relationship between legal and welfare practices in divorce proceedings involving children. It is intended for lawyers and social workers and anyone else concerned with the methods by which law and social policy seek to regulate family life.

When I began to write it my intention was merely to set out the findings of a research project conducted in 1973 and 1974 which sought to discover the way divorcing parents viewed the solicitors who represented them, the court welfare officers who compiled reports about them, those who made judgments in the court, and the legal institutions which authorised these things.[1] Later I came to realise that some evaluation of the whole machinery of divorce was needed. Since the extension of the special procedure to all undefended divorce suits in April 1977 and certain restrictions on the provision of Legal Aid, divorce court practice has undergone a fundamental reorientation in which child welfare considerations have assumed far greater prominence than previously. Even before these new procedures, which in part were influenced by an earlier publication arising from this research,[2] a debate had developed about the way courts of the future should deal with family matters and about the extent of their welfare responsibilities. The fundamental questions are: should the state investigate the way couples exercise their parental responsibilities when they are in the process of divorce? Should the judicial machinery offer divorcing parents help to reach decisions about their family's future? If so at what point? Should the courts in the exercise of their duty to protect the interests of children be empowered to keep families under a degree of surveillance? How are the rights and interests of parents and children to be safeguarded now that judges and welfare officers have greater discretionary power to intervene in and control family life? In recent years the law has grappled with all these questions and the introduction of the special procedure[3] is the latest of a number of piecemeal developments which is determining the character of its response.

The debate is not over. It has great social importance. Since the mid 1960s there has been an astonishing increase in divorce. In 1965 there were 42,070 divorce petitions filed. By 1970 the number had risen to 70,575.[4] Seven years later the total had more than doubled to reach a figure of 167,034.[5] The divorce rate per 1,000 of the married population has increased from 3.1 in 1965 to 6.0 in 1970 and to 9.6 in 1975.[6] One authority has estimated that on current trends approximately a quarter of all marriages now taking place will terminate in the divorce court.[7]

Not only adults but large numbers of children are also involved, since two-thirds of those who divorce have dependent offspring. At current levels, even assuming no further increase, the parents of 152,170 children under 16 are likely to divorce every year, nearly half the children being at primary school.[8] This compares with a figure of only 71,336 in 1970.

These figures imply a remarkable amount of family disruption and reorganisation. Approximately 75 per cent. of those who divorce remarry within four years of obtaining a decree absolute. More than 25 per cent. of all marriages solemnised in 1975 contained one or both parties who had been previously divorced.[9] Divorce is not simply to be understood in terms of ending marriage but also as a licence to remarry. The resulting changes in the family's social structure, as old relationships are given up or modified and new ones established, are not well understood. The evidence presented in this book casts light on the nature of some of these changes, particularly as they concern children.

The rapid growth of divorce has serious implications for the legal institutions that administer family law. Financially the costs are considerable: the cost of civil legal aid and advice rose sharply from £11.5 million in 1971–72 to £34.5 million in 1976–77, the greater part of which was spent on matrimonial cases.[10] Attempts have been made to restrict this monetary expenditure,[11] but the true cost to the community of marital breakdown is obviously much greater. More judges, lawyers, doctors, school teachers, social workers, as well as people engaged in other kinds of social service become necessary as the increasing divorce population enlists the aid of various types of support in their attempts to contain, resolve or escape from the tensions of unhappy and stressful marriage.

Rapidly changing social values concerning marriage, the status of women and the role of the family in society profoundly affect the character of divorce proceedings. In recent years emphasis has moved away from preoccupation with the history of a broken marriage towards a greater concern for the family's future. These days the authorities recognise the importance of ensuring that the parties should reach an acceptable reallocation of their resources and responsibilities, through negotiation or settlement. This is better than apportioning guilt and innocence. Modern divorce is about the division of money and property and the future care of the children. This raises complex and interrelated questions of law, welfare and social policy. The difficulty is that there has been no comprehensive legislation to take account of these changes. In particular the procedural machinery of the law has been slow to adapt to them. It is therefore not surprising that the practice and policy of divorce law has entered an era when it is being reappraised and challenged. A lot of rethinking on the matter was undertaken by the Finer Committee on One Parent Families.[12] Its report may prove to be one of the most important official documents concerning the institutions of marriage and divorce produced this century, not least because it eschewed high sentence and rhetoric and instead sought the facts. It appreciated what McGregor had pointed out in 1957,[13] that without empirical evidence "one cannot pass from the contemplation of unsupported conjecture to the study of reality." The Finer Committee's proposals, which included combining and rationalising the separate jurisdictions of the magistrates court and the divorce court into a new system of family courts, were supported by well-reasoned and compassionate arguments. The Committee's strong endorsement of family courts was the latest of a whole line of similar recommendations from other committees (Payne,[14] Latey,[15] Houghton[16]). It went further than them, both in the strength of its endorsement of the principle and in its examination of feasibility. Yet it did not consider the full implications of the development of the welfare services in the divorce court, partly because this was not fully within its terms of reference, and partly because relevant evidence was not at the time available. The book tries to rectify this.

The recent growth of the divorce court welfare service highlights some of the strengths and weaknesses of the judicial system. It is coming to be realised that the interests of welfare and justice do not always coincide; indeed their pursuit sometimes reveals fundamental conflicts of philosophy. I have tried to explore this issue and to show that failure to acknowledge the nature of this conflict has been one obstacle in the way of reform.

One might think, as Meyer and Timms have pointed out,[17] that administrators and policy makers would need to know at least something about the responses and reactions of those for whom services are intended. Yet, in general, until about 10 years ago there was little available information about consumer experience or opinion. When the research reported in this book was planned in 1970, a review of the available literature showed that it was almost totally lacking in consumer views of the legal and social services associated with divorce. The study of matrimonial proceedings in magistrates courts by McGregor, Blom-Cooper and Gibson pointed to the value of this kind of research, though their own sample was drawn from readers of the *News of the World* newspaper and might have been unrepresentative.[18] Few, if any, systematic studies had made the parties' reactions to the machinery of divorce the primary focus of investigation. Most researchers had approached divorce tangentally, either in the context of poverty studies or in terms of psycho-social adjustment. Similarly, most legal writing had examined divorce in the light of substantive law and social philosophy. Although since the 1939–45 War there had been a strong reformist lobby that drew support from groups of social scientists and lawyers alike, much of their work had been carried out, as Farrar had said:

> "On the basis of *a priori* assertion or intuitive assessments of social facts and consequences."[19]

It is hard to say why lawyers and social workers have been slow to appreciate the value of consumer feedback. Meyer and Timms suggest that as far as social work is concerned there are a number of reasons; first, that social work thinking in the post-war period was heavily influenced by psycho-analytic ideas which encouraged practitioners to discount or explain away any views the client might express; secondly, the drive towards professionalism in social work encouraged the belief that through skills derived from a body of abstract knowledge, practitioners knew better than clients what was good for them; and thirdly, that because social work clients are typically isolated from each other, client grievances are apt to remain private and unexpressed. These last two points apply equally to legal services. Also criticisms from lay persons about legal practice can too easily be dismissed as the result of ignorance. The mystifying effects of legal language and complexity may serve to protect the system from consumer complaint. However, lack of feedback from the public can keep lawyers ignorant of consumer approval.

The consumer views reported in the first 10 chapters of this book were gathered during the course of two surveys conducted for a research into the circumstances of families in divorce proceedings carried out under my direction during 1973 and 1974.[20] The people who assisted the planning of this research, including a small group of chief probation officers in the South-west, thought that the views of those on the "receiving" end of legal and social services associated with divorce were likely to be significantly different from those of the practitioners who provided the services, and would have their own validity. Both surveys sought to sample the impressions and opinions of parents who had recent experience of divorce. The first comprised 102 petitioners (71 women and 31 men) drawn representatively on a one-in-three basis from a total of 470 undefended divorce cases heard in three local county courts. A response rate of 70 per cent. was obtained, 22 per cent. refused and a further 8 per cent. could not be traced. The second sample was more specialist. It was obtained from 41 divorcing couples known to court welfare officers in three South-western counties. It is therefore only representative of those cases in which child welfare reports were prepared for the court. These parents were invited to participate in the research by the welfare officers only after the enquiries for the court had been completed. The welfare officers reported that approximately 70 per cent. of those parents approached agreed to take part.

I have used the evidence of these surveys as the raw material upon which to base my examination of the system. I have also tried to set the research data in the context of more recent trends in family litigation and other documentary material. I am however conscious of the limitations of the evidence; it answers some questions but not others. Although drawn as representatively as possible, the samples were comparatively small and local in character. Petitioner parents were better represented than respondents. The views of children were by no means adequately represented. To get some idea of the range of practitioners' views I have had to refer to published sources. Professional writing by practitioners, while offering valuable insight into some of the problems, may not be representative for obvious reasons. A further difficulty is that the judicial system is dynamic and constantly changing, albeit not as fast, or in the direction that some would wish. Finally, I have been faced with a constant problem of up-dating my material as the book has been prepared. Despite these shortcomings my purpose has been to tease out from the available material those features of legal and welfare practice which seem to have the most important implications for the future. Some of my own professional thinking and subjective value judgments will inevitably influence the conclusions I have drawn. To those who might disagree I would merely ask that they do not judge the weight of the research evidence presented on the basis of my own idiosyncratic deductions. I invite such readers to let the evidence speak for itself and to accept that the book was written in the hope that it would contribute to the debate concerning the manner and means by which family life should be reorganised when marriages break down.

NOTES

1. This was sponsored by the SSRC and carried out from the Department of Social Administration of the University of Bristol. A full report of the project is obtainable from the British Lending Library.
2. E. Elston, J. Fuller, M. Murch, "Judicial Hearings of Undefended Divorce Petitions" *Modern Law Review*, November 1975.
3. The Matrimonial Causes Rules 1977 (S.I. 1977 No. 344 (L.6)).

4. *Civil Judicial Statistics*, Cmnd. 5756 (1973) (HMSO, 1974), Table 10.
5. *Judicial Statistics*, Cmnd. 687 (1976) (HMSO, 1977), Table G.6.
6. Office of Population Census and Surveys, *Marriage and Divorce Statistics* (HMSO, 1978), Series FM2 No. 2, Table 4.1a.
7. R. Chester, *Divorce in the Nineteen Sixties* (Marriage Guidance, March 1972), p. 38.
8. Office of Population Census and Surveys, *Marriage and Divorce Statistics 1976* (HMSO, 1979), FM2 No. 3, Table 4.5.
9. Office of Population Census and Surveys, *op. cit.*, Table 3.2.
10. Lord Chancellor's Office, 26th Legal Aid Annual Report (HMSO, 1976), p. 64.
11. Lord Chancellor's Office, 28th Legal Aid Annual Report (HMSO, 1979), p. 82.
12. Report of the Committee on One Parent Families, Cmnd. 5629 (HMSO, 1974).
13. O. R. McGregor, *Divorce in England* (Heinemann, 1957), p. 187.
14. Report of the Committee on the Enforcement of Judgement Debt, Cmnd. 3909 (HMSO, 1969).
15. Report of the Committee on the Age of Majority, Cmnd. 3342 (HMSO, 1967), p. 68.
16. Report of the Departmental Committee on the Adoption of Children, Cmnd. 5107 (HMSO, 1972).
17. J. E. Mayer and N. Timms, *The Client Speaks* (Routledge & Kegan Paul, 1970).
18. O. R. McGregor, L. Blom-Cooper, C. Gibson, *Separated Spouses* (Duckworth, 1970), p. 48.
19. J. H. Farrar, *Law Reform and the Law Commission* (Sweet and Maxwell, 1971).
20. A fuller description of the objectives of this research and the methods used will be found in the report lodged in the British Lending Library. It is omitted from this book in order to save costs.

Part 1

The Role of Solicitors in Divorce Proceedings

1 The Role of Solicitors in Divorce Proceedings

The Solicitor as Member of a Social System

The legal machinery of divorce can be thought of as a social system which regulates the exit from marriage, changes the social status of those who seek its sanction to divorce, and, if there are dependent children, legitimises the reorganised structure of the family's internal relationships. Therefore divorcing parents and their children can be thought of as passing through this system over a period of time while being subjected to various legal processes. The actual length of time within the system varies. When this research was designed, almost all those who petitioned for divorce did so with the benefit of legal representation. Litigants petitioning in person were rare. Thus we saw the family entering the legal system of divorce when one of the parents, through the agency of a solicitor, started divorce proceedings. They left it only when the decree absolute had been granted and decisions reached about the care of the children, financial support and the division of matrimonial property. For purposes of the research the intervening time was termed the "period of divorce." A solicitor therefore was usually the first member of the legal system that the parent met. He often remained in contact with the parent throughout this period. It is therefore appropriate to start this examination of the "consumers'" view of divorce machinery with consideration of the role of solicitors. It is not my intention to assess their technical competence. My objective is merely to describe divorcing parents' reported experience, and to indicate the general level of satisfaction by using both quantifiable factual information given by the parents, and their more subjective views and opinions of the quality of their solicitors' services. In the process I will comment upon and discuss the implications of the research findings.[1]

The Choice of Solicitor

Solicitors ply their trade in the market place. They are usually the first representative of the legal profession met by the potential litigant. They cannot advertise their services openly. Some have small general practices, others prefer not to take on family law business at all, while others, more usually larger firms, have solicitors who specialise in it. How are potential clients to discover the firm best equipped to serve their needs? All the divorcing parents interviewed were asked how they chose the solicitor who first dealt with their case. Table 1 below summarises the replies from both samples.

Table 1

Choice of Solicitor

	Petitioner Sample n = 102			*Court Welfare Sample n = 41 Couples*		
	Men n = 31	*Women n = 71*	*Total*	*Men* n = 39*	*Women n = 41*	*Total*
	%	%	%	%	%	%
Asked friends' advice	26	29	28	34	59	47
Asked family's advice or used family solicitor	23	21	22	26	11	18
Had used him before – house purchase, etc.	19	9	13	9	8	8
Saw office and walked in	19	8	12	9	5	7
Asked C.A.B. social worker, etc.	–	12	9	17	13	15
Went to court and looked at legal aid list	–	11	8	–	–	–
Looked in telephone book	3	4	4	3	5	4
No choice – only firm in area	10	3	5	3	–	1

*(Two male respondents in this sample did not use a solicitor.)

The totals in each sample are broadly comparable. Selecting on the recommendations of friends and relatives is the most frequent method. Friends were also often reported as having consulted the same solicitor about matrimonial problems. Previous personal experience, either through house purchase or business, is the next most popular method. With the exception of the few parents who lived in relatively remote rural areas and who said that because of this they had little choice, it will be noted that only those who walked in off the street or used the yellow pages of the telephone directory (approximately 20 per cent. or less) chose their solicitor without the benefits of previous experience or personal recommendation.

In certain respects the pattern of choice differs between men and women. The sample of 102 petitioners was asked whether they had had any previous contact with solicitors before consulting them with marital difficulties. Over half the men, 19 out of 31 (61 per cent.) compared to only 11 out of 71 (14 per cent.) women had used solicitors before, usually for house purchase. Thus over 80 per cent. of these mothers had no previous experience of solicitors. Not surprisingly, they tend to seek advice about the choice of solicitors from social workers, Citizens Advice Bureaux or the court itself more often than men.

In the court welfare sample more parents reported using social workers as sources of information about solicitors. This sample as a whole had greater contact with social workers than the representative petitioner sample so this finding was not unexpected. Even so, for the two samples generally social workers are not an important referral source.

Those choosing without the benefit of previous experience or personal recommendation sometimes found the search for a solicitor time-consuming and haphazard. Thus one father remarked:

> "I walked around the city asking solicitors whether they dealt with divorce cases. Most of them didn't seem to – they specialise in different fields. When I got to number four, they said 'we'll take the case for you.' The chap I had seemed to specialise in divorce. Now that's a bit difficult, finding out which solicitors do which."

Choosing by chance can also be discouraging especially if people are already emotionally upset by a stressful marriage. One mother told us:

> "The first one I went to – I was very distressed at the time – I think he just took my name, address and age and noted how long I'd been married. He was totally disinterested. He didn't want to know. I felt as though I was talking to a brick wall. There was no offer of help, no come back and see me next week. I just walked out of that office and burst into tears. I thought 'well, who the hell can I go to?' and that's when I 'phoned up the Clerk to the Justices ... I just didn't know where to turn."

Client Perception of Solicitor's Manner

Parents were asked about the kind of reception they had received from their solicitor and whether they felt they could discuss their marital difficulties with him freely. Table 2 classifies their replies.

Table 2

Whether Solicitor was Considered Approachable

	Petitioner Study *n* = 102 %	*DCWO Study* *n* = 82 %
Yes, approachable, friendly, helpful	51.0	48.8
Yes, felt I could confide in him	19.6	22.0
Yes, felt like a parent figure	2.9	12.2
Yes, approachable, other	11.8	4.9
No, uninterested	2.9	4.9
No, too busy	5.9	2.4
No, legalistic	2.0	4.9
No, other	3.9	–
Did not use solicitor	–	2.4

The great majority of parents in both samples found their solicitors approachable, friendly and supportive. Here are two typical replies:

> "He was the only person I could confide in. I expected him to be very business-like and efficient, but he was relaxed and he made you feel relaxed. He always told me if there was anything I was worried about I could pick up the 'phone and contact him."

> "I was very impressed on my first visit to him. It wasn't an easy thing for me to have to go along and explain to a stranger, but I did find him very easy to talk to and very sympathetic in the sort of questions he asked."

The solicitor's ability to make clients feel at ease was commented on frequently, particularly in relation to the first visit when people were often most anxious, confused or upset. At such times, it was important to them that their solicitor could accept these emotions without embarrassment.

One mother, separated from her children, told us:

> "You can talk to him. I used to upset myself and I used to feel awful, and I said 'Cor, I bet you get used to women crying in your place' and he said 'I do actually.' He said 'Really you have got something to cry for – I'll agree to that.' He really was very nice."

We asked another mother how her solicitor reacted when she used to cry sometimes in his office.

> "Oh, he is very good. He has obviously seen many people like this. He tries to make me laugh. He's very understanding."

A father who had a depressive illness after the break-up of his marriage and the loss of custody of his children spoke in similar terms of his woman solicitor:

> "I think that after what I went through, I was very, very emotional and it made me quite ill. She thought I would harden up, but I didn't. When she realised this she was very kind. I think she can adapt to the sort of person she is dealing with . . . ."

As will be seen from Table 2 above, only a minority of parents reported adversely on their solicitors' manner. Here are some of the more representative comments:

> "He was vague and seemed disinterested. He didn't concentrate on the details of the case enough to bother to remember them. In fact, he sometimes seemed to mix my case up with somebody else's."

A mother involved in a bitterly disputed custody case commented in similar vein:

> "I think in a lot of instances solicitors are extremely busy. They take on far more than they can reasonably cope with. Basically, it's over-work. I mean I can go to him after I've been to see him three or four times and he'll say 'Is it two children you've got?' One feels then you are just a number rather than a person."

Feelings of not being accepted or properly recognised as a person worthy of the solicitor's professional concern and respect was a recurrent theme.

Not to be recognised and respected may be all the more painful when the problem that one seeks advice about has personal and emotional overtones. The contrast between solicitors who were receptive and those who were not is well illustrated by a mother who compared an encounter with her husband's solicitor with the meeting she had with her own:

> "Mine was abrupt, very abrupt. You think he is snapping at you all the time. I feel as if I don't want to talk to him, because he's not listening. Whereas his was kind but firm. He said 'Come on, pull yourself together or we aren't going to get anywhere' and I felt better right away."

Efficiency by itself does not compensate for a lack of empathy, as was pointed out by a petitioner father looking after his five-year-old daughter. The respondent mother was disputing custody.

"I would say he's efficient – he knows the law back to front, but he doesn't understand how a person feels – the strain on me of worrying whether I was going to lose my daughter. I used to say 'do you think I'll win the case?' But he was strictly a solicitor – he wouldn't commit himself."

Changing Solicitors

We wished to know how frequently parents remained with the first firm that they had approached and what proportion changed because they were dissatisfied with the service. See Table 3 below:

Table 3

Proportion of Clients Changing Firms of Solicitors

	Representative Petitioner Sample *n = 102* %	*Court Welfare Sample* *(a) Petitioners* *n = 41* %	*(b) Respondents* *n – 41* %
Stayed with same firm throughout	73	73	56
Changed firm:			
dissatisfied,	12	7	12
client moved area,	7	12	5
firm first approached didn't deal with divorce,	4	5	5
solicitor changed firms,	1	2	5
friend advised another firm,	2	–	10
no reason given	2	–	–
Never used solicitor or stopped using solicitor	–	–	7

Most parents remained with the same firm, the findings for both groups of petitioners being exactly comparable. Only a small proportion of parents (10–12 per cent.) changed because they were dissatisfied.

Table 4 below indicates how often parents saw the same solicitor and how often they dealt with more:

Table 4

Proportion of Clients Seeing More than One Solicitor

	Representative Petitioner Sample	*Court Welfare Sample*	
		(a) Petitioners	*(b) Respondents*
	n = 102	*n = 41*	*n = 41*
	%	%	%
Always saw the same person	58	58	48
Saw two – first left firm	6	5	–
Saw two – passed to more junior person	4	7	12
Saw two – no reason given for change	19	15	5
Saw both solicitor and articled clerk	4	10	5
Saw more than two – others left firm	4	2	–
Saw more than two – no reason given for change	5	2	5
Did not use solicitor/other	1	–	5

Most people only saw one solicitor, the proportions for each sample of petitioners being the same. Surprisingly, this proportion increases in the case of respondents in the court welfare sample. Very few – less than 10 per cent. – saw more than two people.

Most parents preferred to deal with just one solicitor. Referral to someone else in the firm was often commented on as disruptive and impersonal:

> "The first one left, then I had one who dealt with the actual court proceedings, and now I've got another. I didn't like the idea of changing in the first place.... It's a bit off-putting seeing all these different people. Just as I was getting on with one I would have to answer all the same questions with a new man. Besides they had different attitudes. The first one I saw always seemed helpful – the second seemed to look on the black side."

While busy lawyers may have good reasons for passing on some clients to more junior or unqualified colleagues, from the client's point of view such a move may easily be interpreted as implying that his problems are in some way undeserving of the experienced man's attention.

Liaison Between Solicitor and Client

Divorcing parents frequently complain about the length of time legal processes take. They often don't understand the reasons for delays. To some extent, the solicitor controls how quickly the divorce petition is filed, the court hearings arranged, and disputes about the children or money settled. The solicitor acts as a link between the client and the legal system which regulates the changing marital and parental roles within the family. Naturally enough, parents in these circumstances expect to know what is going on, what stage has been reached and how long it will take. Parents in both samples were therefore asked whether they felt that their solicitor kept them informed as their case developed. Table 5 classifies their replies.

Table 5

Liaison Between Solicitor and Client

	Representative Petitioner Sample *n = 102* %	*Court Welfare Sample Petitioners and Respondents Combined* *n = 82* %
Yes, very good – always let me know	64.7	40.3
Yes, quite good – usually let me know	17.6	35.4
No, I had to find things out for myself	3.9	4.9
No, I had to "badger" him and make him do things for me	13.7	15.9
No solicitor	–	3.7

Over 75 per cent. of parents in both samples felt their solicitors were good at keeping them in touch with what was going on. This usually contributed to the client's confidence in the solicitor's general ability. Conversely, the minority who felt that they were being kept in ignorance often became anxious. In consequence, they sometimes badgered their solicitors:

> "I wasn't satisfied really; I felt the solicitor kept stalling it. I 'phoned him hundreds of times, he used to get so het up. He probably had so many cases on his hands."

> "My husband's solicitor sent him copies of letters he'd received from my solicitor! But *my* solicitor didn't and when I went to see him, he didn't even tell me what he'd received. I had to ask him all along the line."

We asked parents in the petitioner sample whether they thought their solicitor got things done as quickly as possible in the circumstances. The majority (60 per cent.) thought that they did; 16 per cent. experienced delays for which they felt their solicitor was responsible; and a further 15 per cent. blamed delays on the court machinery or on the other party. The remainder felt they couldn't judge. Solicitors who explained delays and who were able to give clients a realistic estimate of how long things would take were invariably experienced as helpful and reinforced the client's confidence.

A father who experienced two solicitors told us:

> "The first was very vague – one day hopeful and the next he wasn't. I became very depressed, continually drawing a blank card when I saw him. Whereas the second solicitor was so methodical, business-like and efficient. He had the opinion that there was more than one way to skin a rabbit. I found this very encouraging. I grinned from the first day I came out of there. He would say 'this time next year it will all be over.' In fact he wasn't far out. Took him about 12 months. I didn't get depressed after I went to see him. He lifted me out of it."

Remarks such as these testified to the solicitors' capacity to boost their clients' morale. The opposite was true of unrealistically optimistic solicitors or those who failed to keep clients properly informed. Thus one dissatisfied mother said:

> "I thought the divorce took quite a while. I kept 'phoning him up because I thought he'd forgotten. It seemed to take months. He said it would be through by January but it wasn't. I was still waiting in February. I rang up three times reminding him that I'd heard nothing. He said the courts were taking their time or something."

A father remarked:

> "All these people on the perimeter – solicitors, welfare officers, know what they are doing. I'm in the middle of it and I don't. Where does that leave me? I'm in a void. They could sit down and write a letter to say 'we're still moving' but I suppose it's the expense. I think to myself they must have hundreds of clients. The reason I'm in this position is that I'm just waiting for the law to move itself."

The Solicitor's Stance in Relation to Marital Conflict

Divorcing parents tend to evaluate their solicitor according to whether or not he is felt to be partisan. We wished to examine parents' perception of their solicitors' partisan attitudes closely, since it seemed probable that by doing so we could increase understanding of the way legal machinery contained, resolved or possibly exacerbated family disputes. The questionnaire, used in interviews with the second sample of parents, incorporated questions which tested whether they felt their solicitor had been committed to their interests. Of this sample, 63 per cent. saw the lawyer as clearly partisan – the proportion being somewhat greater for petitioners than for respondents.

Typical reasons given in favour of a partisan role were:

> "If one solicitor is out for a fight, you need another to combat him."

> "Well, in my situation (a mother who was seeking custody, father had left home with children), you're terribly

vulnerable. You need to feel that there is someone fighting for you and doing his best for you."

"If I had plenty of money I wouldn't be fighting for everything and I would understand if my solicitor took a lenient line with the other side. But I have nothing at all, and therefore I must get everything I can. My solicitor realises this and is doing his best."

Twenty-two per cent. of the sample saw the lawyer as neutral, there being in this respect very little distinction between petitioners and respondents. Some considered this stance appropriate to their case. But others implied that it was not, often favouring partisanship:

"Most times he remained neutral. He seemed very pessimistic which made me think he wasn't on my side any more. But of course, this must be expected, I suppose. He knows what's coming, more so than I did. He was cautious."

"Well, he was neutral, I suppose. But he did see me when I was all black and blue. When he saw me like that he was very good. He got the injunction. But I don't know, I think he was neutral."

A small minority, 14 per cent., considered their lawyer uninterested in their case, and invariably mentioned this as a reason for dissatisfaction. Most of these too would have preferred a partisan lawyer.

Overall, the research evidence suggests that partisanship was for most an essential aspect of the solicitor's role. Even so, many were ambivalent about it. This was revealed clearly when parents were asked which of the following two statements they agreed with most in the light of their experience:

(1) "A good divorce lawyer is one who fights hard for his client's interests against the other party."
(2) "A good divorce lawyer is one who tries to reduce the conflict between the parties by getting them to agree wherever possible."

Some parents pointed out that the two statements were not necessarily contradictory, but most saw the point of the distinction between the two and expressed a preference. The unexpected result was that although the majority of parents (63 per cent.) approved of their own particular solicitor being partisan, when faced with the choice between these two hypothetical statements 45 per cent. favoured the conciliatory approach and only 28 per cent. preferred the "fighter."[2] As one would expect those parents who were most bitter and resentful of the other were generally those most in favour of partisanship. By contrast those who remained on amicable terms with each other, or wished to do so, were more inclined to stress the value of a conciliatory approach. One mother said:

> "My husband's been pretty amicable and I think I am, too. The solicitors should have got their heads together and just said, 'Look, she wants that, he wants that, fair enough.' We settled amicably between ourselves, why couldn't the solicitors?"

This sad question highlights the ease with which solicitors can be influenced by the traditional adversary model into aggravating or even initiating conflict. In doing so they may consider they are merely protecting their client's interests.

A number of parents considered that, while their feelings of bitterness for the other might prompt expression through the agency of partisan solicitors, this would not be in the interests of their children. Thus one mother remarked:

> "I agree with the solicitor who tries to get agreement because in my situation especially there's an awful lot of bitterness on my husband's part. It's better to come to an agreement than a heated battle in court, because the terrible bitterness overflows on to the children from the partner that's had the battering in court."

Another commented:

> "It's better to get these things over with as little unpleasantness as possible, especially when there are children involved and you are bound to see each other."

Another frequently advanced reason in favour of a conciliatory approach was the view that unremitting hostility in litigation could have adverse long-term consequences not only for the children but for the parents themselves. One father remarked:

> "I think if the solicitor fights regardless, it can leave one party completely in the cold. Everyone has got to survive, and something taken to extremes sometimes means one person just can't."

A number of parents recognised that under the present system of separate representation solicitors are almost inevitably going to be biased towards the client they represent simply because they do not have equal opportunities of hearing "both sides of the story." Thus one parent said:

> "Somehow the system has to even things out and be fair to both sides, because the solicitors are only seeing one person, they're not seeing two. . . . I sometimes wish they would send for you both and have a talk with you, and meet the other person, before deciding which is the right thing to do. They should hear the proper story from both, and only then try to sort it out."

This comment raises the question whether solicitors shouldn't be more prepared to act as informal family mediators, seeking to minimise the risk of litigation and encouraging the parties to reach settlement. Generally, at present, only the court and possibly its welfare officers can take up a neutral stance and arbitrate in this manner.

The research was concerned not only with parents' experience of their own solicitors but with their views about the part played by the other parties' solicitors. Only a few had actually met them. Their impressions were therefore generally only based on indirect evidence. Most seemed to think that the other solicitor had inflamed the conflict by encouraging their former spouse to be more obdurate. Here are some illustrations:

> "I think he tried to make things worse between us. I honestly couldn't see my wife deciding on her own volition not to cook, wash or do anything for me in the house and make life there so intolerable that I was forced to leave. If she had said as much to me verbally I would probably have believed it was her. But I had a letter from her solicitor containing

instructions. I thought it must therefore be his idea not hers."

"Well, he kept sending pretty demanding letters which were of course answered by demands of our own. The whole thing was pretty nasty and I think increased the bitterness."

A number of parents considered their solicitors had presumed that because they were divorcing they were necessarily in conflict. Yet quite often this was not the case. For example, 13 of the 102 petitioners in the first sample said that they had planned their parting quite amicably. Only a minority of the 102 (32 per cent.) had contemplated serious dispute, usually over property and children, and when it actually came to court only 21 per cent. disputed matters. It therefore seems that in the large majority of divorce cases agreement between the parties is eventually reached, despite earlier periods of conflict and disagreement. I do not wish to minimise the part solicitors play in negotiating settlements. It is nevertheless disturbing to have to report instances where parents felt that the tactical manoeuvres of their own solicitors went against their own inclinations and antagonised the other party. Here are two examples from the 13 parents in the petitioner sample who had remained on amicable terms with the other parent:

"There was one occasion when my husband did get a bit spiteful. That was when my solicitor wrote a letter to his solicitor saying that I hadn't agreed to the settlement and I had."

"My solicitor caused me quite a bit of emotional disturbance by telling me that it was in my interests and urgent that I should send a private investigator down to see my husband, which I didn't want to do, as we'd sorted it all out as amicably as it could be. He talked me into it, but I really didn't want to."

Such comments illustrate how the use of tactics appropriate to the legal combat of ordinary litigation, when applied insensitively to issues that arise from emotional difficulties, in interpersonal relationships, only serve to antagonise the other party. They raise the important question whether family legal issues can be distinguished from other kinds of litigation on account of their intimate personal and emotional components, and whether, because of this, the procedures applied in family law practice need to be fundamentally altered. They also raise the question whether solicitors have a vested interest in perpetuating conflict. Certainly some divorcing parents questioned whether solicitors sought to profit from the breakdown of the client's family relationships. For example, one father commented:

> "In some instances he's got an agreement on things, but I would say the majority of times he's fought only for my interest. You see, it's difficult. When he's going for you, I feel that in the end, through the conflict, his bill is going to be bigger, so it's better for him as well. They're business-men same as anyone else – they have to think of themselves. A lot of people seem to think they're like chaplains but they're not!'

The Solicitor's Role in Relation to Children of the Family

Does the partisan stance adopted by so many solicitors limit their capability to consider the interests of the children separately from those of their client? Although solicitors have no direct responsibility for their client's children it was thought worth enquiring whether they had actually met them. Parents in both samples were asked whether their solicitor ever met the children and ever talked to them about their parents' divorce. In the first sample only three parents could remember their solicitor doing so and in one of those cases the child was being called as a witness. In this sample 70 per cent. of the solicitors were reported as never having seen any of the children, and when they did it was usually by chance because mothers had toddlers with them when they went for interview. In the court welfare sample where the issue of the children was almost always a central feature of the case, 80 per cent. of the parents reported their solicitors never having met the children. Indeed, these data suggest that the older the children become the less likely solicitors are to meet them, even though children over 10 years old often have very decided views about such matters as where they should live and about access.

It follows therefore that most solicitors see the child's interests through the eyes of the parents they represent. Within these terms, how much concern about their children did parents feel their solicitors showed? The evidence about this comes only from the second court welfare sample, and may not be as representative as one would like. Nevertheless, when these parents were asked what had been their solicitor's main concern, matters concerning the children predominated, as Table 6 shows.

Table 6

Main Concern of Solicitor as Perceived by Parents
n=82

	%
Custody and access to children	29.2
Divorce itself	23.2
Matrimonial home	7.3
Maintenance	6.1
Settlement of other property	3.7
Getting their fees paid	3.7
Other more specialist matters	2.2
Solicitor not really concerned with anything	8.5
Didn't know	6.1
Unrepresented	2.4

In order to classify the way parents perceived the role of their solicitor in relation to their children those in the court welfare sample were asked the following questions:

> "If you had any worries about the way that arrangements for the children were working out in the future, to whom would you go – court welfare officer or solicitor, or neither?"

They were asked to give reasons for their choice. Table 7 summarises the findings to both questions.

Marginally more parents said they would rather go to the court welfare officer than to their solicitor, the principal reasons given being that "they know more about the children" and were more likely to be accessible or acceptable to the other

Table 7

Comparison Between the Roles of Solicitors and Court Welfare Officers

	Petitioners *n=41* %	*Respondents* *n=41* %	*Combined* *n=82* %
To solicitor			
he's on my side	24.4	17.1	20.7
he knows more about the case	17.1	7.3	12.2
the only way to take proceedings	2.4	2.4	2.4
Sub-total solicitors	43.9	26.8	35.3
To court welfare officer			
he knows more about the children	12.2	24.4	18.3
in touch with the other side	14.6	9.8	12.2
he's impartial	9.8	4.9	7.3
it doesn't cost anything	4.9	2.4	3.7
Sub-total welfare officers	41.5	41.5	41.5
Would go to both solicitor and welfare officer	12.2	12.2	12.2
Would go to neither – only to friend	–	9.8	4.9
to other	2.4	4.9	3.7
Not sure to whom would go	2.4	7.3	4.9

parent and thus able to conciliate. Here are some comments which reveal some of the limitations of the solicitor felt by parents in dealing with family disputes:

> "Well I would go to the welfare officer. He can be the messenger boy and speak to the other parties. He's more in touch with the children – and besides I don't have to pay him."

> "The welfare officer seems more concerned with the children's welfare. I mean he's met them and talked to them. My solicitor hasn't."

"My wife would take more notice of a welfare officer that visited her than a solicitor's letter, because she knows the implications and the welfare officer has already been in contact with her and is neutral."

"The welfare officer or someone of his staff on duty at the time could go immediately to the scene if something happened whereas a solicitor would have to write letters to the other side, and then it would go back in about a week's time."

"Well in our case the judge made a supervision order. If we have any problems about access, my ex-wife, myself and the welfare officer have to meet to discuss it. If it was just me and the wife – I'd flare up too much. We all met a couple of weeks ago in the welfare officer's office – that's how we came to arrange about the children at Easter."

Those favouring solicitors did so particularly if they doubted the welfare officer's capacity to remain impartial. They realised then that their lawyer might be the best person to protect their interests. One father who had lost custody of his 11-year-old daughter told us:

"I felt the welfare officer's report was biased towards my wife's side. They seemed to feel 'you're a man, you're on your own, you can weather it and the child's already with her mother and contented.' My solicitor on the other hand, she understands the situation and feels that I've been pretty unjustly treated and that my wife got away with a lot. So I would go to her – she's on my side."

The importance of the court welfare officers' impartiality will be examined in greater detail in Part Two. Here it is sufficient merely to emphasise the contrast with the solicitors' partisanship which restricts the solicitors' capacity to represent the interests of the children. The fact that solicitors seldom see the children of their divorcing clients, coupled with their partisan role means that when drawing up the documentary evidence concerning the children for the court (*e.g.* the petitioner's statement of proposed arrangements for the children), solicitors are restricted to adopting their client's view of the children. Solicitors who take a separate, individual perspective of their own, in the context of present adversarial procedure, risk their client asking the question: "Which side is he on?," a point illustrated by the following report:

> "My solicitor said when I first saw him that the paramount interest should be taken in the children. He said 'nobody thinks you're not capable of looking after the children, 'cos if I had thought that I would have taken steps to have had them taken away from you.' That's my solicitor! He didn't sound like the chap that I had just paid a hundred odd bleeding quid to. He's also seen my wife and her old man too, and said that he's very impressed with her. He said he was impressed with *them*! I didn't think that was very permissible – my solicitor meeting the opposition – and being very impressed with them!"

Client Satisfaction with Solicitors' Services

Despite the problems that have been examined, how satisfied were the parents in these two samples with the services of their solicitors? Would they recommend him to any of their friends who might be facing similar circumstances? Would they themselves go back to the same solicitor if they had further legal problems arising from their family life? Parents were asked all three of these questions. The results of the questions: "How satisfied are you with your solicitor?" are given in Table 8.

Table 8

Satisfaction with Solicitor

	Representative Petitioner Sample	*Court Welfare Sample*		
		Petitioners	*Respondents*	*Combined*
	n = 102	*n = 41*	*n = 41*	*n = 82*
	%	%	%	%
Very satisfied	55.9	56.1	31.7	43.9
Satisfied	17.6	22.0	14.6	18.3
Fairly satisfied	20.6	14.6	31.7	23.2
Not at all satisfied	5.9	7.3	17.1	12.2
Did not use solicitor	–	–	4.9	2.4

At least 60 per cent. of parents were either satisfied or very satisfied, and only a small minority were obviously displeased. A comparison between petitioners in each sample shows very close similarities. There is a suggestion that respondents are markedly less satisfied than petitioners, though without a representative sample of respondents with which to make comparison this evidence is weaker.

The answers to the questions whether they would recommend their solicitor to a friend and go back themselves if they needed advice in the future confirm the high level of satisfaction as will be seen from Table 9.

Table 9

Willingness to Recommend Solicitor and to Use Again

	Representative Petitioner Sample	*Court Welfare Sample*		
		Petitioners	*Respondents*	*Combined*
	n = 102	*n = 41*	*n = 41*	*n = 82*
	%	%	%	%
Would recommend and go back	66.7	63.4	39.0	51.2
Have already recommended to friend and would go back	14.7	17.1	12.2	14.6
Would *not* recommend or go back	7.8	9.8	17.1	13.4
Would not recommend but would go back – he knows case	5.9	7.3	17.1	12.2
Would not recommend but would go back because too difficult to change	–	–	4.9	2.4
Would recommend, might not go back	2.0	–	–	–
Don't know	2.9	2.4	4.9	3.7
No solicitor	–	–	4.9	2.4

The proportion of replies from both groups of petitioners are closely comparable, both with satisfied and dissatisfied clients. In each group between 12 per cent. and 17 per cent. of parents had already recommended their solicitor to a friend or relative, thus confirming our finding, reported earlier, that personal recommendation is an important way in which solicitors recruit business.

Discussion

It is sometimes argued that many matters now regarded as questions of family law should be transferred from solicitors working in commercial enterprises to new agencies staffed by social workers.[3] The case against solicitors includes the following arguments: first, that they are not equipped by experience or training to deal with the complex social and emotional factors that invariably underly the legal problems of families. Secondly, that the system of individual representation which results from the traditional adversary model of justice tends to polarise and exacerbate family conflict and does not easily allow lawyers to act impartially for both parties or for the family as a whole, nor does it allow for the interests of children to be adequately represented.[4] Thirdly, that lawyers in private practice have a vested interest in profiting financially from family conflict and are hence less likely to be alert to the possibilities of reconciliation or reaching settlement by agreement.[5] Fourthly, solicitors' middle class values and their use of extended language codes deter people from the lower socio-economic classes from using their services.[6] Fifthly, solicitors are unnecessarily expensive. Their cost bears heavily on the inevitably strained resources of families affected by marriage break-up, and where legal aid is concerned, diverts scarce public funds from other areas where they could be used to the greater advantage of families affected by divorce.

Whatever the merits of these arguments, they don't seem to lead to widely held feelings of dissatisfaction with solicitors' services, at least where these divorcing parents are concerned. On the contrary, overall the level of satisfaction is high, though one must not forget the people who refused to take part in the study. The question arises how representative are these findings? The study was comparatively small-scale and local, being confined to the south-west region. In many respects the samples were representative of the divorcing population as a whole, but it has been suggested that solicitors in this region could differ significantly in their approach to family matters from their brethren in other parts of the country. To prove whether this was so this study would have to be replicated on a wider national basis. The high level of satisfaction reported might be more suspect were it not for the fact that most of the interviewed gave convincing explanations why they were pleased with their solicitor. Therefore in the absence of evidence to the contrary, it is submitted the findings should be accepted.

Indeed, since our survey was carried out, other surveys have reported similar high levels of satisfaction. The study of Users of Legal Services undertaken on behalf of the Royal Commission on Legal Services found that "more than nine out of ten of those who consulted solicitors in 1977 said that they were easy to deal with." Two clients said that they were completely satisfied and only one in 16 expressed strong dissatisfaction. The substance of the Royal Commission's User Survey confirms all the main findings of our survey, in particular the reasons for dissatisfaction.[7]

This research, while showing that in general divorcing parents seem well pleased with their solicitors, may have greater significance for the light it sheds on the way divorcing clients perceive their solicitors and their relationship with them. Without data of this kind it is hard for outside observers to evaluate that relationship since much of the communication between the participants is confidential and protected by legal privilege. Professional writings of solicitors themselves offer valuable insights[8] but are not representative of practitioners in general. They sometimes fail to distinguish between the ideal and reality. The same can be said of individual clients who express themselves on the matter. Research of consumer opinion can compensate for these deficiencies. Even so it has one important limitation. It is an unreliable means of assessing professional competence. Megarry writing of litigation in general rather than divorce practice in particular has remarked[9]:

> "When the advice is given, the job done, the case fought, how does the client appraise his solicitor? Will he sing his merits or deplore his failings? How much of his estimation is based

> on things that matter, and how much on the incidentals that do not – a brusqueness of speech, an attractive or ill-favoured office, or even a blonde typist? I confess I do not rank the average client highly as a judge of solicitors; I would not think myself better as a judge of medical skill."

He then argued that knowledge was essential to understanding, and that understanding should precede judgment. As the client usually had little knowledge of legal matters, it followed he was usually incapable of judging his solicitor's competence.

Nevertheless, this research shows that clients generally do attempt to assess competence. Their efforts are not without consequence since such evaluations affect the solicitor's local reputation which in turn influences the demand for his services. Lacking knowledge of the finer points of law they use other clues as criteria for assessment. Amongst the more important are the solicitor's manner of reception, whether he explains how he is handling the case, whether he can predict with reasonable accuracy what will happen, whether he seems efficient, and whether he treats them with concern and respect. All these factors contribute to the client's trust and confidence in the solicitor's service.

A personable manner and sympathetic handling are obvious tools for good legal practice but they may conceal an absence of legal understanding and the grossest inefficiency, the results of which the client may only realise after the work is done. For example, in this research clients often expressed warm appreciation of the solicitor's efforts to obtain their decree nisi as if they thought that without his skill they would have been unsuccessful.[10] Lacking a realistic understanding of legal practice they applauded solicitors for completion of mere formality. They were often surprised to learn later from the researchers that there was virtually no risk in their being refused a decree.

The research also highlights the extent to which divorcing clients become dependent on solicitors. The lawyers' continuous involvement in the protracted drama of the divorce, often from the point of marriage breakdown to remarriage some years later, makes him a key figure with power both to control the direction of future events, and to guide clients through the uncertainties of complex legal procedure: territory which for many is unfamiliar and potentially hazardous.[11] Whether or not they were being realistic many of the parents interviewed considered their own future and that of the children to be at stake. Having lost trust in their former spouse they often felt vulnerable and considered that their interests required special protection. They frequently passed through states of heightened anxiety not knowing when they would obtain their divorce and be able to remarry, uncertain how the property would be divided or how the arrangements for the children would work out. They often worried about which matters might create difficulties and further emotional conflict and disappointment. Solicitors were generally assumed to be knowledgeable about many of these problems.

As well as being legal advisers they were frequently ascribed a counselling role. In this respect they were, surprisingly, viewed more favourably than most other professional workers with the possible exception of family doctors and the court welfare officers who became involved with cases in the second research sample. Unlike various kinds of social worker – probation officers, local authority social workers and marriage guidance counsellors particularly – solicitors appeared to have the important advantage of being free from stigmatic associations, a matter that will be discussed more fully in Part Three. They were consequently seen as offering a more acceptable form of social support. This might have been due to the fact that the solicitor's counselling role was often performed implicitly. As the Finer Report put it, the legal machinery "treats people ... in the last resort as the subject of rights not as ... 'patients' for whom legal process is just another kind of treatment."[12] It seems as if an approach for legal service, while valid in its own terms, may also act as a face-saving mechanism, allowing people to receive covert emotional support without loss of self-respect.

The partisan role of solicitors, while contributing a lot to the general level of client satisfaction, may also serve particular psychological purposes. There comes a point in emotional conflict when people feel so wounded, threatened or frightened, sometimes by the strength of their own anger, that escape and dependence on partisan support are all that are acceptable. At such times emotion may defeat logic. Some people interviewed said that during their marriage breakdown they had felt driven close to murder. Then a visit to the solicitor had seemed the only reasonable alternative to the use of the bread knife. In such cases a receptive solicitor may well enable a client to ventilate feelings less destructively and may, for example, by offering to write a strongly worded letter to the other party, help the client to feel that his anger has been taken account of. In this respect it can be argued that the traditional adversary system of justice, through the agency of partisan solicitors, offers an important social mechanism for the safe management of emotional conflict, quite apart from its value as a method of determining conflicting legal interests.

Important though the partisan role is, divorcing parents are often aware of its limitations. As has been reported, some saw their solicitors adopting a rigid combative stance which had only aggravated the tensions between themselves and the other parent. Many lawyers are aware of this problem. Thus, Mortlock, a practising divorce solicitor, has written:

> "Too often solicitors write each other letters which sizzle with rancour, or do no more than score points off each other. . . . Nor is there any expectation of benefit to be derived by the parties. Extreme positions taken up by lawyers, frequently render proceedings inevitable.'[13]

Who is the culprit? The client, the lawyer or the adversary system itself? Some people think that it is only when, consciously or unconsciously people are seeking champions to do battle on their behalf, that a battlefield results. Thus Westcott, another solicitor, has recently written.[14]

> "Of course our clients are often extremely angry, outraged and thirsting for blood. They see in the lawyer someone who is going to exact vengeance for them. Unhappily some of us respond to the challenge and we witness the blistering cross-examination in court that seeks to denigrate and destroy the other party."

Individual differences between lawyers always influence the conduct and often the outcome of cases. Their experience, training, personal values, make some into peacemakers, others into warriors.

An unqualified assumption of a partisan stance may well be suitable for normal litigation conducted within the framework of the traditional adversary model of justice. But there are strong arguments that it should be modified for the legal conduct of family disputes. As Mostyn has written:[15]

> "When domestic discord breaks out, it cannot rationally be the aim of the parties to smash each other to pieces. This is the way that angry, humiliated, frightened, bereft people sometimes feel and sometimes talk. They then need advice and help, not fuel. The rational aim is for the lawyers on each side to cool it down, each to endeavour to restore a sense of balance to his client and then for both to look for a sensible solution which will enable the parties to withdraw from the marriage with dignity, and their proper financial entitlement, in order to prepare themselves to get their lives moving again constructively, whether in the context of a new relationship or not. By these means, instead of the children's lives being further strained by bitter litigation, an end is made to pull on their loyalties. This kind of approach calls for patience, sympathy and negotiation which happily may end in resolution. Absolutely the last thing to be introduced here is confrontation. That simply creates another order of problem because, in addition to everything else, the tensions which exist between a winner and a loser will also have to be contained. But if confrontation is avoided, so are its consequences. Nor is appeasement the alternative to confrontation; the alternative is negotiation."

Thus solicitors face the dilemmas of how to protect their client's interests without stimulating further family conflict, and how to foster realistic settlement without making their client feel that the lawyer's allegiance is weakening.

This research also shows clearly that most children of divorcing parents have no direct contact with the system of law that decides their future. The exceptions are the small minority who are interviewed by court welfare officers or judges.[16] Although in principle children's interests are paramount there is seldom any direct attempt to ascertain how children themselves view their interests, even though they may be of school age and well able to communicate independently with the adult world. This may not seem remarkable to practising lawyers, but it surprised a number of parents. It also seems to run counter to the principle behind sections 3 and 59 of the Children Act 1975, which provide that where children are in care or where an adoption is contemplated the court or local authority should as far as it is practicable ascertain the wishes and feelings of the child having regard to his age and understanding.

It is perfectly understandable that solicitors representing divorcing parents do not see it as their place to interview children. They would face divided loyalty which would threaten their partisan commitment to their clients. Yet it is a structural fault in the system that the views and interests of children are often ignored. This has led to suggestions that children should have separate representation.[17] Since solicitors have little experience of communicating directly with children, and may lack the necessary skill, legally qualified court welfare officers or children's ombudsmen as proposed by Justice might be preferable. Yet proposals of this kind, if grafted on to an unmodified adversary system, risk two-cornered family disputes becoming three-cornered ones. To safeguard against this it would be necessary to ensure that whoever represented the children was impartial in the dispute between the parents. This would make them more acceptable and allow for the possibility of conciliation, a point I shall return to when considering the role of the court welfare officer.

It is not always realised either by lawyers or litigants that to concentrate attention on one member of the family to the exclusion of the others is to risk over-simplification and bias, which when acted upon may destroy the complex emotional ties that link all family members even when a marriage is no longer viable. Many lawyers have become so bonded to the adversary system that it is not easy for them to appreciate this point. Yet it should not be forgotten that some weakening of the emotional ties is one of the difficult tasks that clients may have to perform before new partnerships can be properly established. In this sense the adversary system with its over-simplification may actually sometimes help. While many solicitors may persuade clients to reach settlements through a process of negotiation, they do so from a position that is basically identified with the party they represent. As we shall see when discussing the impartial role of the court welfare officer, many parents interviewed in this research distinguished between agreements reached by negotiation and those with the help of an independent conciliator. Curiously, even parents involved in the most bitter conflict seemed to retain a sense of there being an elusive middle ground between them which, with skill and understanding, could be identified by a fair impartial conciliator or, failing that, a judge. I suspect that many children of divorced parents intuitively inhabit that territory and often feel alone and unrecognised there. Yet the implication of this research is that partisan solicitors are poorly placed to do anything about this.

Recent restrictions on legal aid and the extension of the special procedure to all undefended divorce petitions suggests that old procedures based on the adversary model of justice are giving way to more inquisitorial methods designed to protect the welfare of children. Divorcing parents, quite often unrepresented, will be brought into more direct contact with court officials, welfare officers and judges. Judges and social workers will be able to intervene in family life much more. There are advantages but there are also risks to the freedoms of parents and children.

Solicitors will have to adapt to these changes. This research indicates how they might do so. First and foremost, it validates their traditional role as protectors of citizens' interests. Solicitors will have to be even more vigilant when their clients may find themselves in conflict, not only with other family members, but with the powerful welfare institutions of the state, as is increasingly the case in child care matters. Secondly, the restrictions on legal aid in civil proceedings increase the importance of the legal advice scheme, especially for families in the early stages of marriage breakdown. It should be made easier for divorcing couples to seek legal advice jointly from a neutral lawyer. The research findings support the view of the Lay Observer that "there is a need for the public to have more information on the experience and specialised fields of firms of solicitors" so that clients can make effective choice and be confident that the solicitors they approach have the necessary skill and experience to deal with family matters.[18] Specialised and experienced solicitors should know what social services can offer families, and appreciate the role of divorce court welfare officers.

The Royal Commission have recently acknowledged that the increasing complexity of law will inevitably increase the trend towards greater specialisation in solicitors' work. They recommend that the Law Society should take a lead in setting up a system whereby certain solicitors could be designated specialists of one kind or another.[19] In my opinion, family law is an obvious area where this sort of formal specialisation should be encouraged. Linked to an improved system for informing the public about legal services, specialism of this kind could be a real public benefit. A college of family law set up on the lines of some of the specialist medical colleges, as I suggest in the final chapter of this book, could be the most appropriate way of achieving this.

NOTES

1. This part of the book reproduces in abridged form a two part article entitled "The role of Solicitors in Divorce Proceedings," *Modern Law Review*, November 1977 and January 1978.
2. 22 per cent. replied that the stance the solicitor took in the conflict should depend on the circumstances between the parties and the children. Five per cent. agreed with neither statement or else did not use a solicitor so could not judge.
3. B. Abel-Smith and R. Stevens, *In Search of Justice* (Allen Lane, 1968), p. 319.
4. *Parental Rights and Duties and Custody Suits* (Justice Report, Sweet and Maxwell, 1975).
5. A. H. Manchester and J. M. Whetton, "Marital Conciliation in England and Wales," *The International Law Quarterly*, April 1974.
6. B. Abel-Smith, M. Zander and R. Brooke, *Legal Problems and the Citizen* (Heinemann, 1973), p. 224.
7. Final Report of the Royal Commission on Legal Services, Vol. 2, Cmnd. 7648 (HMSO, October 1979), p. 223.
8. W. Mortlock, *The Inside of Divorce* (Constable, 1971). See also J. Westcott. "Family Problems – The Solicitor and his Client" (1977) *Family Law*, 24–29.

9. R. E. Megarry, *Lawyer and Litigant in England* (1962).
10. The research was conducted prior to the introduction of the special procedure in divorce proceedings.
11. B. G. Glasser and A. L. Strauss, *Status Passage* (Routledge & Kegan Paul, 1971), p. 51.
12. Report of the Committee on One-Parent Families, Cmnd. 5629 (1974), Vol. 1, p. 175.
13. Mortlock, *op. cit.*
14. Westcott, *op. cit.*
15. F. E. Mostyn, *Marriage and the Law*, (Oyez, 1976), p. 166.
16. Justice Report, *op. cit.*
17. According to a report published in September 1976 by the Family Law Sub-Committee of the Chief Probation Officers Conference, welfare reports are produced in only 10 per cent. of divorce cases.
18. First Annual Report of the Lay Observer, 1975–76 (1976), p. 5.
19. Final Report of the Royal Commission on Legal Services, *op. cit.* Vol. 1, paras. 27.17–27.23.

Part 2

The Role of the Divorce Court Welfare Officer

2 Preconceptions of Parents

We discovered in the earlier part of the research that many divorcing parents had never heard of the divorce court welfare service. Of the sample of 41 cases which had contact with the service, only 24 per cent. of the parents reported that they knew the service existed before they learned that a welfare officer was to visit them. The most usual way in which parents learned of this was when they received a letter from the officer (49 per cent. of cases). A minority were in court when the judge asked for a report (20 per cent.), or heard about it later from their solicitor (16 per cent.). The remainder (15 per cent.) learned about it in a variety of ways, for example being told by the other parent or in one instance, being told by a neighbour. In 10 per cent. of the cases parents had no time to think about the officer's role in the case or to prepare themselves against the visit because the officer turned up unannounced. Not surprisingly, such visits seemed to upset a number of parents and to arouse their distrust. Here are two examples:

> "I can remember the shock when Mark (cohabitee) came in and said 'Someone to see you.' She said 'I'm a probation officer,' and I can remember thinking 'Ye Gods, what's he done?' That was right because she said to Mark 'I never tell people when I'm coming.' She just likes to drop in in case you're preparing for her. Bit awkward just in the middle of cooking a meal and we all had colds."

> "He knocked on the door, said he was a welfare officer and came in. 'Oh' he said, 'I'm surprised to find you in' and all this. You know they're the type that try to come and catch you when you're not in or something like that. That's what it reminded me of. Like someone had been telling the tale that I'd been leaving the children and all this nonsense."

It is worth noting that the father who made this last comment remained distrustful throughout his contact with the welfare officer.

Welfare officers themselves seem divided on the wisdom of the surprise approach. A study of a sample of 82 welfare officers dealing with 150 enquiries in 1976 taken representatively from 10 county courts showed that in 32 per cent. of instances welfare officers arrived unannounced and that the most commonly mentioned justification for doing so was that such officers felt that parents had "less opportunity to put on a show."[1] Nevertheless, the majority of officers seem to think that it is an imposition for a stranger to call unannounced to discuss personal affairs.

In my own study of divorcing parents known to welfare officers, the 90 per cent. who had time to anticipate the officer's arrival were asked what they had thought the officer was most likely to be concerned with. Their answers varied. Most replies referred to their children's general welfare and happiness at home and at school. Others mentioned more specific concerns such as what the welfare officer would think about the material standard of the home and the quality of their own particular relationship with the child.

All these parents were also asked whether they had been worried by the proposed involvement of a welfare officer in their case. The majority (66 per cent.) reported that they had not, a figure which may be an overestimation since some may have been reluctant to admit to anxiety about the matter or may have forgotten their initial reactions by the time they were interviewed for the research. It ought also to be remembered that recall of their expectations was likely to be influenced by their subsequent contact with the officers. Even so, almost a quarter of the sample referred to fear of being considered unsuitable to have care of the children. Their replies are particularly interesting for the considerable power to influence events that they ascribe to the welfare officer:

> "I was terrified she wouldn't let me keep the children here, we were so cramped."

> "Oh yes, I worried. I went round the house and cleaned and polished everything. I didn't know what to expect you know. She did look round. I think at the back of my mind I was worried that she was going to take my children away from me."

"I spent the day going round making sure everything was spick and span and that. I was on edge right up until he came. I didn't know exactly what he would want to see or do. I talked to my sister but no-one knew what to expect. I told the children he would be coming and why – it wasn't very easy – they couldn't understand why somebody else should decide what was best for them. They thought that either me or their mother should decide what should happen."

More information about parents' expectations was obtained in response to the following question:

"Did you expect the divorce court welfare officer to be helpful in any way?"

The answers are classified below in Table 10.

Table 10

Whether Help Expected from Welfare Officer

	n = 82
	%
No	45
Yes, conciliation – *re* access	10
Yes, conciliation with spouse about other matters	6
Yes, direct practical help – housing	5
Yes, direct practical help – other matters	8
Yes, other kinds of help (*e.g.* talking to children, etc.)	10
Don't know	16

Most of those parents who had time to think about it saw the welfare officer's task as being primarily, almost exclusively, investigative. Thus a father looking after five children on his own remarked:

"No, I expected him to be friendly to a certain extent but not helpful. I thought he would just be coming here to ask me questions and try and catch me out on things – to see if I was putting on a front for him."

Another father, a school teacher said:

"I didn't expect her to be helpful, no. I think really I expected that she would simply ask my views as to the wellbeing of the children. . . . I was pleasantly surprised when it became obvious that she was quite willing to talk about any aspect whatsoever."

Most considered that welfare officers should conduct their investigations impartially. Yet the officers' impartiality was sometimes seen as limiting the amount of help they could offer.

"I hoped he was going to be helpful but I didn't expect it for obvious reasons, because I knew full well before he came that his job is not to be biased towards one or the other."

"Her whole job was to make out a report. It didn't seem as if she intended to give advice. She is dealing with both sides of the family, therefore she couldn't put one against the other by offering help in one direction."

Where help was expected, it was generally anticipated that this would come in the form of conciliation in disputes with the other parent, usually about access. Here are two examples, the first from a mother who hoped the welfare officer might be able to arbitrate between herself and her husband whom she regarded as having too frequent access:

"She [the DC welfare officer] was going to see my husband the following night and I said 'Can't you talk to him and tell him how I feel about him coming over every day?' When he came the atmosphere used to be terrible and there was nothing I could do. I thought it was for my daughter's welfare as well, but quite honestly I didn't think anyone seemed to care."

The second example comes from one of the non-custodial parents, a mother whose former husband was preventing her from seeing the children:

"I think you feel that she [DC welfare officer] could put things to rights, and that she will find out how the children are feeling. I would have liked the children to have been seen."

There were also other relationship problems that some parents seemed to expect help with. Thus one father with the care of two of his own children was planning to marry a divorcee who herself had two children. The integration of the two families was worrying him. He told us:

> "Well, I was expecting a little bit of advice here and there. The thing is we've now got one boy and three girls. Well, I suppose there could be complications later on. The welfare officer could forewarn us what could happen."

All parents who had been expecting a welfare officer to call were asked what kind of person they expected to meet. Here are some typical replies:

> "I thought and hoped it would be a lady – married and with children of her own. This was my idea of a person who could evaluate the situation rather than taking it from the text book angle."

> "They must be understanding. I think welfare officers should be married and have children themselves to give a better understanding. I know they are very well trained, but if they haven't got children themselves I don't think they can understand the problems involved."

> "I had a woman from the Child Guidance Centre here some years ago. Many of these social workers are all 'Miss' aren't they? She was about five or six years younger than me. I thought, 'What does she know about bringing up four kids?' Welfare workers who have kids of their own, *they* can come and tell you what you should do. I mean it's all very well to have Dr. Spock's book under your nose and tell you what to do when little 'un don't sleep – shove this in his mouth. You can't have experience in a college or even out of a book. You've got to have the actual experience of a *parent*. You've got to have had your own and know how tied you can be, how committed you are, have these basic worries. If they've got all these things, then they must be highly qualified to come round and talk. But when they haven't got that, you find it very hard to accept what they say, very hard."

The constant reference to welfare officers themselves needing to be married with children was a dominant theme in the responses. Training itself was seldom disparaged but did not seem to be regarded as important as an officer's personal life experience, maturity and having had children.

Mayer and Timms[2] also found that social work clients typically preferred workers of similar age and marital status. They comment:

> "The clients assumed that only persons who had had a similar experience could possibly comprehend what it was like. . . . This assumption challenges a fundamental precept of the social work profession, namely that social work skills derive from a body of abstract knowledge. The belief that workers must actually *live through* certain situations and events if they are to be helpful, is an implicit challenge to this axiom."

NOTES

1. John Birks, *The Role of the Divorce Court Welfare Officer* (Unpublished M. Sc. degree thesis, University of Bristol, March 1978). I am indebted to the author for permission to use this material.
2. J. E. Mayer, N. Timms, *The Client Speaks: Working Class Impressions in Case Work* (Routledge & Kegan Paul, 1970) p. 73.

3 Encounters with Welfare Officers – Parents' Experience

Impressions of the Officers' Manner

Most people experienced the officer as a friendly person to whom they could relate easily.[1] It was estimated that 85 per cent. of parents viewed their welfare officer in a favourable light. 12 per cent. seemed positively antagonistic and a few others (three per cent.) appeared indifferent. Later in the interview, parents were also asked whether there was anything in their encounter with the officer that they specifically disliked or found unhelpful. 67 per cent. had no adverse comment to make. 21 per cent. mentioned some aspect of the officer's manner and approach to his task. Eight per cent. objected to bias or inaccuracy in the contents of the report that they had been fortunate enough to see[2] and four per cent. to the nature of the questions they had been asked. Most of the parents were therefore satisfied with their individual welfare officer, although there was criticism of the organisation of the court welfare service and its procedures.

Typical explanatory remarks from those pleased with the officers were:

> "She was very sympathetic, marvellous with the children, very homely, very understanding."

> "Very pleasant, just about right I should say. Friendly enough but not friendly enough to get too involved emotionally. I think she's got the right approach."

> "Totally different from what I expected. She was friendly and nice. I felt I could trust her. This is important. I suppose these people are very carefully picked to do their job. You automatically feel you can trust her."

> "His manner put me completely at ease."

Another characteristic much favoured by parents was the neutral stance evidently adopted by many officers. This seemed to be a crucial aspect of the welfare officer's role. Here is a small selection of illustrative remarks, some of which were made independently by both parents in a case. Thus a father remarked:

> "He seemed to be very impartial. He chose his words carefully. He always said the right thing. He was pleasant."

While the mother, interviewed elsewhere, commented:

> "I was pleased he was impartial and would be unbiased. He was sympathetic, interested and friendly, but he didn't take sides."

It was clear that many welfare officers at the beginning of their contact with families stress their neutrality to parents:

> "He said right out that he wanted to see both sides of it and that it would be difficult and take a great deal of time."

Neutrality was often associated with the position of the children. Thus one mother commented:

> "I was surprised when we got talking. He wasn't on my husband's side and he wasn't on mine. The main concern was that the children were going to be all right."

In similar vein a father remarked:

> "He was helpful. He was not always for my wife. He just wanted to get the facts and see where the child would be best suited. He was putting her interests before anything."

Another mother told us:

> "I welcomed someone really in the middle because Simon had always told me one thing and his father another. I know children often tell you what they think you want to hear. But when the welfare officer came the children were saying something to a completely independent person."

Some parents described the neutrality of the welfare officer more in terms of his being concerned for the family as a whole rather than a particular section of it. Thus one mother said:

> "He seems to really care what happens to *all* of you. . . . I feel he's involved with the problems and is caring very much and wants to sort them out for the best of everybody. . . . I don't think he's on my side or my husband's. He just sees things as they are, and you tend to have confidence in him."

Yet neutrality that is not coupled with concern can be experienced as coldness. Thus one mother remarked:

> "I found her very middle of the road and awkward to talk to. She wanted you to do the talking and I didn't quite know what to say. I knew I was being assessed as a person and it was very awkward and uncomfortable. Usually when you meet someone you feel they're being sympathetic to you or they're not. But she was neither. It was peculiar and I found it difficult."

Another mother said:

> "I found it difficult to assess what he was thinking and whether he thought I was right in my opinions. If my solicitor disagrees with anything I say he will tell me. But the welfare officer sat and listened and didn't pass much comment. I suppose he was trying to be extremely fair and trying to see both sides of it. He can't afford to take sides can he? But I think I would have had more confidence if I'd known he agreed with the way I felt sometimes."

Divorcing parents often endure periods of self doubt in which their emotional need seems to be for a certain amount of validation from others. This is part of the value of partisan support which is generally provided in almost institutionalised form by solicitors. Court welfare officers have to decide whether they are able to provide validation of this kind while striving to remain neutral.

Reactions to Interrogation

Because the welfare officer is preparing a report he normally has to ask a lot of questions. How do parents react to this? To find out we asked whether they always understood the reasons for the questions they were asked, and whether they felt they could talk easily with the officer. The majority (80 per cent.) replied affirmatively. Most parents appreciated that welfare officers have to ask questions, and many commented on the skill and sensitivity with which they did it. For example:

> "He's the sort of person you can talk to easily. Some people who ask you questions give the impression that they only want to find out your business. But with him although he asked lots of questions he said 'If you don't want to answer them you needn't.' That makes a lot of difference. He didn't hurry me or put me in a difficult position."

> "To be honest with you, the type of questions she asked and the way she put it to you, well you just found yourself talking, you know? She could draw things out of you."

> 'He didn't question very much at all. He just left the doors open for me to talk on and on."

> "I thought he would have been more nosey. But he didn't pry at all. It depends on the type of person you talk to what you tell them. If someone gets your back up before you start, you tell them nothing. If you think a person is really interested and wants to help you don't mind sharing your experience with anybody. Mr. D. (welfare officer) was very quiet. If you hadn't much to say, or didn't want to talk, he wouldn't push you. He would take his time and maybe call again. Whatever you say it must come from you on your own accord."

The majority of parents seemed to have found the welfare officer's approach to the investigation open and straightforward. This seemed to reinforce trust:

> "Oh, he explained himself very well. He put questions to you plainly and clearly."

> "She always put it the way she wanted it answered. When she wanted to know about my daughter Jane, she always put it that she only wanted to know for certain reasons. Do you know what I mean?"

"I didn't feel as if he'd use things I said unfairly. I could tell him things freely. I didn't feel he was asking me things to trick me."

Although only a minority of parents viewed their welfare officer unfavourably, a number of those who did referred to being subjected to persistent, forceful and insensitive questioning. For example, one father said:

"He was sort of cross-questioning rather than just asking. It was like as if you were in court. Instead of talking *with* you he was cross-questioning you. You had already told him two or three times what you thought and what's happening, but he'd still come up and push the same questions down your throat. He kept saying, "Well, why do you think that?"

Another said:

"He kept asking questions which were impossible to answer at the time – like where was I going to be living and what would be my plans. There just wasn't much I could tell him so he kept coming back. He kept giving me the impression that I was withholding things from him, but I just couldn't give him answers at that time."

Even parents who got on well with their welfare officers sometimes found the inquisitorial aspect of their work difficult to cope with. Some evidently were made to feel quite defensive. For example:

"All through I felt a little uncomfortable. The feeling you're being looked at and assessed."

"I was always a bit wary with him. I imagined him going away and writing down what I'd said. I always felt that once I'd said something I couldn't go back on it. It would be in his report and that would be that."

Sometimes parents had mixed feelings about the skill with which they had been interviewed:

"She just talks generally, but she brings things out of you you don't even know you said at the time. She doesn't fire questions at you, but before you know where you are you've told her something. You don't realise it until you sit back and think after she's gone."

"You don't realise she's asking you questions. Very shrewd woman, she's very clever. You know some people can find out anything they want from you if they put it in the right way. You don't even know you're telling them what they want to know. She'd make a good psychiatrist – she's so inoffensive the way she puts things."

Remarks such as these indicated that these parents had been left feeling that they had been tricked by the welfare officer's skill. They were on guard for future encounters.

Several parents said that they had been quite puzzled by questions that the welfare officer had asked them. This was particularly so when their own history and background rather than their child's circumstances became the focus of the investigation. For example, one mother told us:

"I thought he was completely mad! He was *so* interested in when I was more or less born and what happened to me then and things which, to me, didn't have any relevance to the children. He was more like a psychiatrist."

Similarly, a father remarked:

"There were some questions that seemed quite irrelevant – like when it came to my home background or what jobs I've had from the time I left school, what my mother's done and whether my mother was divorced. I mean that's nothing to do with *my* marriage – nothing to do with *my* family. My mother is not living with me, she doesn't keep me, so that's irrelevant to the case."

It seems that some welfare officers forget that parents do not always understand or share their belief that early childhood experience determines later behaviour. This can lead to a major failure of communication. The need for officers to explain the reasons for some of their questions was apparent from remarks such as:

"When he explained what he was here for I felt more relaxed and didn't try to avoid his questions or anything like that."

"I would have spoken more freely if I had understood what she was getting at."

Interviewing Children – the Parents' View

In almost every case the enquiry for the court involved the welfare officer in seeing the children. The kind of contact they had with children was very variable. Some were seen alone, others in the company of parents or other siblings. The older children are, the most likely it appears that they will be seen on their own. Some parents seem to accept this quite easily – a few even welcomed it as the father who said:

"It was a good thing. It proves if one's telling a lie and the other one's trying to cover up and things like that."

One father, a solicitor's clerk, who was quite pleased that his son was seen on his own, remarked:

"They ought to get more from the child – far too often they consult everybody but the child himself."

Many parents find it emotionally upsetting to talk to their children about the marriage breakdown. Even though it may well be in the children's interest to be told the facts of the situation in order to dispel the unrealistic fantasies they may have about it, many parents avoid doing so if they can.[3] Some of them in this sample welcomed it when the welfare officer offered to talk with the children. Thus one father reported:

"He put the boys more at rest you know. I think they were under the impression they would have to go back to their mother. After he'd spoken to them – as I say he was a friendly sort of chap – they seemed more at ease, more secure. They've been a lot better since."

Nevertheless, there were parents who were bothered by the welfare officer seeing their children on their own. One mother reported quite vividly how her ten-year-old son had been upset by being asked about his relationship with his father:

"We came here to live and forget all about the nastiness with his father. Then the welfare officer came here and asked him all the questions – brought it all back. He cried, he couldn't sleep that night, and the next morning he cried again. He brought all the horrible things back you know. He couldn't sleep very well – crying his eyes out thinking. He'd been asked all these questions about his father. Naturally he thinks the world of his father, but he came to live with me."

Interviewer:

> "Do you think it would have been any different if the welfare officer had spent longer getting to know him?" "Yes, perhaps if he'd known him it might have been different. He didn't know him. It was like a stranger really come to ask him all these questions."

A number of parents thought that welfare officers should take more time getting to know children before talking to them about emotionally fraught subjects. Thus one mother was very surprised that her children aged 10 and 12 had been asked which parent they wished to live with on the first occasion the welfare officer visited – reporting that "she was probably with them 20 minutes at the most." Seeing children on their own and creating a sufficiently trusting and relaxed context in which to do so requires sensitivity, skill and careful preparation. It must take account of the children's age, sense of security and capacity to sustain a conversation with an adult about a subject easily producing anxiety. It was clear from parental accounts that occasionally officers went to great lengths to win children's trust and confidence before seeing them on their own. On the other hand, we heard of a number of instances when the preparation for the interview seemed minimal and the encounter was brief, formal and awkward. For example, one father reported:

> "I suppose he was talking to them for a quarter of an hour or 20 minutes. We never questioned them about what he said, but they said he was quite a nice man. They didn't laugh about it. Quite serious about it they were. Richard didn't want to see him again. He said: 'Oh, I ain't going to have no more of that – keep asking questions.' The others they didn't mind at all."

In similar vein a mother reported that her nine-year-old daughter in the care of her father had been interviewed individually:

> "She said Mr. T. [DC welfare officer] had been. She didn't like it very much. She didn't like being questioned – she's shy. I think if she didn't know the answers it would worry her."

Many of these parents were anxious lest they might lose care or contact with their children as a result of the court's decision. Most parents seemed to appreciate the welfare officer's need to see the children on their own so that they might speak freely and independently. But it is not surprising that some parents worried about these interviews, not knowing what had happened. Interviewing children is clearly delicate. Only officers with suitable skills ought to be selected to do it.

Reactions to the Extent and Scope of the Enquiries

Parents were asked whether they thought the welfare officer should have made more or fewer enquiries about the children's circumstances. Most (60 per cent.) thought the extent of the enquiry was appropriate. A sizeable majority (34 per cent.) however thought that they should have got to know the children better and obtained corroborative evidence about their parenting qualities from relatives, friends, or neighbours. Parents were most likely to say this if they knew that the welfare officer had interviewed such people connected with the other parent. In this respect divorcing parents often need the assurance of symbolic even-handed treatment from the welfare officer if they are to have confidence in his impartiality and fairness. Only six per cent. felt that the enquiries were unnecessarily extensive. It is striking that so few of these parents seemed to have resented the welfare officers' intrusion.

Help to Families Provided by Welfare Officers

All the parents were asked whether they could remember whether the welfare officer had offered to help them in any way. Table 11 classifies the answers.

Table 11

Whether Help Offered by Divorce Court Welfare Officer

n = 82

	%
No	50
Said I could contact him if needed	24
Yes, conciliation concerning the children	18
Yes, practical help – housing, welfare grants, etc.	2
Yes, other help with relationships	4

Parents were also asked whether on reflection they had found their experience with the welfare officer helpful, and if so in what respect. Table 12 summarises their replies.

Table 12

Whether Divorce Court Welfare Officer was Experienced as Helpful

n = 82

	%
Helpful – someone to talk to	40
Helpful – useful advice	12
Helpful – practical help	8
Nothing helpful	20
Neutral – just did his job	20

It will be seen from both these tables that in about half the instances welfare officers were reported as not having offered parents any particular help. As we have already seen (Table 10) many parents did not expect it. Nevertheless, in a number of instances it is clear that welfare officers went beyond investigating matters for the court and actively offered help of various kinds. Whether they were right to do so is debatable. Some officers think they cannot conduct objective impartial enquiries and give active help at the same time. Others argue that it is never possible to be objective and that a welfare officer's duty to place the interests of children above all else requires him to offer families any help that he can. As it is, the research evidence suggests that this help is more likely to be in terms of relationship than in the provision of practical services. The researchers

were told of many instances of casework help by the welfare officer during the course of the enquiry. Here are several illustrative accounts:
A depressed mother:

> "I think if ever I had any irrational ideas about just packing my bags and clearing off she [the DC welfare officer] would stop me. The things she would say and her attitude would stop me. She comes to convince you that you don't really mean the things you sometimes say. I've said things like wanting to clear out, and she has told me it's just the state I was going through – give me six months and I'll be feeling different. She made me realise that I had had a hell of a strain. You need someone to tell you these things."

Another mother with the care of teenage boys who were reacting badly to their parents' separation:

> "He helped me accept a situation which was perhaps not as unique as I had thought. The mere realisation that there are similar cases occurring all the time with various outcomes did help me accept the situation. The fact that he knew so well that boys of this age do react in a certain way, and that my children were not acting as outrageously as I thought helped. He explained many things to me so I could see the psychological implications and the reasons behind a certain type of behaviour. I certainly understood it a lot better after I talked to him than before."

A mother who had left her husband when she formed a liaison with his best friend told us of the welfare officer's attempts to conciliate between them. The father was jealous and suspicious of the mother's attempts to see the children; she suspected that he was intimidating them against seeing her.

> "I saw her [DC welfare officer] once. Then we were still having terrible trouble with access so I phoned her several times. . . . She went to see my husband first and then she came to see me and Jack [cohabitee]. I thought she really ought to see the children with me. She had seen them with their father and wanted to see them on their own. She went back but he wouldn't leave the house. He went into an adjoining room

> where he could hear the conversation, so she couldn't speak to them on their own. She went round there on another evening and asked 'Would you be willing for the children to come and see their mother? I'll take them, spend the day there and bring them back – so you'll be sure there'll be no funny business.' She was very good but he refused. So then she felt she had better get her report finished as quickly as possible. She felt it was urgent. Well, she has done her bit!"

Other researches by Wynn,[4] Marsden,[5] George and Wilding[6] as well as the Finer Report give ample testimony about the many serious practical difficulties faced by parents bringing up children on their own. Our own research found the same. Reduced income, accommodation problems, and difficulties in finding day care for children had faced many of the parents we met.[7] Yet, the divorce court welfare officer seldom seems to have been turned to as a source of help with these problems. This may have been partly because by the time the court welfare service became involved, the family had already overcome, or at least come to terms with, some of the immediate practical problems that arose when the parents separated. Perhaps many welfare officers did not see it as part of their task to help families with such problems. Their own view of the extent and limit of their responsibilities might have been communicated to and accepted by the parents. Welfare officers themselves agree that this happens. One of them indicated that he thought he was unusual in ensuring that parents were receiving their full welfare rights entitlement. In one of these cases the father with care of four school children told the researchers:

> "One of the main things he [DC welfare officer] was concerned about was the children at school – as regards to helping them with school uniforms and things like that. I never got no grants nor nothing – did it out of me wages. Then Mr. B. [DC welfare officer] came along and got these things for the children. He also sorted out some squabbles we had with the school. Elizabeth [13 years] got upset because the headmistress had told the children in her class that this sort of thing between mums and dads does children no good. Elizabeth got upset and came home to me and was in the house for three weeks. She talked to Mr. B. about it and I let

> him sort it out. He found out exactly what was wrong. He took it completely off my hands."

In case it should be thought that this welfare officer was being partisan to the father, it should be mentioned that he had also helped the mother, caring for a fifth child, secure council accommodation. But accounts of social work help of this kind were exceptional.

Parents who had experienced the welfare officer as helpful most frequently defined this help as being able to talk about their family problems and worries to a concerned neutral and understanding person. Although most parents had received support from their solicitors and quite often from their doctors as well, many commented that the welfare officers' visits gave them particular opportunity to ventilate their anxieties about the divorce and its effects on family life. This was often warmly appreciated. Mayer and Timms refer to satisfied social work clients in their study obtaining

> "considerable relief by unburdening themselves to the worker. Because they felt at ease with the worker, they were able to talk freely, their tensions were eased, at least temporarily."[8]

This applies equally to many parents who had dealings with divorce court welfare officers. As one parent said:

> "You know you bottle it all up inside you. When he comes here you can let it all out, whether he likes it or no!"

Another remarked typically:

> "I should just talk easily to him, even if it was only talking about mortgages and things like that. He seemed to understand about children – he had children of his own you see."

Reactions to the Timing of the Welfare Officers' Intervention

A welfare report can be asked for by the court at any stage in the proceedings. In this particular sample there was almost no pattern in the length of time between the separation and the officers' entering the case:

Table 13

Time From Final Separation to First Contact with Welfare Officer

n = *82*

	%
Within 3 months	4.9
3 months –	12.2
6 months –	22.0
12 months –	14.6
18 months –	14.6
2 years –	2.4
2½ years –	12.6
3 years or more	14.6
Can't remember	2.4

All that can be said is that the vast majority met the welfare officer at least six months after the final separation and nearly a third after two years.

In the parents' view what was the best time for the welfare officer to become involved? Most (76 per cent.) considered that it should have been earlier than it was. The remainder thought the timing appropriate, and only one thought that it should have been later. The reasons for earlier intervention can be deduced from such typical replies as:

> "He should come in as soon as possible. As soon as one party approaches a solicitor I think a welfare officer should go round and see if there's any chance of patching up the marriage. Then they could write their report on what they've seen and heard and it could be used at the first hearing."

> "They ought to come as soon as you definitely know you can get a divorce to see if you can cope all right."

> "If he came in earlier the whole job could have been done in one operation. Whether that would take up longer time in court I don't know. When it's a straightforward mutual agreement case it should be done in one operation."

> "In my case I think they came in about the right time, but I don't think it would be a bad thing if they got in on the scene right at the beginning and feel their way. I think children can be – how can I put it – can be bribed up to a point. I mean

with one of our daughters we had to play cards very coy with her for a while. She's a girl who if she had a row up here she'd have gone back to her father, and if she'd had a row with him she'd have been back up here. She's that type of girl. It might have helped to ask the welfare officer's advice about that."

"They should come in earlier – to act as liaison officers between two parents who are fighting over children. I feel they are needed to keep things peaceable – to keep the parents in touch with reality. This would help children tremendously. In most marriages when they split up like us, there is bitterness on one side or the other and it must pour over the children. If these people were brought in right at the beginning then with luck it would be stopped or at least some of the heat taken out of it."

"When break-up of marriage occurs it would be very helpful if one could feel there was a body of these people available to whom one could quickly and easily turn for help rather than be left hanging in the air until one is beginning to despair. They certainly should be available if asked for at an earlier stage – not wait until some calamity or tremendous difficulty arises."

In advocating earlier intervention, most of these parents were regarding court welfare officers as a potential source of help for the family as it adjusted to the consequences of marriage breakdown. My firm impression is that this role was regarded as more important than that of being an investigator of the children's circumstances for the court. In this context, most of the parents we spoke to regarded the time either before or after separation as the most stressful and critical. These are the times when parents as well as children are most likely to encounter accommodation difficulties and disruption in the pattern of family finance. It is also usually the crucial period during which arrangements for the children's care are decided. Parents would welcome some neutral family conciliation and advice service, linked with the court, to be available to families as soon as they separate.[9] In the earlier part of this research we asked the representative sample of 102 petitioner parents whether they thought it would be a good idea to have a special person attached to a family court of the future to whom divorcing parents and their children could turn for advice and help. Seventy per cent. of them welcomed the idea.[10]

NOTES

1. It is not possible to say whether such findings would be typical of all parents having dealings with divorce court welfare officers, since this sample was comparatively small, chosen from a particular region, and had a refusal rate of 30 per cent. There is no way of telling whether those who declined to take part were satisfied with their officer. We tried to limit bias in the sample by asking officers to approach all parents that they had dealings with over a given period. We had no independent way of checking that this had happened, but accepted the officers' word that they had in fact done so.
2. See Chapter 7.
3. See Chapter 5.
4. Margaret Wynn, *Fatherless Families* (Michael Joseph, 1964).
5. D. Marsden, *Mothers Alone* (Allan Lane, 1969).
6. V. George and P. Wilding, *Motherless Families* (Routledge & Kegan Paul, 1972).
7. See Chapter 11.
8. Mayer and Timms, *The Client Speaks* (Routledge & Kegan Paul, 1970).
9. See Chapter 16.
10. E. Elston, J. Fuller, M. Murch, "Judicial Hearings of Undefended Divorce Petitions," *Modern Law Review*, Vol. 38, p. 632, November 1975.

4 Family Reorganisation: Access

Most parents dealing with the divorce court welfare service found it helpful to talk about their own and their children's response to the marriage breakdown. The welfare officer was seen as an important source of neutral support and advice as the family adapted to the consequences of separation and divorce.

There are two major child welfare issues which can cause divorcing parents particular anxiety. First is the question of access – should the children see the absent parent, and if so, when and how often? The second concerns the children's understanding of their parents' broken marriage – what should parents tell them about the reasons for the breakdown and when should they be told? Since I will argue later that there is a need for a specialist family conciliation and advice centre linked to the court and available to help families deal with such questions I want now to consider and illustrate these matters more fully.

Access is a tremendous problem and creates a lot of anxiety. People sometimes try to cope with its complexities and distress by oversimplifying and pretending that the problems are merely legal rather than emotional. Parents, solicitors, court welfare officers and judges collude together in this pretence. This is not to say the law has no part to play.

Professional opinions about access are divided. This is partly because there is, as yet, insufficient empirical evidence upon which to formulate reliable guidelines for practitioners. That practitioners and parents are searching for guidelines can be seen for example by the provision in the Justice Report of a "Proposed Visiting Code" evidently drawn up by a distinguished paediatrician.[1] Court welfare officers too have recently begun to formulate some general principles based on their experience.[2] Valuable though these documents are, they are largely based on clinical experience which may contain bias by over-emphasising the risks of harm. They lack the confirmation that might have been available had long-term studies been made of representative samples of families affected by parental separation and divorce. Such studies are much needed and they would have to take account of many variables, which could have direct influence on the access issue and others, such as frequent moves following marriage breakdown, which might disturb children's behaviour.[3] In the absence of such information practitioners cannot answer with confidence the difficult question how the absence or otherwise of contact with the non-custodial parent is likely to affect the child's future development. Indeed we are lacking even very basic information about the way access orders work. Maidment has pointed to some of the unanswered questions. She asks:

> "What actually happens to access orders once they are made? Are they complied with? Do visits lessen in frequency or come to an end and if so why? Is it because of the attitude of the custodian or for reasons of convenience to the non-custodian? What types of relationship exists between the children and the visiting parent? The questions are legion."[4]

In the absence of information, unsubstantiated conjecture flourishes, fueled, for example, by the assertions made on the subject by J. Goldstein, A. Freud and A. Solnit in their monograph.[5] Basing their arguments on an untested psychoanalytic hypothesis, they assert that:

> "Children have difficulty in relating positively to, profiting from and maintaining contact with two psychological parents who are not in positive contact with each other. Loyalty conflicts are common and normal under such conditions and *may* (my italics) have devastating consequences by destroying the child's positive relationship to both parents."[6]

They advocate giving sole custody to the "psychological parent" who has day to day care of the child. That parent should have the right to deny access to the non-psychological parent. (This could include both biological parents in some cases.) In this way they consider that threat to the child's attachment to the psychological parent is reduced and the child's emotional security enhanced. Disregarding the possibility of children being faced with divided loyalties when two unhappy parents are living together, no-one would deny that children can be disturbed when parents are in disagreement about access. But the vital question is in what proportion of divorce cases are children likely to be so disturbed? Is it sufficient to merit a change in the substantive law regulating access? In my opinion before we make such drastic alterations to parents' rights and duties, we need to know much more about the realities of access provision in the divorcing population as a whole. In particular, we need to study more carefully those families where access works well, as well as those where it may be disturbing children.

Research Findings

Because access seemed such an important feature when considering families affected by divorce, we decided to investigate how it was actually being dealt with by the families to be interviewed in the research. We also intended to discover whether the parents themselves might have important things to say, based on their experience, which could contribute to general understanding of access and shed light on the part lawyers and court welfare officers might play in resolving access problems.

The research investigated three basic questions; namely, whether or not the non-custodial parent was having continuing contact with the child; how the decision about access had been arrived at; and whether the parents interviewed were satisfied with the arrangements. The following three tables classify the replies to these questions:

Table 14

Access – How Often Non-custodial Parents see Children

	Petitioner Study n = 102 %	DCWO Study n = 41 %
Access more than once a week	16.7	20.5
Access once a week	16.7	21.5
Access once a fortnight	7.8	19.2
Access once a month	5.9	15.4
Access 3 or 4 times a year	12.7	9.0
Access once every 6 months or less	7.8	3.8
Access on holidays only	2.0	2.8
Access taking place – sub total	69.6	92.2
No access – court denied	–	2.6
No access – other	30.4	5.2
No access – sub total	30.4	7.8

This table reveals marked differences between the two samples. In the court welfare sample access was taking place in more than 90 per cent. of the cases whilst in nearly a third of those families from the representative petitioner study there was no access. An important point to note is that in most of the non-access cases the children concerned had been very young when their parents separated. If children are of school age, it seems more likely that the non-custodial parent will wish to continue to see them. It should also be noted that whereas in the court welfare sample 48 per cent. of the children were reported as sometimes spending nights with the non-custodial parent the corresponding figure for the petitioner study was only 26 per cent.

Table 15

How the Arrangement About Access had been Arrived at

	Petitioner Sample n = 102 %	*DCWO Sample n=41* %
Agreement with husband/wife alone	30.4	30.5
Agreement made into court order ("by consent")	14.7	29.3
Court order – reasonable access	10.8	12.2
Court order – specified access	1.0	15.9
Sub totals	56.9	87.9
Irregular access – no definite arrangement	12.7	6.1
No access – by agreement	18.6	2.4
No access – without agreement	11.8	3.7

The proportion of cases in which parties reach a positive agreement to exercise access, without court orders confirming it, were almost exactly the same in both samples – almost a third. The element of consent is also present in a third of cases where parents either agreed not to see the child or where courts subsequently confirmed their agreement about it. The respective combined totals are 63.7 per cent. and 62.2 per cent.

Table 16

Satisfaction with Access

	Petitioner Sample n = 102 %	*DCWO Sample n = 82 Parents* %
Having access – very satisfied	15.7	4.9
quite satisfied	19.6	25.6
the best in the circumstances	14.7	30.5
Sub total: those with access satisfied	50.0	61.0
Having access – not very satisfied	15.7	22.0
not at all satisfied	3.9	3.7
Sub total: those with access unsatisfied	19.6	25.7
No access – satisfied	26.5	6.1
not satisfied	3.9	2.4
Combined totals		
Satisfied with arrangements	74.4	67.0
Not satisfied with arrangements	22.5	28.0
Other	1.0	4.8

In evaluating the information, contained in Table 16 above, it should be remembered that only one parent, usually the one having care of children, was interviewed in the representative petitioner sample. Therefore in this sample it is possible that the replies of respondents would have differed significantly. In the court welfare sample both parents were interviewed. The table presents combined totals for parents with and without care of children from both samples.

Analysis was made to see whether those who expressed dissatisfaction with access arrangements fell into any particular grouping. Although there is a slight suggestion in both samples that parents having care of the children are more inclined to be dissatisfied than those without, the figures did not exceed 25 per cent. in either sample, no obvious distinction between mothers and fathers being revealed. Two-thirds of parents were satisfied with the arrangements at least at the time they were interviewed. In the absence of follow-up studies it is not possible to determine whether the level of satisfaction alters with the passage of time.

Parental Views About Access

Such a bare statistical analysis gives little idea of the nature or complexity of the issues that families faced. Therefore in the remainder of this chapter, I present a number of illustrations which reveal what a difficult matter access can be.

(i) *No access*

The following quotations advance reasons for the decision not to see the child; the first from a non-custodial petitioner father of an infant child:

> "He was so young he didn't know me from Adam. All he could say was goo-goo.... I think it would be wrong to interfere with any other arrangements that my wife had made with any other man that comes along. I think it would be immoral to butt in and say 'I want to see my child.' Whereas if that child had been older it would have been different. I might have requested access then. I still pay £2.50

a week for him. Not a lot these days I know. It's obvious he's there, but to me he is just a memory."

A number of fathers, particularly in the petitioner sample, had made a deliberate decision not to seek access, sometimes even when they had formed a close attachment with the child. For example, the father of a six-year-old boy, a professional, middle-aged man whose wife was much younger, told us:

"He's an intelligent child, and I'm not saying that because he is my son. I used to take him to school in the mornings in spite of the fact that my wife was running a car. I liked walking down with him, used to get some air. Did us both good. He preferred to walk with me than go in the car. We used to talk like grown-ups."

Interviewer:

"Yet I think you told me you decided – it must have been a difficult decision to make – that you were not going to have any contact with him until he was old enough to make up his mind about things?"

"Well at the moment I don't want to have him torn between us. It's difficult to face but what good would that really do? I don't think he's old enough – perhaps about nine. If I go to see him now what's the point? You see he won't be living with me. He'll be living with my wife and I suppose this chap, so I don't want to cause any friction. I don't believe in a child being pulled one way and then the next way. That's no good for a child at all. It's just your selfish way of going on. After all a son of six-and-a-half should be with his mother, not with me. If he was 10 or 14 it would be another matter."

A mother with care of two children aged three and two when she separated from her husband:

"He never sees them. We haven't seen him for months. The woman he lives with has two children of her own. At the beginning when he first came to see the children we nearly got back together again. I'd got a new council house and we were going to make a fresh start. Then she [new wife] persuaded him not to come back and said that if he saw me

> and the kids again she'd leave him. He just sends a pound now for their birthdays. In a letter to my solicitor he said he'd disowned them. Fancy saying that!"

Another mother of young children:

> "He has never bothered to see them. The woman he's with doesn't want him to. She's got no time for children. I think I prefer it as it is now really. I think they'd be torn both ways and he'd be spoiling them if he just had them once a fortnight. But if he wanted to see them I wouldn't stop him as long as the children wanted to go."

Father with care of two children:

> "She's seen them three times since she left and each time she has left a great big mess behind her. So I've said I don't want her to see them. Since then she hasn't tried to do so. I think that's how things will stay, because it's better for me, and what's better for me is better for the children."

Some parents cease to see their children because they find the experience too upsetting. In the court welfare sample there were several mothers who gave this as their reason for not seeing their children. Thus a mother suffering from a schizophrenic illness who hadn't seen her eight-year-old son for two years remarked:

> "I was quite upset for the first couple of years. I was looking after my new husband's kiddies but I still thought is he all right; is he pining for me? When my first husband had him (child subsequently cared for by paternal grandparents) we went to see him and took him some sweets and that and when it came time to say goodbye I wished I could have took him home again with me. But I never went there again because I upset myself so much at the time. I thought if I don't see him I shall not miss him or want him so much."

Another mother who subsequently resumed seeing her children:

> "I was very upset when I first moved away; then I got used to not seeing them for a couple of weeks. I found it more upsetting going to see them again than staying away

altogether. But now I look at it from the children's point of view – that they would feel neglected if I went away altogether and it's better that they should see me occasionally even if it is a bit upsetting for us all."

One mother having left her husband for someone else went six months without seeing her children. One day she met them when her married daughter arranged a surprise meeting with the younger children. From that time onwards she saw them regularly and eventually resumed care of them after a disputed court case. She described the reunion with her children:

"My new husband and I were going to my married daughter's for a few days. Well she arranged it. You see I didn't know but she had arranged for the children to be there as well. That's how I came to see them. She had kept trying to make me see them but, as I said, it wasn't that I didn't want to see them, but I knew I would break down if I did. I kept putting her off saying 'Well, one day I will' but I didn't think I could face it. So that's how it was – we went down there to stay and there they were."

Interviewer:

"That must have been an unforgettable day?" "Oh yes, yes. They all cried and I cried buckets. The next day when we went back to Brighton I couldn't say goodbye to them. They all went out to play so I said to my husband 'Come on, we'll go now.' I couldn't say goodbye to them again you see. Well, after that I told my solicitor that I had seen them and he said 'Well now you've done it would you like to see them again?' I said, 'Oh yes, but I can't see them once a week because I can't afford it' (journey some 120 miles). He said 'Well, then, how about once a fortnight on a Sunday?' Well, that's how the access started."

(ii) *Irregular access and infrequent access*

Irregular access was almost always a source of irritation particularly to the custodial parent. One mother asked by the interviewer whether she had ever thought it best for the father not to see her small son, Philip, replied:

> "Yes, in the beginning when Philip was waiting at the windows. This was Sunday mornings. Philip used to get up early and just sit there waiting for his father to come. He used to be looking at the clock and of course eleven o'clock would come – no dad – quarter past eleven – no dad – half past eleven, the kid was absolutely out of his mind, in tears and pale, just generally screwed up thinking his father wouldn't come. After six months of this sort of thing I approached my solicitor about it 'cos it was driving me up the wall and I don't think it was doing Philip any good. The solicitor said, 'Right, we'll come to some other arrangement' and sort it out with him. Since then he's come on time and everything is okay."

Poor communication between parents such as this may prevent them talking over even a comparatively simple problem. Although in this case the matter was dealt with by the solicitor, in other similar ones welfare officers were reported as having conciliated successfully as well.

Another mother complaining about the effects of casual access said:

> "I'd rather he did see them with a proper arrangement. The children shouldn't forget him unless he makes a clean break. As it is now he comes to visit one of our neighbours, a friend of his. The little boy runs to the bottom of the garden to see him, but he doesn't visit him properly."

Likewise another mother remarked:

> "I don't think it's fair, him just coming when he feels like it. They don't know when he's going to come and see them. The children kept asking 'When Daddy's going to come and see us?' He's got a car, he should come and take them out. The way he's going now I wish he'd make up his mind – either stay away completely and not see them at all, or else come and take them out, but not just come when he feels like it."

Chopping and changing access arrangements can create resentment. Either parent can be responsible. Thus one non-custodial father said:

> "To start with we had them once a week. Then she came up and wanted them every Saturday. We had them every Sunday for a while because it was more convenient with my wife. But then she came and said she wanted them on Sundays because she wanted to visit her sister. I couldn't put up with all this changing about so I took her to court over it. They worked it out there that I should have them two Saturdays and two Sundays per month and one evening a week. I think the solicitors came to that agreement for us – but it's all very confusing."

Custodial parents were sometimes upset that the other parent saw so little of the children, particularly if they had established an identification with the absent parent. For example, a mother of a six-year-old boy remarked:

> "He does ask about his father. He says things like 'When I'm grown up I'm going to work with Daddy and I'm going to live with Daddy.' I don't discourage the child because I think I won't ever put him against his father. As it is their father doesn't really bother with the children. Although he says he loves them he doesn't come up and take them out. That really hurts me. When our little boy gets older and wants to go and live with his father I wouldn't stop him but I think then it would help if he could talk about it to somebody else 'cos it upsets me, his father being like he is with him."

Another mother having discipline problems with her two sons (10 and eight) said:

> "Quite honestly I would be quite glad if their father did decide to see them because they used to do exactly what they were told for him. He was quite strict. Being boys I would prefer them to see him even if it was only once a fortnight for a few hours just so that they know he is still their father. But he doesn't bother with them."

A mother of two girls aged four and five who had not seen their father since he left the home two years before remarked:

> "The children would like to see him. The younger one is less bothered but Karen (aged five) was very close to him and it

upset her a lot. This is especially because she is now at school with the daughter of the woman my husband now lives with. She sees the other child in smart clothes that he bought her. At first she used to tell me that she hated me because he had gone and that she would rather be with him. I had to explain to her that he wouldn't have her. She is under the Child Guidance because of it all."

Another mother exclaimed quite simply:

> "How can he be in the same town and not come and see his children?"

This father's assumed rejection of his children may have made the mother's own feeling of being rejected more intense.

(iii) *Regular but problematic access*

(a) *Divided loyalties*. A number of parents referred to the problem of their children's divided loyalty being aggravated by access. For example one mother described a conversation with her nine-year-old son about the father:

> "He's continually asking the boy to go and live with him. He's also continually asking the boy who he loves more – me or him? The child comes home and tells me. I say to him 'What do you say?' and he says 'I don't answer him.' I said 'Well, come on love, I'm not going to be cross with you.' He then said 'Well, I tell him I love him best because he lets me go to see him.' I said 'Well, it doesn't matter, it doesn't matter at all.' And do you know what he said? He said 'I'm frightened to tell him I love you best.'"

A father of two girls described the uncertainties they felt in telling him about the circumstances at home when they visited him:

> "I think the two girls haven't been too sure exactly how much they ought to tell me about what's going on at home. There have been occasions with both girls when one of them has started to say something and the other has looked at her as if to say 'you're not supposed to tell Daddy that.'"

Their father added:

> "I think this is where you have to be very careful about questioning them so that you don't put into the child's mind confusion, division of loyalties and so on. It's a very difficult situation. You naturally want to express an interest in the children, in what's going on and what's happening to them, without it appearing that you are questioning to find out if there is anything 'bad' going on."

A custodial father made a similar point:

> "She sees them once a fortnight . . . but I don't know what happens really. It was put plain by my solicitor when they reached agreement about access that the children were not to go anywhere near her new chap. But whether they've kept that up I can't say. I don't know what happens. I don't ask the children because I'm not that type of person. I don't go into what happens when they go to her and they don't talk about it. We leave it as a fallen tree."

Some children seem happiest when the worlds of each parent are kept distinct, even though through access the children themselves "keep a foot in both camps." It becomes threatening for them only when both parents meet. The mother of a 14-year-old boy who lived with his father described such a problem:

> "The boy was still terribly attached to me but of course still had loyalty to his father. He didn't quite know where he stood. He dreaded the first time when his father and I should actually meet accidentally. It did happen the other day. We were both shopping in the supermarket. He was with him and I saw them both first. I could see in the boy's face he was absolutely dreadfully embarrassed about what might happen. When we did in fact smile and said 'hello' he looked tremendously relieved. It seemed to me to mean quite something to him – the fact that something dreadful didn't happen."

For this boy the idea of his parents' meeting seems to have been worse than the reality.

Children may also protect themselves from conflicting

loyalties by carrying on a "secret" relationship with the non-custodial parent. Thus a boy living with a possessive and jealous father was reported by his mother as making "extra" visits to her which the father knew nothing about.

> "I think he misses me because he knows he can only visit me once a week. But he has taken it into his head to ride down here on his bike, pop his head round the door and say 'Hi mum, I've come to see you but don't tell my Dad 'cos he'll stop me coming.' I sense insecurity there and think it's a real shame. I wonder what they are thinking and how it's going to affect them."

There was another case where a 12-year-old girl in the care of her mother was reluctant to visit the father and his new wife. This woman, seeing it in terms of divided loyalty, tried to explain the girl's point of view to the father who felt rejected by his daughter.

New wife:

> "I don't think it's so much that she doesn't want to come. I think my husband has made her out to be more anti us than she really is. I think she is reserved and aloof, but I've seen her very close with her father. You see now she is in a very difficult position of feeling that if she shows any affection for her Daddy she is being disloyal to her mother. . . . She feels she must show her first loyalty to her mother and she feels she can't show any love for him in front of her."

Father:

> "Yes. The court welfare officer has said that it is most important that each parent should make the child feel there is nothing wrong by still loving the other parent. Unfortunately I think a lot of the trouble is that my ex-wife has given her the opposite idea."

(b) *Conditions under which access takes place.* The actual circumstances in which access takes place can be difficult and a source of resentment. There can be a world of difference between visiting children at the former matrimonial home and seeing them elsewhere. For example, one father found it difficult to visit the children in the former matrimonial home because it involved meeting his ex-wife's new husband. He said:

> "They would probably like to see more of me but it's difficult when there is another man living there. I'm lucky I suppose to have 'reasonable access' but it does make it awkward with the other chap there. He goes upstairs or into the kitchen but it's not very satisfactory. I don't feel free and easy to do what I like while he's there, and he's there most of the time unfortunately."

For people on low incomes the cost of access can be a real constraint. Not only is there the expense incurred in entertaining the children, there is the cost of travel to be considered and the time that that may take. A non-custodial mother only allowed specified access every Sunday, when asked what she did with the children, said:

> "Well I can't go far with them because up to now I haven't really had any money, but I take them fishing in the park and things like that. They always want to go farther afield but one thing is I haven't got any money and another thing between 10 in the morning and 6 in the evening isn't very long. By the time I get them down here they've only got time for their dinner and it's almost time for them to go back again."

Another non-custodial mother said:

> "The reason I stopped having them during weekday evenings is because by the time I've left work, walked to fetch them, and hadn't had time for a meal, it was such a rush. They were only at my place for just over half an hour and then I had to walk them home again for eight. Couldn't afford bus fares. I felt they were being pushed back and forth too much."

Shortage of time can act as a constraint in other ways. A non-custodial petitioner father when asked whether he knew what his children felt about the arrangements in the family remarked:

> "I haven't had the opportunity to discuss things like that in depth with them. When you are living apart from them you cannot get that sort of communication going because it

becomes a visit. I mean you want to hear everything they have been doing and they want to hear everything you have been doing, so that by the time you get down to wanting to discuss things in depth with them it's time to be away. Therefore there just never seems time. Furthermore they may well feel that things are best left unsaid – you don't want to risk stirring up emotional problems again. Provided they seem happy enough and well fed you do tend to back away from things like that. One has to be honest about it, there is also a risk of stirring up your own emotions and once that happens you can't be rational or logical in talking to them. They might not want to come again if you did that."

(c) *Spoiling and exploiting.* Another similar access problem is the suggestion, usually made by the custodial parent, that the children get spoilt when they go on visits to the other parent. In one case both parents, interviewed separately, referred to this problem, seeing it in different terms. The mother had left to live with someone else and after a few weeks the children, both teenagers, went to her. Thereafter the father saw them regularly. The mother put her view in the following way:

"He used to try and bribe them to go back with him and to say that they didn't like it here. Take the girl – weekends he used to bribe her by taking her out and buying her things. . . . He also tried to bribe the boy by buying him a bike. He said to the boy 'You can come back and I'll buy you a bike.' That made our boy stop and think, but he said 'All right. You can buy me a bike but I'm still going home to Mummy.' But they still go to their father at weekends. They go down Friday evenings and stay until Sunday evening."

When the father was interviewed he put things rather differently:

"The girl got very moody at times when she lived with me so she went up there to her mother's. Whether it's a good thing or not I'm not sure – living up there and coming to me at weekends. They treat it like a holiday or somewhere to go. It's rather difficult for me to correct them too heavily if they misbehave for fear they won't come down here so often. It's a bad influence on them in a way. You know they come down here and I tend to make a fuss of them and buy them things which sometimes I think I shouldn't, yet I'm so pleased to see them here."

Some custodial parents even encourage the child to "exploit" the non-custodial parent. For example one mother rather bitterly said:

> "No, I wouldn't deny him access. Honestly I've said to my little girl 'If you meet your Daddy, you please him; you get out of him what you can. You say you want this and that, because if you don't spend that money he'll spend it on that woman.' I mean I would never stop her seeing her father. If he wanted her for a week's holiday, he can have her, because it gives me a break and I know she is safe with him."

Similarly, another mother said she had advised her ten-year-old boy who was reluctant to see his father:

> "You go and see him for a couple of days and get out of him what you can. My younger daughter also said to her brother, 'If you don't go you won't get anything, John.'"

(d) *Continuation of the marital struggle via access.* Control over the access arrangements can be used by the custodial parent as a way of punishing the other parent. One mother who had left her husband because of his violence illustrated this:

> "Because I've applied for access every Sunday from 10–6 he has made it awkward. I've gone up on a Saturday and said to him 'It's a nice day and my Dad says he'll take the children out with me in his car.' He's just said 'No, you applied for them on a Sunday and that's the only time you can see them.' I've also asked if they could sleep with me one night. He said 'No' to that too. It's not allowed. So it's just Sundays from 10 a.m. to 6 p.m. and no changes at all."

This was the same case in which the mother reported her son making secret visits to her.[7] One quotation does not adequately illustrate this point. It was difficult to find material to use, probably for two reasons. First, it may be hard for parents to admit, even to themselves, that they are using the child to punish the other parent. Secondly, when they do realise this is a problem, they generally talk about it at great length.

(e) *Emotional disturbance of children attributed to access arrangements.* There were many instances in which parents reported disturbances of one kind or another in their children's behaviour. More usually these referred to general disturbance caused by the parents' separation or even to the marital tensions that had preceded it. Only a few parents attributed disturbances specifically to access arrangements. Nevertheless here are several illustrations:
Father looking after five children, aged six to 13:

> "I did have a problem with our Carol (aged nine). She and her brother, Timmy, used to wet the bed but we got them out of the habit before the wife left. Then all of a sudden Carol started wetting the bed again. It was about the time the wife used to come up and take them out, and it must have upset her. Whether the wife was saying anything to her or not I don't know, but after that Carol stopped going out with her mother. The mother went back to work and Carol stopped wetting the bed."

Father on visiting his children at the mother's home:

> "Well, whenever I'm with them Margaret (daughter aged five) is a lot more rebellious and cheeky to my wife than she ever used to be."

Parents often say that children show distress when they are being handed over to the other parent. For example one parent:

> "The oldest girl clings to me – she's the sort who expresses her affection you know. But the boy, he goes very quiet when I have to leave him, he's often asked to stay overnight and it's upset him when he's not allowed to."

Parting with their children and meeting the other parent in the process may be a time when parents themselves feel vulnerable.

(f) *Problems arising from children forming relationships with new partners and their children.* The children's relationships with new marital partners is nearly always a tricky matter. Yet where communication between the former partners is reasonable and trust persists it can work satisfactorily. It may also be vital that the parent can accept and trust the former spouse's new partner. The quotations suggest that the critically important relationship may be between the old and new spouse, although this may not be fully acknowledged by the parents concerned. One mother described how her new husband's children by his former marriage got on with her own children:

> "They come and visit and they love it. They talk on the 'phone and play like brother and sister.... The children are happy and mix well together. We've got a fairly good communication with his ex-wife. At first it was pandemonium; she wasn't going to allow us to do this and that. We said we wanted reasonable access, his son was pining for his father then, but it's all right now. The son is being page-boy at our wedding and his ex-wife is being really marvellous about it now. You see she accepts it a bit more."

This mother makes the point that the passage of time is often needed before the "rejected" spouse can come to terms with the marriage breakdown and develop enough emotional security to risk the children forming relationships with the former spouse's new partner.

The threat, real or imagined, that new partners can pose to the former parental coalition was often mentioned by parents who were dissatisfied with access arrangements. One father whose wife had taken the only child of the marriage, a boy aged six, when she went to live with another man remarked:

> "It really feels like not having a child. Although I see him every week it's just like taking somebody else's child out for the day. I mean I look at him and see myself in him but I've had a struggle on that one day to keep a mutual relationship going with him. You see, as I've said, she [former wife] goes with other men and that. He [child] will look up at me and say 'Oh, so and so [new man] is coming today.' Then after a few weeks she'll be with somebody else. Then he'll say 'Oh, so and so is working now all the time.' You see that's what she says to the little boy. I notice he goes very quiet when she's been having rows with the man she's been with."

Ambivalence and uncertainty about new partners and their role in relation to the children of the family is revealed in the following comment from a mother separated from her children by a possessively jealous father who was denying her access:

> "I think he [former husband] is more worried now he knows I'm getting married. I think he'll do something. He just doesn't want the children near my new chap. I don't know quite what he could do."

Interviewer:
> "How would you feel if *he* gets married again?"

> "It would depend on what sort of girl she was. If she was a nice girl, kind to the children, it would be all right. I can accept that nobody can replace Mum. I wish in some ways he really would get married. He's had several girl friends but no-one seems to stick very long. I feel things would be a hell of a lot better for me if he did have someone permanent."

Uncertainties and complexities posed to family structure by remarriage are well illustrated by the following conversation between a petitioning father and his new wife, herself divorced with the care of children by her previous marriage. The children of the other marriage remained in the care of the respondent who had recently remarried. The extract reveals some consequences for the non-custodial parent's relationship with the new partner's children which may occur when access to the children of the former marriage is denied: Petitioner father:

> "I think in possibly two years or less my son will be making murmurings that he wants to come here. My former wife remarried two months ago and a lot will depend on how it works out. I don't know anything about the chap – only that he was in the Navy for a number of years and is about 40. He might grow more antagonistic towards my children. They're not his and he's got daughters of his own. He'd be less than human if he didn't think his were the most important in the world and mine were just somebody else's no matter how

nice or nasty they were. Being in that same position myself I know how he feels. My new wife's got two children. I like them, but they are not mine. My own children I love dearly. Is that a terrible thing to say?"

New wife:

"No, I know how you feel. It's very much more difficult than for the children. Well no, I suppose it's most difficult of all for my little girl. She was just over two when my first marriage broke up. She doesn't remember her own father. The only daddy in the world she knows is Tom here (reference for interviewer to petitioner father). She knows he is not her daddy. I don't think it would be half so difficult if he had easy access to his own children. Instead all day long he's got two children around him who are not his own and his own he cannot see. That makes for a lot of difficulty and tension which shouldn't be there."

Such a case illustrates well some of the problems that arise when a couple each of whom have children by a former marriage, live together. Some kind of enlarged and ill-defined family structure is created.[8]

New partners too can find access a threat and difficult to cope with. They sometimes feel that important aspects of their partner's former marriage are being kept alive through the access arrangements. This can arouse envy and resentment. The new wife of a divorced policeman made the following comment about her new husband seeing his children two or three times a week:

"They seem to be in continual contact all the time. It's a continual reminder to me of his link with his wife. I think it would be better if we had them just a day a month just to keep in contact so that they know who their parents are."

Although access arrangements can create problems for children because of complexities formed by the new patterns of relationships, if these matters are well handled by the adults children can be helped to come to terms with them. They may even discover that the new family structure offers a network of emotional support and security. For example, a non-custodial

father and his new wife recounted the following episode about a six-year-old boy:
Father:

> "He seemed to have got it that either his mother was going to leave him or his Daddy. He has said once or twice 'Why did you leave us Daddy?' didn't he?"

New wife:

> "Yes, he said 'Mummy said you don't love us any more.' But I said to him 'Of course your Daddy loves you, he loves you very much and so do I.' And he just said 'But Mummy loves us.' So I said 'Well that's right your Mummy loves you too but you can love lots of people and lots of people can love you. You don't have to be loved by just one person.' I said 'If I love you as well you're lucky you've got someone extra, instead of having lost someone because your Daddy still loves you.' You see I was trying to get over this feeling he'd missed out on something. I tried to get the feeling over to him that instead of having been abandoned by one person, he'd actually got someone else to love him as well."

Father:

> "Since then he seems to want to come more often."

New wife:

> "Yes. He says he wants to stay a bit longer. But doesn't say he doesn't want to go home. He still regards this home as his home, but he's just more relaxed being here now."

(g) *Access and the inarticulate child.* Sometimes children can't easily explain to the parents why they find access arrangements difficult to cope with. This may increase tension between the parents as is illustrated by the following account. The father was a professional man who had gone to live with his secretary whom the children knew. The twelve-year-old son reacted against seeing his father but found it hard to tell either parent precisely why. The mother explained what happened:

> "At one stage it was having an adverse effect on Paul [son] seeing Mrs Jones [secretary] and his father together. Both the

children said to me they wanted to see their father alone. Paul never did like Mrs Jones anyway and gradually he came to not wanting to go. It got to him not going two or three times. It didn't go down very well with my husband and he used to get cross with Paul about it. That made things worse – I think he felt insecure and felt more secure staying at home with me. I tried to persuade him to go, I tried to tell him his father was still fond of him and that he ought to go, but the child was adamant. This made it very difficult because my husband was blaming me for it – I know he was – I know he thought it was my fault."

The father put his view of the problem in this way:

> "Well, Paul seems to have reacted against me. He's given various reasons to the court welfare officer and through his sisters. He's said in the past he didn't want to come because I'd asked him a lot of questions or because he doesn't like Auntie Jane [new wife] or he's anti me because I don't like Mummy. All kinds of reasons have come out – even that he doesn't like coming with his sisters because they are silly. All kinds of excuses."

Interviewer:

> "And how have you felt about all this?"

> "Very unhappy initially. Even now I feel hurt that this should have happened because I'd always believed we had a good relationship. We were close and had a lot of fun together. I suppose it's a bit of a blow to me that he doesn't still feel the same way. I'm trying to be patient hoping that the thing will sort itself out. But I realise it's not good my insisting that he stays in my company."

In this case the court welfare officer helped to resolve the difficulties. Having spoken with the boy the welfare officer was able to explain to the father how the child was seeing things. Three months later when the parents were reinterviewed by the researcher the mother reported that the father had taken the boy out on his own several times and that the children "were now accepting the situation beautifully."

(iv) *Regular and satisfactory access*

Although I have been illustrating some familiar access problems it should not be forgotten that the majority of families in which it was taking place reported it as being satisfactory. Some had had initial difficulties which had been overcome as members of the family adjusted to the new circumstances.

As one would expect, those parents who had remained on reasonable terms seemed to experience the least difficulties. For example, one father described the arrangement he had made with the mother of their eight-year-old daughter:

> "I don't know whether we are different from most people about the way we have done things. The child's mother has her during the week and I have her at the weekends. If I go away for a weekend or out on a Saturday night then I arrange beforehand with my wife for Susan [daughter] to stay at home that weekend and vice versa. Sometimes I have her for an evening during the week if my wife is going out. It just seemed the logical way."

In another case where both parents had met new partners, but still remained on good terms the father usually saw his two daughters (aged seven and five) three or four times a week including most Saturday afternoons. Both parents seemed happy about this arrangement, the mother remarking that she believed "that it was in the children's interests to carry on with both parents. They like him and Saturday has become the highlight of their week." Her only reservation was lest the children should get too fond of the father's new girl friend. It is perhaps inevitable that arrangements made when a family is in a state of flux, do not always work in changed circumstances. Thus in another satisfactory access case with both parents on friendly terms, a father commented:

> "Well, if she got married that would change the situation, but I would still keep in touch with the children. This is one of the things that worries me – what would be my rights to the children if she did remarry. If I found the bloke extremely unsuitable to bring up my two children what would I do about it?"

In the satisfied group there were a number of parents who had allowed older, usually teenage, children to make the decisions about access. The custodial parent sometimes didn't know or even wish to know when or how access was taking place. Some of these parents found that this enabled them to disengage more easily from each other, without in the process denying the child's links with the other parent. For example a mother looking after three children aged 16, 15 and nine remarked:

> "He doesn't come here, not since the divorce. Our daughter [fifteen years old] goes up to him but she never tells me when she goes. She just lets it slip now and again that she's been up. Our older boy has taken his girl friend up to see him, but I think only once. The older ones can please themselves when they see him, but he's got to come here to see the youngest and he hasn't since the divorce. I'm not complaining. As I said I ain't got no hate in me for him – he just hurt me and I just want to finish it."

Another mother explained her view about access and the decision to leave the choice to the children in these terms:

> "I didn't mind them seeing their father. After all our argument is not *their* argument. I think they should keep in contact, provided they want to. I've got two children: Christine who will go with her father Saturday and Sunday, Peter who will just go on Sunday because he has other interests which he does on Saturdays. I don't force them. If they want to go they go. It depends on the individual child."

It seems curious that these illustrations seem to show that things may work well when, or because, the parents are *not* communicating.

Access and the Long-term Welfare of the Child

This research did not intend to investigate how access or non-access might affect the long-term development of children. Nevertheless, we met several parents who, as children, lost contact with one parent when their own parents' marriage collapsed. Although it would be unwise to read too much into the effect of this on their own marriages, we noticed that each of these parents expressed strong and sometimes ambivalent views about access. Here are three illustrations: Mother of a three-year-old girl:

> "There's no arrangement about access at all. After we split up he came and saw her a couple of times. Then he didn't see her for seven months. Since then he has never made any effort to see her or enquire how she is. I think now because of his attitude it's best for her not to see him because just seeing him occasionally for five minutes will be perhaps more upsetting to her as she gets older and begins to realise who he is. Obviously she is going to wonder as she gets older. Well then it will be up to her whether to see him. But I worry about it. You see my own parents were separated and I didn't see my father for nine years. I know what she'll perhaps feel."

A mother of a five-year-old boy told us:

> "I'm lucky his father doesn't seem to take any interest in him. If he did I would do anything to prevent him seeing the child until he is 15. You see from my own experience I've been lucky because my own father protected me until I was 15 from seeing my mother. Even then I wasn't ready for it and it has sort of hurt. I don't get on with her maybe because of not seeing her all those years. If my little boy misbehaves what I try to avoid is to say 'You're just like your father.' When my own father was disappointed in me he used to say 'You're just like your mother' and that used to hurt me so."

A mother of four children who was letting the children decide about access despite a bitterly contested custody dispute remarked:

> "I resent what happened to me, not being allowed to see my father. My mother would *not* let me see him. And yet she left us on our own in a convent for three years in Wales so that she could go to London and work."

Interviewer:

> "What were your feelings about not seeing your father?"

> "The divorce was over and about a fortnight later Dad came to the house. I'll never forget it. I remember we had a glass

door. I remember trying to push past it. I broke the glass. But she wouldn't let me go to him. They had a terrible row about it and I can never remember my parents arguing like that before. I was nine at the time."

Interviewer:
"How had you got on with your father?"

"Oh, very well. I thought he was marvellous. He had a lovely voice and was always very good to me. Being a soldier he was a disciplinarian and we were brought up to respect authority but I didn't mind."

Interviewer:
"Have you ever tried to contact him since?"

"No, we moved and then we went to the convent. He went away with the regiment and we never saw him again. I promised my mother I would never see him or try to see him. I've no idea where he is and it's nearly 20 years. . . . Anyhow you can see why I'm happy that in our case the children should decide when they want to see their father."

Conclusion

The general conclusion to be drawn from all these illustrations is that access problems are often symptomatic of a fundamental dilemma facing divorcing parents. This is how to disengage from the broken marriage while preserving a sense of being a parent with a part to play in the children's future. Some can not resolve it and give up their parental role, others strike an amicable balance between these conflicting demands, and yet others argue and fight. Parenthood normally assumes a coalition between spouses. Arrangements about access reflect the way the family's social structure is reorganised, how parental responsibilities are redefined and new boundaries drawn around family relationships. These adjustments take time. They often proceed by painful trial and error before the family as a whole and its individual members can discover an acceptable equilibrium.

What it all seems to come down to is that divorcing parents must work out for themselves how much each parent is going to see the children. If children are old enough they too should have an important say in what happens. Solicitors, welfare officers and judges may have skill, knowledge and experience to help parents and children decide. Sometimes they can suggest ideas the parents haven't thought about. Thus it might be more appropriate for workers in the system to think about access in family reorganisation terms and to be prepared to adopt a fairly pragmatic approach aimed at assisting this reorganisation process. In my opinion this is preferable to thinking solely in terms of enforcing rights or of making families abide rigidly by a particular code of practice. Even so, I acknowledge that decisions enforced by court authority may on occasion introduce a much needed element of security into previously turbulent states of uncertainty. When things go wrong the calm neutral voice of reason, experience and understanding often seems to be missing. Someone should encourage the parties in the dispute to communicate in a more balanced, less anxious and defensive manner. At present in our system of family law we have generally no-one better than the court welfare officer to do this. In the future, family conciliators might do equally as well provided the powers-that-be placed greater emphasis on the value of this sort of conciliation. Much family stress might be avoided. As one mother remarked:

> "The strain on the children was pretty bad at that stage (after separation) because of the behaviour of myself and my husband. At that time there didn't seem to be very much that anyone could do about it. In fact I wish now we had gone to the court welfare officer off our own bat, but at that time we didn't know he existed. He could probably have done more than the solicitors did. I just didn't appreciate that at the time."

NOTES

1. *Parental Rights and Duties and Custody Suits* (Justice Report, Sweet and Maxwell, 1975).
2. Chief Probation Officers Conference, Divorce Court Welfare (Report by Family Law Sub-Committee) pp. 24, 25.

3. See Appendix I.
4. Susan Maidment, "Access Conditions in Custody Orders." *British Journal of Law and Society*, Vol. 2, No. 2.
5. J. Goldstein, A. Freud, A. J. Solnit, *Beyond the Best Interests of the Child* (Free Press, 1973).
6. *Ibid.* p. 38.
7. See quote, p. 80.
8. In practice, judges under the new special procedure often seem now to enquire into the children's relationship with new partners and any other children they may have before deciding the question of satisfaction. It may be that the law is moving towards a wider conception of the term "children of the family."

5 Family Reorganisation – Telling the Children

Another difficult issue facing separating parents is the question of telling the children about the break-up. Most of those interviewed in this research seemed aware that even if they had not already done so there was likely to come a point when they would have to decide whether to say something about it to the children. Those that thought it right to do so faced the added questions of when to tell them, how best to do so and what to say. Their decisions were influenced by, for example, the age of the children, what the other parent may have said, and what the children could be assumed to know already if, for example, they had witnessed major rows or fights between the parents. In the court welfare sample a small but significant group of parents (10 per cent. of the total) specifically mentioned that they had been so perplexed by the question of "telling" that they would have welcomed early advice from the welfare officer about it.

Other research evidence from studies of families affected by parental separation have reported that parents often find the loss or absence of the other parent a difficult matter to explain to children. For example, George and Wilding in their study of motherless families showed that although the majority (83 per cent.) of deserted fathers did talk to the children, many had found it difficult and their approach had ranged from "gentle and forgiving explanations to the harsh and punitive."[1] Marsden reported that about a quarter of the mothers in his sample had not said anything to the children.[2] In Gorer's study of bereavement, half the sample of surviving parents had avoided talking with the children about the death of the other parent.[3] In any case culturally many British parents find it difficult to talk with children about emotive subjects such as death or marriage breakdown. Even so the question remains; should parents grasp the nettle and try to explain their version of the break-up to the children as soon as they are old enough to have some understanding? Or is it best to avoid the risk of "upsetting" the children by ignoring the subject? That was the dilemma that many parents in our samples faced. Before considering in detail how they approach it, I wish to digress and look at a similar problem that arises in the context of fostering and adoption.

At one time in professional child care circles the dominant view was that the less a child knew about his family history and antecedents the better. The opinion was that a child should be allowed to forget painful memories of rejection and separation in order to settle down to a new life in a foster home or with adopting parents. But in the 1960s professional opinion began to change, largely as a result of several research studies of children in care.[4] These suggested that the more a child knew and understood about his past, and about the reasons why he no longer lived with his natural parents, the more likely was it that he would accept the new situation. Although the research evidence was not totally conclusive it suggested such a hypothesis. Today almost all the standard texts on adoption and fostering take the view that reliable self-knowledge is important for most children. Without it, a child's self-image may be distorted and identity formation may be handicapped by a feeling of incompleteness. As far as adoption was concerned, strong support for this line of reasoning came from McWhinnie's study[5] and Triseliotis' investigation of 70 cases of adopted adults who sought evidence about their origins from the Register House in Edinburgh, most of whom learnt of their adoption only in their teens and then often by chance.[6] The results of these researches influenced the Houghton Committee's recommendation that English law should be altered to permit adopted children on reaching the age of majority to discover details about the circumstances of their adoption provided there were safeguards for natural parents.[7] Even before Triseliotis' work, most books on adoption policy stressed the need for adopting parents to tell their adopted children as much as possible about the circumstances of the adoption and to do so from the earliest point that they are able to understand. Parents were also urged to provide frank answers to any questions children might ask about their origins, mindful that as they grow up their capacity for understanding expands.[8] Acknowledging that this is difficult for many adopting parents, adoption agencies invariably see to it that their social workers discuss the question of telling with prospective adopters and increasingly offer consultative support and advice about it.[9]

It may be premature to suggest that divorce court welfare policy and practice should be brought into line with adoption policy, even though there may be something to be learnt from it; divorce and adoption are different. It has not yet been fully established that the welfare of children of divorced parents is necessarily enhanced by knowledge of the facts. Further research is needed. We sought in the Bristol research to learn how divorcing parents themselves actually approached the issue of telling the children and how they viewed it generally. In this respect our approach complemented George and Wilding's more specialist study of fathers having care of children.[10]

Research findings

All parents were asked whether they had spoken with their children about the marriage break-up. Table 17 below classifies their replies.

Table 17

Whether Parents had Talked with Children About Marriage Break-up

	Representative Petitioner Sample	*DCWO Petitioner and Respondent*
	n = 102	*n = 82*
	%	%
No, left too quickly	3	1
No, it might upset them	8	16
No, best left to the other spouse	1	3
No, better left until children older	16	17
No, better left until children ask questions	6	4
Sub-total	34	41

	Representative Petitioner Sample *n* = *102* %	*DCWO Petitioner and Respondent* *n* = *82* %
Yes, on my own before separation	4	1
Yes, on my own at separation	13	10
Yes, on my own after separation	33	33
Yes, together with my spouse before separation	3	6
Yes, together with my spouse at separation	2	1
Yes, together with my spouse after separation	1	4
Yes, both parents known to have talked separately to children at different times	10	4
Sub-total	66	59

Approximately a third of the parents in each sample reported not having spoken to the children, fear of upset or the age of the children being advanced as the main reasons. Of the remainder who reported speaking with the children, the largest group (a third of each sample) did so on their own some time after the separation. The small group of parents who got together to talk with the children usually did so before separation had taken place. Our impression was that most of these parents remained on amicable terms with each other. We did not discover how many children were not told the facts by either parent.

As a check to the findings and in order to allow for the possibility that parents may have assumed that the child already had sufficient knowledge of the break-up and reasons for divorce, all parents were asked whether they thought their children understood about the divorce. Table 18, below, classifies their answers:

Table 18

Parents' View of Child's Understanding of Divorce

	Petitioner Sample n = 102 %	DCWO Sample n = 82 %
Sub-Group 1: Families in which children considered not to know		
False reason given for other parent's absence	2	—
Subject avoided when raised by children	6	5
Children thought to be too young	21	13
Sub-total	29	18
Sub-group 2: Families in which some or all children considered to know something		
Told a limited amount	21	24
Everything explained	16	7
Only told when they asked questions	9	2
Children saw it all happen	10	11
Children understand generally but not details	1	20
Some understand, others too young	13	12
Sub-total	70	75
Sub-group 3: Parent doesn't know what children understand	1	7

More parents in the court welfare sample thought their children would know about the divorce. This is attributable to the fact that the average age of children in this sample is higher. Apart from this the two groups are broadly comparable.

All parents were asked whether their children had ever asked questions about marriage break-up. Table 19 classifies their answers.

When interpreting these findings allowance must be made for those children considered by their parents to be too young to comprehend the break-up – 21 per cent. of the petitioner sample and 13 per cent. from the court welfare sample.[11] Nevertheless the table suggests that, according to their parents' recollections, nearly a third of the older children in each sample had not asked them any questions. We can only speculate about

Table 19

Have Children Asked Questions?

	Petitioner Sample	*DCWO Petitioner & Respondent*
	n = 102	*n = 82*
	%	%
Never	45.1	30.5
Some have asked, others not	10.8	22.0
Seldom	6.9	7.3
Sometimes	23.5	32.9
Frequently	5.9	2.4
No, children don't want to talk about it	5.9	3.7
Not known	2.0	1.2

the reasons for this. Some children no doubt had the impression the subject was too disturbing and was best avoided. Most of these children seemed to have had parents who had decided not to talk to them about the break-up.

The statistical information given in Tables 17, 18 and 19 gives an inadequate picture of the diverse issues raised by the question of telling and of the wide range of views that parents held. The remainder of this chapter therefore presents some illustrative material taken from recorded interviews.

Families in Which Children had not been told

As can be seen from Table 17, there were a number of parents who had not spoken to the children about the separation who were afraid to do so in case they upset them. Typical of this group was a father who, when asked whether the age of the children had influenced his decision not to speak to them, replied:

> "Well, no. They never seemed to question anything at the time, so I thought it best to let things just go on. It might have upset them otherwise."

Similarly, young children were sometimes given false explanations about the absence of the other parent. Thus the mother of four children, ages six, four, three and two, remarked:

"They are not old enough to understand. They think their father is away working. They ask for him but I just say he is away working, because they won't understand what divorce is all about, not at that age."

Another mother of two children aged five and nearly three said:

"I shall explain to them as soon as they ask me, as soon as they notice a difference. My husband has always done shift work and so they've never seen a great deal of him anyway. Quite honestly, I don't think they've noticed any change. At the moment, it's just a case of Daddy being at work and that's that."

The prospect of sometime having to explain things to the children worried a number of parents. For example one mother of a three-year-old said:

"He was only 18 months old when I left his father. Now my worry is, will he throw it up at me when he gets older? At the moment when other kids come here with their mothers and fathers and he says 'Where's my Dad?' I just pass it off like. He accepts it at the moment, but later on I'm going to have to say 'I had to leave Daddy because he wasn't nice.' I'm dreading this time when he can talk properly and understand."

Some of the parents who had not spoken with the children remarked that their children sometimes seemed confused by the family's arrangements. For example the mother of a three-year-old boy said:

"He is a bit young. He don't really know what have happened. I don't think he understands anything because his father pops in now and again. All he knows is that his father is living somewhere else and I'm living here with Mr. A. I think later on when he gets a bit older I will be able to explain it better. At the moment I suppose he's a bit confused really."

A mother of two boys, aged nine and five, who had separated from their father, an American airforceman, four years previously, when asked whether either child had asked her questions replied:

> "Well, my oldest one has occasionally. He said to me, 'I suppose we'll have to forget him, we don't see him any more.' I said 'Who's him?' 'That man we used to call Daddy.' But other than that he's said nothing. But I'll tell you a funny thing, our baby he'll see an aeroplane and he'll wave and I'll say 'Who are you waving to?' and he'll say 'I'm waving to Mike.' Mike and Daddy are two different people as far as he's concerned – he doesn't connect one with the other. So I don't even mention him to them. We've got rid of all his photographs. It's just a thing that's not thought about any more. I think it's better for the children that way, otherwise their minds tend to get into a turmoil."

Several of the parents who had not explained things to the children, when asked whether they thought their children understood what divorce meant, referred humorously to episodes in which their children seemed to have been testing out their appreciation of divorce in play. Thus one mother reported:

> "Well, one day we were passing the court. My son, who was seven-and-a-half at the time, said 'That's where you get divorced, isn't it?' although we had never mentioned to him where we went. One day he came downstairs and he had all the papers in his hand. 'Let's play divorces' he said to our little girl. 'You can be the secretary and you take all the particulars down and I'll be the judge.'"

Another mother said:

> "I don't know if they know what divorce means, but a funny thing happened one Saturday afternoon coming home on a crowded bus. My little boy saw a couple coming out of church just married. A little girl turned round to her mother and said 'What do you do after you get married Mummy?' My little boy said 'You get a flaming divorce, of course!' The bus went into hysterics. You see I think at that age they just think it's part of life."

Families in Which Parents had told Children

A number of parents who had spoken to the children about the marriage breakdown told us that doing so was one of the hardest parts of the whole separation process. We were given a number of graphic accounts of how children learnt of the separation. A mother with a boy aged nine and two girls aged 12 and eight, told us:

> "They were very upset when I first told them. Extremely upset. Well, I had to tell them the next morning when my husband went you see. They had seen me upset at his mother's and wanted to know why. I said that he had gone. They were very upset. Later they calmed down and they came in here [sitting room] and we sat and talked. I explained that Daddy loved someone else and that I wasn't quite sure what was going to happen. They said 'Do you think Daddy will come back?' I said 'Well, I don't know.' It was all shattering to them. They cried. It was dreadful, and I was in tears also. It was awful. Well, any way . . . I calmed down, and told them that Daddy still loved them, that he was still their Daddy and that they would still see him. But although it was a shock, they had noticed and realised the atmosphere that had been in the house for quite some months – a year or so – which had obviously affected them."

> "I had a little note from Jean [aged eight] given to me on the same day. It was typical of several they gave me at that time. It was stuck on the kitchen door. Here it is – you'll have to open it. You see what she says, 'I love you Mummy. I love you Mummy – you're the best cook in the world, Mummy.' This was the sort of thing they gave me. They felt they had to reassure me you see. . . . They were very good. They realised that I needed help as much as they did. They kept saying 'We can still be a family, Mummy, we can still have fun.'"

This extract also illustrates a point made by a number of parents, namely that children, perhaps especially when young, can be an important source of support to a parent in an emotional crisis. Shared upset can also be experienced as mutual comfort.

The majority of parents seemed to feel that it was important to give children some information about the break-up. Some did this regularly as the situation developed. For example, a fireman left with two school-aged children (nine and seven) said:

> "In a small village like this you can't keep anything quiet so it's best to tell them. I've kept them in contact with nearly everything as it's gone on."

Interviewer:

> "Did you find it difficult to talk to them?"

> "Not particularly. I thought it over carefully in my mind – how I'd approach it, what I was going to say to them, how much I'd say to them at the time, those sort of things. You see if a child found you out on a lie about something important like this just once, they'd never trust you again. If they found out from someone else in the village, and some people can be very spiteful, and if you hadn't told them, it would be an awful lot for a child to worry about."

Similarly a mother with three children, aged 11, eight and six, remarked:

> "I've never kept any secrets from them. I've moderated things a bit, obviously, but I've always been very frank with them. If the question of their Mummy and Daddy living apart is brought up, I tell them."

Some children accept things more easily than others. Thus one mother said:

> "I've always believed in telling them what is happening from the beginning and then they can accept it. Just the same, I found Cynthia [13 years old] has always been older in her ways and more prepared to accept it than her brother John [10]. He's been more upset and generally slower to accept it."

Some parents find it easier to talk only to those children who are likely to be sympathetic to their view of the break-up. Thus a mother of three said:

> "I've talked about it particularly to the girls. But as I've said, David – he's all his father. I don't say too much to him. He

> understands we're finished and that's it. But our Laura and Susan, I've had a good talk with them."

Those who talk to the children may do so in order to recruit them to their side and thus make life easier. Thus a father looking after two children and finding it a strain said:

> "I think you've got to win the children over to your side to get their co-operation. If you're lucky enough to have the sort of children you can explain the whys and wherefores to, you're half-way there."

Several of the non-custodial fathers thought that the mothers had spoken in this kind of way to the children. Interestingly, they did not challenge the other parents' accounts because they did not want to divide the children's loyalty. But there is a sense of unfairness and bitterness in their remarks. Thus one father when asked whether the children had ever asked him questions about the break-up replied:

> "No. They used to tell me why it had happened. They've said 'Mummy left because you shouted at her.' I'd say 'Oh yes, well never mind.' Mind you if there was something they wanted to know, I'd try and answer the best way I could and I'd put my view of it all."

Another father said:

> "I think the wife has explained her version of it. That seems to have satisfied them, so I've left it at that. After all they've got to live with her, not me, so I haven't told them my view of it."

One mother, when asked what she thought was the appropriate age for a child to be told about divorce, shrewdly pointing to one of the problems about telling, replied:

> "Any age, but not to bring in all the bitterness. There's a right way and wrong way to tell a child. I've told both of mine the truth. I've stuck to the facts and haven't run down their father. They believe in me now. . . . The children have known what was going on. But we haven't used them as battering rams or anything like that. I don't think either of us has ever tried to use them in our battle."

One parent in the court welfare sample had had a friend who had helped her appreciate some of the problems that can be created if children are given biased information. This friend had herself been the child of divorced parents:

> "This friend of mine said to me that she had reached a stage, about 16 or 17, when she wanted to know the truth and not be told biased stories. She asked her mother for anything in writing concerning the divorce and it had all been burnt. She said to me: 'Don't burn anything – petitions, the answers to letters, anything – when they are adult they might want to read them.' She said 'I've always had a terrible urge to know the truth and to know exactly what happened. I've only got my mother's version of it and I don't know who my father is. I've never seen him.' She said she couldn't explain this biting urge to know what really happened. She said they might never ask but if they do and they are insistent on knowing then it's there. So I've put it all in a fireproof box – everything. They'll have to ask to see it mind you – I'm not just going to give it to them one day and say 'Read that!'"

Children's Confusion about Role Changes

A number of parents reported children asking questions about the non-custodial parent's change of role. These questions revealed the kind of confusion that children may face when parents separate. For example, one mother said of her eight-year-old son:

> "When I came home from the court, he asked me if I was divorced. I said 'Yes.' He said 'Does that mean he's not our Dad any more?' I said 'Of course he's your Dad.' He said 'Whew, I was worried that if he wasn't our Dad no more he won't buy us our clothes or give us any more money.'"

Some parents seem to mislead children about the nature of these role changes. Thus a non-custodial mother asked whether she knew if her husband had talked to the child of the marriage that he was caring for, replied:

> "I think he has, yes. He must have done 'cos he's under the impression that now we're divorced I'm not his Mum no more. This is what he's been told by his friends at school as well."

Another non-custodial mother involved in a protracted custody dispute reported:

> "I think I'm the best person to talk to the children. Anyhow I had to talk to them. My ex-husband went so far as to say to them that because I had walked out and left them I was no longer their Mummy and they weren't to call me Mummy. About three weeks after getting access to them my little girl [five] wouldn't let me near her. Every time I went to pick her up she'd push me aside. So I knew I'd have to talk to her. I managed to get her on her own when she was trying to put her shoe on. I sat her on my knee and said to her 'Why don't you let me pick you up and cuddle you any more?' At first she didn't answer me. So I said 'You always used to like to sit and cuddle.' Then she said 'I'm not allowed to. Daddy said you went off and left me because you didn't love me any more and I wasn't to let you pick me up and cuddle me.' So I had to tell her that if anything I loved her even more now, because I hadn't got them during the week. I told her how her Dad and I didn't love each other any more, that we used to argue all the time and fought. I explained that when two people get to doing that they have to decide to break up. I said 'Although you probably don't understand now, you'll probably realise when you are older that it was better not to have been brought up with all that going on.'"

In Chapter 11 I examine more fully the role of the court welfare officer in helping families with the task of informing children about marriage break-up.[12]

NOTES

1. Victor George and Paul Wilding, *Motherless Families* (Routledge & Kegan Paul, 1972), pp. 56–59.
2. Dennis Marsden, *Mothers Alone* (Allen Lane, 1969).

3. Geoffrey Gorer, *Death, Grief and Mourning* (Cresset Press, 1965).
4. Gordon Trasler, *In Place of Parents* (Routledge & Kegan Paul, 1960), pp. 78–86. See also Robert Holman, "The Foster Child and Self-Knowledge" *Case Conference*, Vol. 12, No. 9, March 1966.
5. A. McWhinnie, *Adopted Children: How they grow up* (Routledge & Kegan Paul, 1967).
6. John Triseliotis, *In Search of Origins* (Routledge & Kegan Paul, 1973).
7. Children's Act 1965, s. 26.
8. See for example: (*a*) Jane Rowe, *Yours by Choice* (Mills and Boon, 1959).
   (*b*) Margaret Kornitzer, *Adoption* (5th ed., Putnam, 1976), p. 115.
   (*c*) H. D. Kirk, *Shared Fate* (File Press, 1964).
   (*d*) Iris Goodacre, *Adoption Policy and Practice* (George Allen and Unwin, 1966), p. 118.
9. See Houghton Committee Report, p. 84.
10. *Op. cit.*
11. Fifty-six per cent. of the children in the petitioner sample were under five when their parents separated. The corresponding figure for the court welfare sample was 41 per cent. By the time divorce occurred these figures had gone down to 32 per cent. and 22 per cent. respectively. See Table, Appendix I, *post.*
12. See p. 162.

6 Dissatisfaction with Welfare Officers

Only 12 per cent. of parents interviewed were positively dissatisfied with the court welfare officer. What they had to say gave further support for the view that the officer should be neutral and open minded during the course of the enquiries and subsequently, if conciliation is to be attempted. As one might expect, some of these dissatisfied parents probably had an aggravated sense of grievance because they had "lost" their case. Yet there were also others who complained strongly about the welfare officer's approach even though they accepted the decision of the court.

I have chosen two cases to quote from. Although unrepresentative of the majority, they expose the risks involved in allowing welfare officers a large measure of unstructured discretion, and they illustrate dramatically a number of critical points that I wish to discuss more fully later. It should perhaps be noted that neither of the welfare officers involved was a specialist divorce court welfare officer. Being ordinary local probation officers they may have lacked experience in this kind of work.

In the first case, the petitioner father successfully challenged the objectivity of the welfare officer's report, the court ordering a new custody hearing and a new report from a different officer. There was a dispute about four children, two girls in the care of the mother and two boys with the father. He complained about the first welfare officer on two grounds; first, that the officer's strong religious beliefs prejudiced his ability to make a balanced evaluation of a father's capacity to look after young children; second, that this particular officer had a close professional and personal relationship with the co-respondent which suggested that the officer's report might be biased. The mother, although pleased with the officer, made many comments during the interview with the researcher which in effect supported the father's allegations. Thus she said she saw the officer as "definitely on my side." She felt she could "use him for reassurance whenever upset," she "had had regular contact most weeks" during the stages of the case and had paid "at least 10 visits to his office." She told the researcher that she was "banking everything" that the welfare officer was on her side.

The following extracts are taken from the father's accounts:

> "I think it disgusting that this man had anything to do with the court. One qualification they should have is total objectivity and some legal training on the lines that the judges and solicitors have. They should not be strongly religious. I object that he is a member of...... Church [reference here to a non-conformist evangelical church]. Anyone who is so religiously committed cannot be objective. He shouldn't be able to tell me that I shouldn't get divorced because of what it says in the Bible, which is what he did. It's nothing to do with him, giving me lectures like that. Biblically, he says, the children should be with their mother. By looking after the children myself I'm going against the Bible. He also wanted to know straight away whether I was practising a religion or not. Actually I'm a Catholic so knew enough about what the Bible says to know what he was talking about....
>
> Another thing I didn't like was that this man was a friend of the man my wife went off with. I didn't like these two being so close. The welfare officer said that he would have to talk to him. He pointed out that although he knew him a lot through his work, he would still have to talk to him about our case. Now I don't like that, it's getting an opinion from one on her side not mine. So there you are, you see I didn't feel I could trust him [DC welfare officer]."

The next case was one in which the welfare officer had recommended that the care of the children, aged 12 and nine, should be transferred from the mother to the father and his new wife who had herself recently been divorced. The father was a serviceman and, during a period overseas, the mother had formed a liaison with another man. The children knew about this but had been asked by the mother not to tell the father. Subsequently he found out, moved to another locality and began divorce proceedings. By the time the welfare report was being prepared the father was planning to remarry, but there was no clear prospect that the mother would marry the co-respondent.

I have chosen to quote fully from the case for several reasons: it shows how once a welfare officer becomes biased, he cannot help the family so much. It illustrates the kind of stressful crises that can occur when families are split by decisions of the court. It also raises a number of policy issues.

When first interviewed by the researcher the mother was depressed. The event she recounted had occurred a few weeks previously. She explained how various aspects of the legal proceedings had reinforced her sense of guilt, particularly the use of a private detective who had asked her to sign a statement admitting that she was guilty of committing adultery. She commented:

> "After all these months I still feel that I am guilty. Even Mrs. Jones, the welfare officer, makes me feel guilty. I feel she's been judging me morally. I feel as though I'm walking around with guilt written all over me. My family rejected me at first too, but it's not so bad now."

Such a comment suggests that she saw the welfare officer as part of the social apparatus that labelled her an adulterous mother. The welfare officer filed her report recommending that the children should be placed in the care of the father. The mother's solicitor wrote asking her to call to see him so that he could explain the contents of the report. It was a shock to her. She remarked:

> "I must admit when my solicitor told me about the children being taken away I was so upset I didn't really hear much more of what he had to say about anything after that. I was staggered. You see when she [welfare officer] came to visit me I didn't have any idea what was going on in her mind, whether she thought the children would be better off with their father or what. I had no idea what was going to be in her report. I expect it's their training to be like that. She didn't show me anything. It was such a shock getting it from the solicitor. When I heard about the report on the children I

cried in front of him. He carried on reading and talking as though nothing had happened – he was young – I probably embarrassed him."

As a result of the welfare officer's recommendations the solicitor suggested to the mother that it might be wise to agree that the children go to their father. The mother in a confused state went home to talk with the co-respondent, Paul:

"In the evening Paul came over. He was angry at some of the things that had been put in the report. I think Mrs. Jones felt that my husband was settled in a house with this other woman and was more stable there than I am here with the children. Paul doesn't live here all the time and we haven't decided whether we are going to get married and buy another house and that sort of thing. All this was in the report. That evening I was upset again, but Paul was of the opinion that I should let the children go to their father for a while and try again for them when things are a bit more settled."

This was how things were when the research worker first interviewed her. A second interview was arranged to follow shortly after the court hearing. This is the story the mother told them: Several days after hearing of the welfare officer's recommendation she spoke to the children. Her son, Michael, aged 12, said that he wanted to go and live with his father. The nine-year-old daughter, Tina, seemed undecided:

"I've talked to them and so has Mrs. Jones. I think it was silly for her to do so. She put too much weight on what they said. She asked them who they wanted to live with . . . one moment the nine-year-old wants to live with her father, the next she wants to live with me. But Michael seems set on living with his father I must admit. I was not trying to persuade them either way. They could probably see that I was upset. They said 'We'll all come and see you lots of times.' Tina said she didn't mind who she lived with. I don't think she wanted to make a decision. I don't think it's fair to ask children to have to make a decision of this kind between parents."

Some of her friends advised her to dispute the case and go to court, but her solicitor counselled against it saying that if she lost it might prejudice a later claim for custody. He also advised that the court was unlikely to go against the firm recommendation of the welfare report. During this further interview the solicitor again read parts of the welfare report to her. This time she comprehended more of it:

> "He read more parts of it out to me – it sounded pretty awful – but it wasn't given to me to read."

Interviewer:

> "Do you think it should have been?"

> "Well, I think I should have been entitled to it. It was about me and my children. If there was anything to be said surely it could have been said to me, rather than written down for other people to read."

At this interview she accepted her solicitor's advice and withdrew her claim for custody and did not attend court. A few weeks later the court ordered that the father should have custody, care and control. Although the children had three weeks of the spring term left at their schools before the Easter holidays, the father made arrangements to move them to his house some 80 miles away two days after the hearing. The mother described the way the children were handed over, and the part the court welfare officer played:

> "It was awful. I've never known such an absolute shambles. I had a 'phone call. They went to court on the Thursday. On the Friday I 'phoned the solicitor and he said 'Well, your husband's got the custody of the children, he'll be wanting to take them. He can take them really whenever he wants.' And I'd just assumed that he'd let them finish out their term at school, they only had two weeks to go to the end of term. I had a 'phone call from my husband that afternoon. 'Pack the children's suitcases, have all their stuff ready, I'll be there to collect them 12 o'clock the next day.' I just couldn't believe it – it was a shock to them. Anyway I did get their stuff ready. There was nothing else I could do – I was in a daze. I couldn't believe it. So I had the Friday afternoon off because the children were at school and the teachers didn't know – I mean they had to be told and I was in such a state I didn't

know whether I was coming or going. Paul and I drove out here to make sure my husband hadn't come to the house. I was a bit worried he might try and empty the house while I was at work which he could have done. And I went to Tina's school and I couldn't even see the headmaster because I couldn't have talked to him you know I was that upset. I went back into the car and Paul told them Tina would be leaving that afternoon, and she wouldn't be back again. The headmaster was furious, he was so angry. He was angry with Mrs. Jones too because he'd already told her that it would be a bad thing for Tina to be taken from the school. She's a backward reader – and he thought it would be best if she was left at that school. Mrs. Jones obviously ignored it completely – I think that wasn't even in the report. Then we drove to Michael's school, that headmaster was pretty furious as well. He said he'd never heard anything like it, that he should be just taken one day. So, of course, everything had to be packed and they left school all in a rush."

She then described the hand-over of the children to her husband. To her surprise Mrs. Jones, the welfare officer, was present:

"I had their things ready. I had done some shopping and Paul and I came back in time with the children to have their stuff ready. Paul said 'I won't stay.' He didn't want to stay because it was really something between me and my husband. So Paul went off to the local in the village. He walked in the door and who should be there but my husband, a friend of his and Mrs. Jones, the welfare officer, all sitting in the pub. So they all came out. Paul said he had a go at her saying 'What on earth do you think you are playing at taking the children from their mother within hours without any preparation whatsoever and without letting them leave at the end of term or anything.' She evidently said she thought it was the right thing to get it over with quick. Anyway Paul came back to me saying 'I'm not leaving you on your own with the three of them here.'

I was quietly in the bedroom with Tina packing her things and there was such a rumpus when they arrived. I turned round and there was Mrs. Jones. They were all there just straight in the house you know. I thought this was something between me and my husband, what on earth was she doing? She said 'I came in case there was trouble.' But what trouble? I had agreed. I was hardly likely in front of the children to start shouting and rowing with him. . . ."

At this point there was a pause in the narrative because the mother started to cry. A little while later she was more collected and the story continued:

"And yet she came into the bedroom and said 'Come along Tina.' She said 'I'll take Tina with me.' She said 'Say good-bye to your mother.' Of course Tina became hysterical. She was breaking her heart. Mrs. Jones took her and put her in the back of her car and left her parked outside there. Michael by this time was crying too. So she said 'Get your things Michael. I'll take them off down the road away.' Michael obviously wasn't moving fast enough. She said 'Come along Michael, hurry up.' I mean, poor child he didn't know what he was doing. It was so rushed. He said 'Oh, I need my football boots – I need this, I need that.' It was an absolute shambles."

Interviewer:
"And then they left?"

"There was a man I'd never seen before emptying my garage of children's stuff – packing it in the car. He never so much as looked at me. I went out to the gate. Tina was crying and jumping up and down in the back of the car. I wanted to get out to her. Mrs. Jones stood with her arms across the gate. I had to move her arms out of the way to get past. I thought none of this need have happened if she hadn't come. Paul said something to her about moving to let me get out to Tina. She was breaking her heart in the back of the car. I thought there she is shut in the car and no-one taking any notice of her. So I went out and spoke to her. Anyway they got everything into the car and Michael into the back of his father's car. Mrs. Jones drove off with Tina in the back of her car on her own.

"After it all I thought what was Mrs. Jones doing having a drink with my husband? I felt if she hadn't come the children would have gone without all the upset. I mean I had agreed. It wasn't as if they had to be taken forcibly. Mrs. Jones just spoke to me and made out her report. She never said to me she would be making such and such recommendations – nothing at all. It was just a case of talking to me, then going away and making up her mind. Then I didn't see her again until the day they took the children. I felt she was completely in favour of my husband. I don't think she knew him well enough to know his real reasons for wanting the children. She said the pressures on the children here were too great – but what pressures? Are the pressures here any greater than those there with his woman's divorce underway and the pressures of her children? I don't really know what she means by all that."

Three weeks after this episode the children returned to spend their Easter holidays with their mother. They had told her they liked their new schools. The mother reported that the children seemed to have settled well but that Michael particularly seemed more pleased to see her than Tina.

This case highlights three important and contentious questions about divorce court welfare work. They are as follows:

(1) Should parents see the contents of the welfare officers' reports?
(2) Should courts invariably follow the recommendations made in the welfare officers' reports?
(3) Should divorce court welfare officers be drawn from the probation service?

These questions will be examined in the next three chapters.

7 Welfare Reports – Should Parents See Them?[1]

If divorcing parents are in conflict about their children or even if they are not, the court has a duty to be satisfied that the arrangements for the future welfare of the children are satisfactory or the best that can be devised in the circumstances.[2]

The Matrimonial Causes Rules 1973 governing, *inter alia*, proceedings for divorce, judicial separation and nullity are clear. Rule 95(1) enables a judge or registrar at any time to refer to a court welfare officer for investigation and report any matter arising in matrimonial proceedings which concerns the welfare of a child. Rule 95(3)(*b*) says that after the court welfare officer has filed his report, the registrar shall "notify the parties that they may inspect it and may bespeak copies on payment of a prescribed fee."

What then was the intention of the Senior Registrar's Direction No. 4 of June 1973 which states that:

> "Copies of reports by Court Welfare Officers which are supplied to parties or solicitors must be boldly marked: 'Confidential Report to the Court – Not to be Published' "?

It could hardly have intended that the report was not to be published to the parties because both the Matrimonial Causes Rules and the Direction itself specified to the contrary. Yet that is the interpretation which has been adopted by many lawyers and welfare officers.

During the pilot work we discovered a number of instances where one or both parents had not only not received a copy of the report but had even been denied sight of it. In some cases, the parties' solicitors were reported as having told their clients that it was against the rules of the court for them to see the report because it was "the property of the judge." This was confirmed during interviews of our court welfare sample of 42 couples. It was found, at least in the places where the research took place, that such practices were widespread:

Table 20

Numbers of parents who did or did not see the Welfare Officer's Report

Total sample: 84 parents (42 couples)	
Parents who did not see the report	60
Parents who saw report	
(a) shown by solicitor	19
(b) saw it by chance	3
(c) unrepresented respondents receiving report direct from court	2

Of these 42 couples there were 14 where one parent only saw the report and only five cases in which both parents had seen it.

Even the minority of parents who did see the report did not always do so with the approval of their solicitors. One mother explained how she had seen it by chance at the court on the day of the hearing:

> "Well, I saw it yesterday because my solicitor went off for a chat with my husband's solicitor and I had a good read. But you're not supposed to. It's for the judges' eyes only, so he told me. But being inquisitive, if things are left there – why not? I thought it very fair from my side anyhow."

Her husband, when asked whether he had seen it, replied:

> "No, you're not allowed to see it by law. I saw it upside down on the solicitor's desk (I can read upside down, although he didn't realise it). I asked if I could see the report and he said no. He read something out, and then put it down, and I thought – that's funny, I'm sure I'm allowed to see it. But it said 'Property of the Court, not to be communicated in any way, shape or form.' If it was found that it had been communicated to me then my solicitor would be in trouble with the court."

A number of parents explained that their solicitors had told them they were not permitted to show parents the report, but could read bits from it or summarise its content. Thus one mother said:

> "No, I didn't see it. He said he wasn't allowed to show it to me but that he could tell me what was in it if I wanted to know."

Her husband had not seen it either but had its contents summarised by the court welfare office. Another mother said:

> "My solicitor had it today and he explained it was confidential and of course he couldn't let me see it. I was disappointed."

In a subsequent interview she said that the welfare officer explained that she did have a right to see the report and had offered to come and show it to her.

A father who was interviewed twice had been told on the first occasion by the research worker that he did have a right to see the welfare report. At the second interview he recounted what happened when he told this to the solicitors:

> "I said 'I've been given to understand I can see this report.' He said 'You're not – I've told you.' And I said 'Well, why not?' and he said 'Because it's private and confidential. There could be things in here written by the probation officer that could be libel to your character and you could prosecute.' I said 'Well, that's a bit hard on me if I want to comment when I to go court.' So I was a bit upset about that. But I didn't see it and he refused to let me see it, so I said 'Oh well, I don't know where I stand now.'"

These excerpts illustrate the confusion about this matter. Many parents do not know whether they have a right even to see a welfare report. The note about confidentiality attached by the court to the top of each report seems to be interpreted by some solicitors as meaning that parents are not allowed to read it. One mother, when asked whether her solicitor had explained why she was not allowed to see the report, said:

> "No, I don't know why you're not supposed to see it. It's a bit silly if you can't see it yet he can discuss it with you. I don't understand it. I mean it's the same thing as seeing it. He could read it word for word and say he was discussing it with you – as long as you don't look at the piece of paper."

We asked the 84 parents whether they thought they should have a right to see reports. A clear majority, 53, thought that they should, whereas only 14 thought that they should not. A further 17 parents were undecided about it. Typical of the many who would have liked to see the report was a mother who said:

> "No, I didn't see it and I think I should have done. I think if you see these things and there's something you don't agree with, you have the chance to explain it. If there is anything in these reports that you have to answer to, you should have the right to see just what it's about."

Another said:

> "If there is anything detrimental to me I would rather know, because I'd rather put my mistakes right."

Other parents said they should see the report because, after all, it concerned them. As parents they asked why shouldn't they know what was being said about the future of their children? Yet it was characteristic of most of those whom we interviewed that they accepted the inevitability that the report was secret and confidential. As one ex-sailor put it:

> "It's very like in the navy in a way. You get two lots of documents on your behaviour while you're in the navy. They show you one and tell you you've got a 'very good.' The other you don't know the details of. But I think you ought to know what's in the report, yes."

Some parents who did not see the report regarded it as positive concealment which reflected adversely on the character of the welfare officer. One rather bitter father said he thought it was typical of his welfare officer's "hide-and-seek" personality. But there were also a number of parents who had a fair idea that the report had positive things to say about them who would have liked to have seen it in writing as useful confirmation of their good parental qualities. Parents after divorce probably need encouragement of this kind. A father who had had the report read to him by his solicitor said:

"I wish I could get my hands on it actually – you couldn't have wished for a better report really. What he put in for us ... I mean it would be a good reference. You'd get a job anywhere with a report like that!"

It should not be forgotten, however, that there is another side to this coin. Parents might be discouraged by seeing adverse comment at a point when they are vulnerable and in need of encouragement. The minority of parents who felt they should not see it mostly took the view of the mother who said:

"I told the welfare officer the truth and I'm prepared to trust the authorities."

We interviewed no-one who, having seen the report, regretted having done so. Several were glad to have had the opportunity to correct factual errors which they had noticed. For example, there was one case where the report incorrectly referred to a mother having had an abortion before she married. The mother's solicitor had not questioned this, but the mother did when she read it.

If solicitors are unfamiliar with the Matrimonial Causes Rule 95(3)(*b*), it may be that the Senior Registrars' Direction in June 1973 and the note attached to the report saying "Confidential Report to the Court – Not to be published" gives them pause and invites misunderstanding. Parties are entitled to expect solicitors to know their job. An expanded note would have avoided confusion.

One can understand very well that some solicitors may find it embarrassing to discuss with the parent the welfare officer's views particularly if they expose some of the parent's shortcomings. A solicitor who keeps a report of this kind secret would, of course, protect himself from this embarrassment. An alternative approach would be to send on the reports direct to their clients, as some solicitors do. One mother, who had been shown the report by her solicitor, disagreed with the comments of a school teacher contained in it:

"He painted a picture that my children were proper little tearaways, which was very upsetting for me. I felt like going down to the school and having it out with the teacher, but my solicitor said 'Don't, these things are fully confidential.' He said 'I feel you should see this, but this is their opinion' so, anyway, I just forgot about it."

Whatever reasons solicitors may have, welfare officers seem to be divided about the wisdom of allowing parents to see reports. Practice Direction No. 4 was issued only after the Chief Probation Officers' Conference had expressed disquiet that the information contained in reports was being disseminated beyond the parties. Conversations with welfare officers reveal that some support a policy of openness, while others argue for secrecy. Only a minority consider that parents should have an absolute right to inspect the report. Thus research by Birks in 1976 revealed that the majority of officers in his sample (78 per cent.) of 82 favoured giving parents a "general impression" of what they intended to report to the court, but that when it came to giving parents sight of the report officers were far more divided. Birks reports "a definite reluctance" against the idea of the officer who prepared the report giving it to the parents. The majority felt that parents should only be shown it at the discretion of either their solicitor or the court.[3] Sixty-eight per cent. opposed the idea of parents having an absolute right to see the report.

The Case for Openness

The main argument for openness is that it is a fundamental principle of our traditional adversary mode of trial that the court should only act on evidence which is presented to it and which the parties themselves or their legal representatives have had the opportunity of testing. There is no place in such a system for secret or private information available to the judicial authority denied to the parties. As Edmund Burke said "Where mystery begins, justice ends."

This is, of course, the principle which, in criminal proceedings, governs the normal practice of probation officers showing their social enquiry reports to offenders. A number of them apply the same principle to their divorce court practice. As one officer put it:

"I never put anything down on paper that I'm not prepared to let people see or challenge."

Some officers go further than this and argue that the first person to show the report to the parties should be the welfare officer and not, as at present, the solicitor. They would argue that a policy of openness not only accords with the principles of our mode of trial but is also the best way of establishing the trust of the parties and helping them to accept what might be unpleasant court decisions. This can be particularly important if the court welfare officer is to be needed later for conciliation purposes or supervision.

One mother reported to us how the welfare officer had told her, before the court hearing, that he was going to recommend that her children should stay with their father. This had caused her deep anguish. Yet by being told what he was going to say in his report, she was enabled to anticipate the court's decision and to accept more easily the reasons for it. She was asked whether she thought it a good thing for the welfare officer to have done this:

"Yes, I do. I felt it was good because I wasn't going into court raw. I was going to court prepared because I knew what was going to happen. I had a terrible battle with myself, trying to decide whether to fight or whether to go ahead with the claim for custody or whether not to."

Interviewer:

"Do you think it was easy for the welfare officer to tell you what he was going to say in his report?"

"No, I don't think it was because he's a sensitive man. I like him very much as a person. He said 'You probably won't agree but I have my reasons for doing it' and he told me the reasons. He said 'I'd rather you kick me now than when we go to court.' I think he's very shrewd. That night I could have killed him. I hated him when he went. But he definitely did the right thing by telling me. It put me in a position where I had to make some sort of decision as to what to do at court. That took a lot of heartsearching because obviously I wanted to fight to the bitter end to get custody of the children. But I

> knew that if I fought there'd be an awful lot of bitterness and loads of affidavits, nasty, cruel affidavits. It causes a lot of ill feeling. There's enough of that as it is."

In this case, the court subsequently ordered joint custody with care and control to the father. When access was later disputed, the welfare officer was brought in by both parties as a conciliator.

The Case for Secrecy

As Birk's research shows, a number of welfare officers take the contrary view – namely, that provided the parties' solicitors see a copy of the report, it is better for the parents themselves not to do so.[4] They substantiate this by arguing first that it guards against the possibility of the information contained in the report being used later by a vengeful disappointed parent to hurt the child. Also people may talk more freely if they feel their information will be confidential to the court. This applies to school teachers, doctors and family friends, for example. But it applies particularly to parents and children who may feel that the remnants of their relationships would be put in jeopardy if their views were disclosed. As one parent said:

> "My solicitor did quote small passages that he thought were relevant, but the actual report itself I don't know what it says. That is something purely for the assistance of the court. He's making a highly confidential report on two separate parties. The welfare officer might say something which, if it came out, might cause far more friction than good and he's supposed to be doing good – not creating friction."

It is also argued that only by reports being regarded as confidential can strict control be exercised over their dissemination. One chief probation officer wrote to me that:

> "a number of instances had occurred – a particular one in a Plymouth pub where the Welfare Officer's report became the subject of pub gossip, a copy of the report having been sent to the client by his solicitor. There was a genuine fear that a lot of harmful gossip – if nothing worse, for instance the risk of

> blackmail – might arise if the circulation of reports was not in some way restricted to the court."

Court officers too have told me of occasions where harm has resulted from disclosure of things in the report: for example, in one case a man in prison learnt this way that his wife was having an affair with another man. As another chief probation officer has said:

> "The problem is not so much what you say about A, but rather what A sees you have written about B."

Another reason sometimes advanced for not letting parents see the report is that some welfare officers might feel inhibited from offering the court a frank assessment of their opinions if they knew that parents were going to read it. This may be especially so where an officer is apprehensive that his views might give offence to a parent with whom he wished to remain on good terms. These officers claim that if welfare officers have to be cautious about what they say and how they say it, the court may be deprived of the clear, unambiguous statements that it needs if it is to discharge its duty to protect the interests of the children.

This research in three South-western counties suggests that the Senior Registrars' Direction No. 4 of June 1973 confuses people and leads them to ignore the Matrimonial Causes Rules. It appears to be exceptional for parents to see welfare reports about their children. This removes the parents' right to challenge or test the veracity of the report's contents. A solicitor cannot know as much about his client's circumstances as the client himself. If parents have not read the report they cannot tell their solicitor about any factual errors.

Another objection to the practice of secret reports is that it can so easily be used as a device to protect, not so much the children, as the welfare officers. As one of the officers interviewed by Birks very honestly said:

> "I discussed the general content of the report but did not show the report because I did not have the courage."

This practice shows that our system of justice, when applied to family matters, is not as open as it purports to be. As this investigation has discovered, this can contribute to a cynical mistrust of the judicial system felt by some parents or the sense of apathetic helplessness at the hands of authorities felt by others.

Whatever the arguments for a policy of openness or secrecy, there is no justification for the present inconsistent practice. At present the advantage lies with unrepresented parents since they are always sent a copy by the court. Such circumstances seem tailor made to aggravate a sense of injustice, since parents are not being treated in an even-handed fashion.

It is true that in the wardship case of *Official Solicitor* v. *K.*[1965] A.C. 201 and the adoption case of *Re P.A.* [1971] 1 W.L.R.1530 it was held that interested parties do not have an absolute right to see confidential reports. In those cases it was established that judges have a discretion to refuse parents the sight of the report if real harm might result to the child from the disclosure. Thus in *Official Solicitor* v. *K.* at page 211, Lord Devlin said:

> "In my opinion confidential reports should not be submitted as a matter of routine, but only in exceptional cases where disclosure of certain information would be harmful to the infant."

Two points follow from these cases. First, they suggest the discretion of the court to restrict a parent's right to see a report is to be exercised with caution and only exceptionally. Second, these precedents only apply to adoption and wardship since in divorce the wording of the Matrimonial Causes Rules states that the parties have a right to see welfare reports.

Behind the divergence between the rules and the practice lurks a fundamental clash of principle and approach. The basic argument is between those who believe in open justice and those with a more paternalistic philosophy who want the welfare authorities to be trusted with the responsibility of preparing reports that should be for professional eyes alone.

There might be a fairly simple practical solution to this problem – a solution which both respects the rights of the parents and acknowledges that on occasion undesirable disclosure of a report's contents can adversely affect the interests of children and perhaps third parties as well. Instead of writing one long continuous report, evidence given by individual parties as well as the welfare officer's conclusions should be reported on separate sheets. Then at the very least parties should have the opportunity of checking the evidence attributed to them and seeing the welfare officer's conclusions. Parts of the report could be detached if the judge thought in exceptional cases that the interests of the child would be harmed by full disclosure of the whole report to a particular parent, subject to the safeguard that solicitors should be entitled to argue for or against full disclosure. That part of the report could be withheld but only by order of a judge following the recommendation of the welfare officer. The judge would have to give his reasons. Welfare officers themselves should be encouraged to show and discuss their reports with both parents whenever possible before the court hearing. The person who writes a report is best placed to explain it. In any event a more explicit practice direction is urgently needed.

Since the extension of the special procedure in 1977, an informal practice has developed, whereby welfare officers make confidential enquiries to various social agencies. The parents do not know. As a result of this practice in certain courts judges may have before them at the children's appointment secret information about the family. I discuss the implications of this practice more fully in Part Three.

NOTES

1. This chapter was first published as an article in the *New Law Journal*, 31 July, 1975.
2. Matrimonial Causes Act 1973, s. 4 (1).
3. J. Birks, *The Role of the Divorce Court Welfare Officer* (Unpublished M.Sc. thesis, University of Bristol, March 1978).
4. Ibid.

8 Implementation of Welfare Officers' Recommendations

It is commonly assumed that courts with jurisdiction in family matters proceed on the basis that it is for the judge to decide cases coming before him, according to the nature of the evidence and his interpretation of the law. It is for the welfare officer, when requested by the court to do so, to investigate the circumstances of the children and to provide a report containing evidence about them. It is now normally accepted that welfare officers can express their own opinions about this evidence in their report. Although it is still a debatable issue, many courts accept the practice of welfare officers recommending in their reports that the judge should follow a particular course of action. All this falls short of the welfare officer assuming the role of judge himself. Yet this research and one at Oxford have uncovered practices which suggest that that is what is beginning to happen.[1]

The Oxford study of court records revealed that of all cases in which welfare reports were prepared 70 per cent. in the English sample contained clear recommendations about the children's residence and all the Scottish reports did so. The authors noted that judges usually followed these recommendations. They comment:

> "Where judges follow the suggestions of Welfare Officers, it is not clear what function they are performing: when, as occasionally happens, they depart from the suggestions, it may be asked whether they are better able to make the judgement than the officer."

The Oxford analysis of court records confirms our finding that many parents had good reason for believing that the court would follow whatever the welfare officer recommended in his report. Some claimed that their solicitors had told them that "what the welfare officer says goes" and on the strength of this had been advised to settle out of court. Thus one father told us:

> "The report was called for by both our solicitors before the custody. What they decided was rather than go to the expense of a custody hearing, get a welfare report and depending on its recommendations go from there. As a result of this I then dropped the case. That was the only reason I stopped the case."

In another case a father, seeking the care of two school-age children, was not told the altered date of the court hearing by his solicitor. This is what he said happened:

> "Well, he didn't even let me know. The next thing I knew was that I got a letter saying the children were to stay where they were with my former wife and I had joint custody. He [solicitor] told me later that even if I had been there I wouldn't have been able to do anything. It was all done on the welfare report and they do what the welfare man says. Apparently the two solicitors having seen the report had worked it all out together before the court. I was very annoyed about it I can tell you. The judge went on the written evidence and the welfare report. Whether this is usual I don't know. According to my solicitor it was. They don't necessarily interrogate the parties concerned."

If this man's account is correct the practice of the solicitors concerned was grossly improper since the father had every right to be heard.

It is not possible to say how widespread is the practice of settling on the basis of the welfare officer's report. No doubt sometimes when it occurs it is perfectly acceptable to the parties. Yet, as in the two instances quoted above, there are occasions when the practice leaves at least one parent with an unsavoury taste of having been denied open justice. Injustice may be aggravated in other ways. First, the parents may be denied opportunity to see what was in the welfare officer's report. Secondly, they may not be present at the court hearing or present when solicitors reach settlement on their behalf. Thirdly, they may be deprived of the chance to cross-examine the welfare officer about the evidence because the officer in question did not attend court. Fourthly, delays may occur and things may have changed since the welfare officer wrote the report.

In the sample of 41 cases known to welfare officers we were given illustrations of all these points; sometimes they occurred in combination. For example, in one contested custody case we were told independently by both parents that the court had decided to allow their boy to remain with his father, after an adjournment for welfare report, on the basis alone of that report and further written affidavits. Neither parent had seen the welfare report. The mother told us:

> "I didn't ask to see the report, because I expected a hearing to take place, and I thought that the report would be read out to both parents then. But of course this never materialised at all. I certainly thought I would be given some information. I would have liked to have known what the boy himself had said. Perhaps it would have been rather painful. But I was absolutely flabbergasted when I realised it had all gone through with no hearing. I wasn't even informed of the decision. I was still waiting. In fact if it hadn't been for my going to the solicitor again about the property I still wouldn't have known."

I have been advised that, given the facts as stated by the parents, the mother might well have had grounds for appeal.

It will be seen in this case, as in another already quoted (see p. 130), that the decision was reached after an adjournment for further evidence. In each case the parties were not recalled when the court reconvened. No doubt, from the point of view of the judge and the lawyers, it was unnecessary for the parents to be present once they had given their evidence even though they had a legal right to be there. But the parents were left feeling they had been excluded from their own case, left ignorant of later developments and finally presented with the decision.

A sense of injustice may also occur if the welfare officer is not present in court to be cross-examined about his report. A number of parents were clearly surprised and disturbed that the welfare officer having made the enquiry, was absent when the case was heard. Thus one father remarked:

"If I had to go to court over the children I think he should be in the court too. They should not just have to read off a bit of paper what he's put down. You can't always exactly put down what you think on a piece of paper can you? It sounds a lot better if you are there."

In another case we were told of an instance when the judge in chambers asked for a further report, because the welfare officer, who was not present, had given no indication in his report what the child in question thought about the dispute between his parents. The father remarked:

"The upsetting part is that had he [the welfare officer] either turned up at the hearing or given a fuller report there wouldn't now be another delay and another hearing. I think that was a very grave omission. Having given a report on something so important they certainly ought to be at the hearing. Suddenly double the cost because the probation officer didn't turn up! Everyone expected him to be there but no-one knows quite whose job it was to ask him."

In our sample there were other reported instances of adjournments in order to ask a welfare officer to be present to testify in person, thus adding to the cost of the case.

In how many cases does the welfare officer attend the chambers hearing? By the time the research was completed 31 welfare reports had been considered. Twenty-one of the welfare officers had not been in court.

Probation officers spoken to about these cases point out that attendance at court can be a very time consuming business, and, as it is, they are carrying an ever increasing burden of reports. Therefore they cannot be expected to attend court on every occasion. If court hearings were better organised so that people always knew approximately when a case would be heard, welfare officers might be able to attend more often.

The principles of welfare practice in this respect were explored in the 1936 report of the Departmental Committee on Social Services in Courts of Summary Jurisdiction. At that time it was clearly expected that in matrimonial hearings before magistrates the probation officer would be in court to present his report in person. The report stated:

> "The court should be entitled to receive a full report from the Probation Officer. The report should be in writing and copies should be supplied to the parties. In order to ensure that the parties are given their right to challenge the report, the Probation Officer should go into the box and be sworn and either read his report aloud or state that its contents are true. He should be liable to be cross-examined by either party. . . . Any statements in the report that are challenged should be disregarded unless they are within the Probation Officer's own knowledge or can be proved by some other means."[2]

One can easily understand why courts wish to spare busy welfare officers the cost of unnecessary attendance at courts. But the evidence of this research suggests that this is not the only reason for non-attendance. Welfare officers have told us that they are often not informed when the hearing is taking place,[3] and often don't know the result of the case until by chance one of the parties informs them. There may also be other reasons. It may be tactically advantageous to solicitors if the welfare officer is not in court to be cross-examined. We have spoken to some solicitors who take the view that unless their client has a very strong case it is likely to be counter productive to dispute the welfare officer's findings or challenge his impartiality, objectivity and professional judgement.[4] This may particularly be the case where the welfare officer is a familiar figure in the court, where his motives are assumed to be benign, and where he is known and trusted by the judge.[5] The absence of the welfare officer at court may also sometimes make it easier for solicitors to persuade their clients to accept the officer's written report as a basis for settlement. They could argue that to summon him to court would involve further adjournment, delay, extra cost and prolong the worry and uncertainty about the outcome. Judges are hardly likely to complain even if the basis for the consensus between the parties is wafer thin. The absence of the officer in court prevents the judge himself from examining him on his report. It is not therefore surprising that some judges should act out of faith in their officers and follow the recommendations of the report, unless its contents are strongly challenged. This challenge is less likely if the parties have not had an opportunity to see it.

In 1968 a report on divorce court work by the Conference of Principal Probation Officers expressed concern at the varying practices between courts about the attendance of officers at court. An earlier nationwide investigation they had conducted showed that in only four of 46 probation areas was the officer expected to attend on all occasions when a report was being considered. In most other areas the officer attended occasionally, usually when there was dispute or when the judge specifically requested it. There were eight areas where officers never attended. The chief probation officers themselves gave cautious approval in principle to officers attending court as a normal practice. They comment:

> "What is contributed by the Officer is determined by relationships within the court. Some judges welcome the Officers' attendance in court and in Chambers throughout the whole day. This seems to resolve many difficulties which could arise through lack of information. A number of situations appear in court which cannot be included in formal documents. Furthermore the judge may expect some help in deciding whether or not to request enquiries."[6]

More recently, a report by a group of divorce court welfare officers from Devon argues for the officer's attendance at court on the ground that it has important symbolic value, quite apart from other services that he can perform in court when present. It can show association with the court and hence enhance the officer's authority, offer a chance to display to both parties neutrality in relation to their conflict, and above all demonstrate care for the children and the family as a whole. The Devon welfare officers write:

> "This would show a degree of care sometimes ignored, and whilst not always possible with present resources, it should be recognised. Failure to be at the court can, to some extent, be alleviated by letters to the client, showing a continued interest and leaving the door open for further assistance if this is required."[7]

I think these welfare officers are absolutely right. Even so, the fact remains that it is the exception rather than the rule for an officer to be in court when his report is considered. This research has found that many parents take a poor view of it, particularly when they have the impression that their case had hinged on the officer's finding.

Delays in considering the Welfare Report

A further unsatisfactory practice concerns delays between the filing of the welfare report at court and its consideration at a chambers hearing. Parents were asked when the welfare officer last visited them and when the chambers hearing had taken place. The following table summarises their replies:

Table 21

Period Between Last Visit of Welfare Officer and Chambers Hearing or Settlement
n = 82 (replies of petitioners and respondents combined)

	%	
Less than one month	17	
One month	28	
Three months	17	36
Six months	11	
Nine months	4	
One year	2	
Case still unsettled	8	
Don't know	13	

The startling figure here is the 36 per cent. who reported last seeing the welfare officer at least three months before their case was heard. To these must be added some of those whose cases were still unsettled at the end of the research period, amongst which was at least one case that had been waiting a year for final determination, and a further three that had been waiting over nine months.

We heard all kinds of explanations for these delays – difficulties in settling the disposal of property being perhaps the most common. It seemed clear that some solicitors wanted to get the fate of the matrimonial home settled before dealing with the question of the children. There may be some point in this, but it is not an adequate reason for the court not considering the officer's report and deciding, on the strength of it, what needs to be done in the children's interests. One exasperated welfare officer told us that she had had to re-interview and rewrite the contents of her report three times.

Some parents reported to us that the circumstances of the children had changed substantially since their last contact with the officer. Several children had moved homes. In one case, where the care of a child had changed from one parent to the other, the research worker persuaded the parents to inform the welfare officer, since it was likely to affect the contents of the report. Other parents had done this on their own initiative. For example, a father who had found out that his former wife and children had moved house told us:

> "They had moved house. As a matter of fact I rang up the welfare officer on Friday, and asked where they had gone. She didn't know. I told her as a welfare officer she should know. She said she was only asked to make out a report, not to keep in contact."

It cannot be satisfactory that courts sometimes receive reports containing information that is seriously out of date. Prompt consideration of the report after it is completed is the only way of preventing inefficiencies of this kind.[8]

Welfare officers are concerned about such delays. The 1976 Report on Divorce Court Welfare prepared by the Family Law Sub-Committee by the Chief Probation Officers Conference remarks:

> "A report may be ordered, an investigation carried out and the report prepared and filed. Then for reasons usually associated with the content of the report, the solicitors for the parties take no action to revive the case. This may mean that justified and sometimes needy intervention for the children can be withheld in the interests of the parties."

The Devon court welfare group also drawing attention to the problem comment that even when a court welfare officer considers the children to be at risk the local authority social service representatives may be hesitant to act under child protection legislation until the current proceedings are complete.

According to our research evidence, these welfare officers are justified in their concern. An illustrative case is that of a mother quoted already.[9] The court hearing, at which the judge asked for a report, took place in November. The welfare officer completed her report the following February. Three months later at the end of May when we interviewed the mother she told us:

> "The welfare officer felt she had better get this report finished as quickly as possible. She felt it was urgent. She had done her bit, but I don't know why it is taking so long. You know we have only just finished taking affidavits and statements. There is one witness – a cleaning woman who was with my husband. She's a witness for me, but she's only just been interviewed. The solicitors haven't even applied to court yet – and the welfare report went in ages ago. In the meantime I'm losing all contact with the children and it's going on so long. That was one of the things the judge stressed last time we went to court for access [previous November]. He said that it was most important to keep up regular contact with me until the custody case is decided. . . . I can't understand it. They ought to take notice of someone like the welfare officer because she's acting in the interests of the children, rather than the solicitors who don't seem to give a damn."

It is not always possible to say where responsibility for delays of this kind lie. Solicitors may sometimes exploit them for tactical advantage. In these cases welfare officers should encourage the parties to complain to the Law Society. But welfare officers too may contribute to delay. It has been suggested that some are too thorough in their approach and spend too long trying to conciliate between parents when it would be better to get the case back to court; a point solicitors might bear in mind.

In our view the system itself is seriously at fault because reports are often called for only after the case has been to court. The Oxford study produced some disturbing information about the time it can take from an adjournment to final settlement of the case[10]; in 45 per cent. of contested custody cases in which welfare reports were sought the adjournment lasted for more than six months. By contrast adjournments for affidavit evidence were considerably quicker, usually no more than two or three months. Even in 28 per cent. of uncontested cases reports took at least five months to be prepared and considered. Curiously in uncontested cases affidavit evidence took even longer to produce, possibly suggesting that an uninterested parent can be a source of delay.

Proper preliminary scrutiny of the papers as practised in some areas, and as advocated by Judge Jean Graham Hall[11] would allow registrars to anticipate the need for prompt investigation so that the judge has a report before him when he considers the case. As we have seen, 75 per cent. of the parents would have preferred the welfare report to have been prepared much earlier. Adjourning a case for a welfare report inevitably prolongs uncertainty about the outcome. The majority of parents considered the most appropriate time for the welfare report would have been soon after they had separated or had started divorce proceedings. As one father commented about current practice:

> "It's not help really. It's just pure enquiries at the moment. It's this suspense all the time – what the hell's going to happen? That's what worries me."

There is a further consideration. As uncertainty created by these delays may cause strain and anxiety both to parents and children, welfare officers are sometimes assessing behaviour and emotional states that have been directly produced or aggravated by the system of which they are part. In any case it is almost bound to be a tense situation for many families when reports of this kind are being prepared. Surprisingly, welfare officers themselves often fail to appreciate this when making assessments of behaviour in their reports. Unless they do so their reports could be unreliable.

NOTES

1. J. Eekelaar, E. Clive, K. Clarke and S. Raikes, *Custody after Divorce* (Centre for Socio-legal Studies, Oxford, 1977).
2. Report of the Departmental Committee on the Social Services in Courts of Summary Jurisdiction Cmnd. 5122 (HMSO, 1936), p. 31.
3. This is clearly contrary to the Matrimonial Causes Rules 1973. Rule 95(3) (*c*): "... the registrar shall give notice to the officer of the date of hearing of the application or other proceedings."
4. For critique of the use of reports in juvenile courts see Andrew

Sutton, "Reports for the Juvenile Courts – Rituals or Revelations" L.A.G. Bulletin, July 1978, p. 155.

5. Philip Bean, *Rehabilitation and Deviance* (Routledge & Kegan Paul, 1976), p. 113. In a chapter on the use of social enquiry reports in criminal courts, Bean, a former probation officer, identifies the way courts have developed informal practices to protect probation officers from having the contents of their report rigorously scrutinised and challenged, even though research has shown that the reports themselves often contain inaccuracies, unsubstantiated fact and moral judgements dressed up in social science jargon and offered as professional opinion.
6. Conference of Principal Probation Officers, Divorce Court Welfare (Discussion Paper No. 2). Report of meeting held at Cavell House, London, 25 October, 1968.
7. Devon Probation and After Care Service; Report by Divorce Court Welfare Study and Support Group, March 1976.
8. It should be remembered that court decisions do not necessarily stabilise the family's child care arrangements. Thus however good the information available to the court, it may not matter much if circumstances go on changing rapidly.
9. See p. 61.
10. Eekelaar, Clive, Clarke and Raikes, *op. cit.*
11. Judge Jean Graham Hall, "The future of the Divorce Court Welfare Service" *Family Law*, Vol. 7, No. 4, 1977.

9. Should Divorce Court Welfare Officers be Drawn from the Probation Service?

Early in the research we discovered that a number of parents disliked the idea of the probation service being associated with divorce.

Petitioner parents in the first representative sample were asked what kind of social worker, if any, they would like to see attached to the family court of the future. The table below indicates their views:

Table 22

Type of Social Worker Preferred in Family Court
Petitioner Study only
n = 108 (6 cases of double counts)

Local authority social workers	32
Someone independent, specially trained and attached to the court	31
Health visitor	14
School counsellor	8
Probation Officer	5
Marriage Guidance Counsellor	1
Others	5
Doesn't matter	4
No social worker should be involved	1
No opinion/information	7

The answers to this question produced a surprising amount of material which shed light on the ways in which social workers and counsellors are regarded generally. For example, only five parents considered probation officers to be appropriate for work in the family court, the majority preferring either a social worker from the local authority or a specially appointed worker linked closely to the court.

Clear trends emerged why certain kinds of social worker either were or were not considered suitable for this work. The overwhelming majority who discounted probation officers did so because of their connection with the criminal court. Typical answers were:

> "I don't think it should be a probation officer that comes to see the children. I'd mind that. What if the neighbours saw a probation officer visiting – they'd think someone in the family was in trouble."

> "I don't think it should be a probation officer, that wouldn't be right. Say he was visiting the lad across the road who was in trouble. That would make your children think they were in trouble too."

> "No, probation ... that's too much to do with courts with regard to people had up for criminal offences being on probation. That sounds too officious."

> "If somebody comes and says 'There's a probation officer at the door' you think 'Oh, blimey, what's happened?' If my mother came round and said 'There's a probation officer here to see you,' I'd say 'Christ, I've left me car lights off' or something."

Many parents in our first sample had no idea that the probation service provided welfare officers for the divorce court. This was not surprising since very few had had previous dealings with a divorce court welfare officer. It was thus decided to ask all parents in the second court welfare sample whether they knew which organisations employed the officer they had met. Parents were given a list of seven possible employers. The table below quantifies the results.

Table 23

Knowledge of Employing Authority of DCWO
n = 82

	%
Probation	41.5
The court itself	17.1
Local authority social service	15.9
Health service	2.4
Marriage Guidance Council	–
Local Education Authority	–
Some other organisation	–
No idea	23.2

If they did not already know, parents in both samples were told of the welfare officers' association with the probation service. They were then asked whether they thought it appropriate. The table below classifies the replies. Only 70 out of 102 parents in the first sample were asked this question:

Table 24

Reaction to Welfare Officers' Association with Probation Service

	DCWO Sample	*Representative Petitioner Sample*
	n = *82*	*n* = *70*
	%	%
Very appropriate	2	7
All right – makes no difference	45	31
Not appropriate – stigma of criminality	31	36
Not appropriate – other reasons	16	26
Don't know	6	–

It can be seen that in the court welfare sample opinions were fairly evenly divided between those who objected and those who did not. Comparison with the earlier representative petitioner sample in the right-hand column shows that the court welfare sample is rather less antagonistic to the probation connection. Nevertheless, the probation officer's stigmatic association with crime remains prominent, being referred to by about a third of each sample. There is a suggestion that the actual experience of meeting welfare officers sometimes moderates the strength of the distrust that the stigmatic overtones of probation arouse. Even so, only a small minority of parents in both samples reacted quite positively to the connection, all of them fathers who were without the care of all or some of their children. Because they lacked contact with the children they seemed to want the probation officer to act as some kind of family policeman to keep the mother and usually her new partner under some kind of surveillance to ensure their children were all right.

For example, one father without care of his children who was himself a policeman remarked:

"I would have preferred it if the welfare officer had had more contact with her [former wife] and the children earlier; that he didn't let her know when he was going there. The thing is that circumstances have altered since he last went up there. I mean her boyfriend is living with her now even though she told me it was all finished between them. I think the court should keep an eye on the children, because I can't go to the house now even though it's jointly owned by myself and her."

Even parents who had no specific objection to the probation service and did not feel stigmatised by association with it sometimes expressed puzzlement at the assumed connection between divorce and crime. For example one mother remarked:

"I can't really see where the court welfare man and probation go together. Unless the break up of a marriage is the cause of a lot of delinquents. Well, not so much delinquents, but maybe children of broken marriages are that little bit less secure and more likely to get into trouble. Is that it?"

Another from the court welfare sample said:

"Well, it's all the same really isn't it? Although I must say I couldn't find the connection between a probation officer and my kids. Probation officers deal with people who've committed crime."

There was no doubt that most parents would have preferred not to know of the welfare officer's connection with the probation service. Nevertheless it appears that quite often officers openly tell them about it or give them clues, for example, through their letter heading, as in the case of the mother who said:

"I don't really know where he came from, but I should guess the probation service because his letter had 'Probation Service' crossed out."

Most parents seem to prefer the term court welfare officer. As one father said:

"It sounds a bit frightening when you hear it first – probation officer. I prefer the name court welfare officer – it sounds more a family thing. Probation officer sounds more like a policeman. That's the first thing you think of when you hear of probation officer – being in trouble with the police. Mind you, now I've met Mr. B. [DCWO] I've a different opinion of them than what I had."

10 The Future – Towards a Family Court Welfare Service

All the parents interviewed were told that the government was considering setting up a new system of family courts.[1] They were asked to suggest ways it might differ from the present system. Their answers shed light on important policy questions, namely:

(i) Should a family court be part of a new social welfare organisation?
(ii) Should there be a family court with a primary role of adjudication and a clearly defined welfare responsibility?
(iii) What should be the extent of the court's welfare responsibility?[2]

The Characteristics of the Court

We found that far from having no opinions on the hypothetical family court parents have plenty of ideas and comments. All the 102 petitioner parents interviewed in the first sample had had to go to the county court under the previous divorce procedure. Fifty-two of them wanted a more private and less formal setting.[3] Most (67) thought that lawyers should continue to have control over the proceedings particularly when there was dispute, but 52 felt that judges would be helped if social workers prepared more reports (in this sample fewer than 10 per cent. had had reports prepared) and attended the court in person. Many thought that judges should be specially trained to understand better the social and emotional aspects of divorce and its effect on family life. Some suggested that it would be a good idea to have more women judges. Only a minority (14 per cent.) thought that social workers should replace lawyers and judges.

The Interests of Children

The majority of parents in both groups took the view that in divorce proceedings the interests of children needed watchful protection. The following remarks are typical:

> "I don't think it is the past history of the marriage which should be of interest to anyone; it's the future arrangements for the children that matters."

> "I think the main thing about a divorce is not what's gone on between me and my wife, it's the children. If some of the children are going to suffer, that's what should be taken care of."

> "The welfare of the children must come before the feelings of either party."

In the first representative group of petitioners, only a small number of whom had met a court welfare officer, the majority (75 per cent.) considered that the court should make more enquiries about the children than in their particular cases. Most thought this should be done by a social worker from the court visiting the home and meeting the children. In the court welfare sample the majority of them (60 per cent.) were satisfied with the amount of investigation that had taken place. It seems therefore that few parents object in principle to enquiries about their children being made. The problems arise over how it should be done in practice.[4]

The independent investigation of a welfare officer was seen as only one of a number of steps that could be taken to protect the interests of children. Thus parents were also asked their views about the idea of children of divorcing parents receiving special protection from the court by being placed under some kind of supervision for a period. Over half rejected this suggestion although some (15 per cent.) thought that it might be a good idea in special circumstances, a view held mostly by fathers without care of their children. Even so, most of these qualified their support for supervision. For example one said:

> "Well, it's certainly an invasion of privacy. This is the big snag with it. But take my case. I wasn't speaking to my wife, I wanted no communication with her at all. Her family and

relatives weren't speaking to me either. I had no intermediaries who could reassure me the children were being looked after all right. Although I saw them every few weeks and they were all right, I did on occasions have doubts. Reassurance about them, that's all I wanted."

Most parents took the view that supervision would be unwelcome and demoralising both to the parents and the children, as for example the mother who said:

> "I think it might make you feel a bit edgy, knowing you were being checked up on. It is interfering again, isn't it? You don't get it when you're married, do you?"

A father commented:

> "A lot of children, if they were subjected to this sort of thing, would feel – well, perhaps not exactly outcasts – but they would be very much aware that they are not like other children. That would be unfortunate. It's very important that they should feel there is nothing wrong. It's not their fault – it's just something that's happened."

A mother in similar vein remarked:

> "Not supervision, no, because I think they feel different from the rest anyway. To make a particular effort putting them on supervision would make them feel more different than they would on their own."

Parents in the first sample were also asked whether they thought it would be a good idea to have a special person attached to the family court to whom divorced parents and their children could turn for advice and help, perhaps in preference to supervision.

Table 25

Advice and Help

n = 102

	Number
Yes, it would be a good idea	80
Not a good idea, supervision better	11
Not a good idea	8
Other (no comment, no information)	3

It is striking that so many petitioners while rejecting formal supervision welcomed the idea of a place attached to the court to which adults and children could go for advice. Some people suggested that in this way their children could go to an independent person if they had worries or wanted help in discovering an explanation for their parents' marriage breakdown. As one mother put it:

> "Obviously there is going to be confusion in a child's mind for a considerable time. I think it would be very, very helpful if a young person could feel that they have got another objective person whom they have already met – somebody they can turn to, somebody who will listen."

The problems of divorce involve a good many interrelated questions in particular of law, economics and social behaviour. One difficulty facing parents is that it is extremely difficult to obtain help that is genuinely interdisciplinary in approach – social workers may have specialist knowledge of behaviour but are often shockingly ignorant about the law. The reverse is often the case with lawyers. Our impression was that many parents are seeking a less compartmentalised but no less competent response to their problems:

> "In so far as you could go there and discuss any problems you had appertaining to the children, the divorce, the financial position and they could advise you personally and tell you where to go, so you weren't stuck at home thinking 'Who can I contact?' It would be good if the family court could cover a wider sphere rather than just coping with divorce."

Such views lend weight to the argument for a new specialist welfare service for the family court, as will be seen by examining more closely parents' views about particular characteristics of various kinds of social worker. Nevertheless it is perhaps only fair to say at the outset that my overall impression is that people are wanting a collection of archangels to do this kind of work. Just the same, an idealised vision may indicate what should be aimed at.

Social Workers and the Family Court

I have already considered parents' reactions to the idea of probation officers being attached to the family court.[5] Most saw it as stigmatic, confirming the Finer Committee's opinion that courts of criminal jurisdiction should be kept quite separate from those which deal with family matters. Most of the parents we interviewed seemed particularly aware of images and associations that could be stigmatic to them or their children. They were especially sensitive to being regarded as "bad" or delinquent, as non-coping dependent people, and as poor. From the evidence of this research it seems that many of the existing social work and counselling services carry stigmatic associations of this kind or are just seen as inappropriate. By contrast, doctors, lawyers and health visitors have no such associations. They seem more acceptable and popular because an approach to them does not involve loss of face or the risk of feeling stigmatised. Unfortunately, going to a social worker sometimes seems to involve people in the acceptance of a submissively dependent role, a consequent loss of self-respect or a decline in social status.

1. *Marriage guidance counsellors*

> "Marriage guidance would probably be all right to stop the marriage breaking up, but I shouldn't think they would be suitable when it has."

> "If you've got to the point where you're separating, the marriage guidance counsellor has done what he can so you can't go back to him or her, so you've got to go on to somebody else who can really just sop up the tensions and advise and guide you."

These two typical comments testify to what is apparently a widely held view that marriage guidance counsellors are primarily concerned with the preservation and repair of existing marriages. The research gathered a good deal of evidence to show that the large majority of couples do not begin divorce proceedings until one or both are firmly of the view that the marriage has broken down. We found no evidence to suggest that solicitors encourage people to resort to divorce. Once people have decided upon divorce, many find suggestions that they might consider reconciliation offensive, since it implies that they don't know their own minds or should not determine for themselves what is in their own interests. As it is, most people have decided on divorce by the time they approach a solicitor about it. In our first sample of 102 divorce petitioners, only 15 had had a period of reconciliation after their first contact with a lawyer, and this may have been some months or even years before the final separation or breakdown of the marriage. Evidence that we submitted in 1975 to the Home Office Working Party on Marriage Guidance shows convincingly that the legal provisions in the 1969 Divorce Reform Act to facilitate reconciliations are quite ineffective simply because so few people are prepared to consider it once they have decided to divorce.

Marriage guidance was often discounted for work in the family court for other reasons as well. A number of parents seemed suspicious of its "amateur, middle-class" image. As one said:

> "To put it unkindly, these are the local do-gooders who haven't had any special training for the job."

Many parents were under a false impression that because counsellors worked voluntarily they had not been suitably trained. Another widely held view was that marriage guidance counsellors were inappropriate to deal with the problems of child care and parenting that arise from broken marriage:

> "As far as I know about the Marriage Guidance Council, I think this just involves the husband and wife and not the children. You know if they can fit up the husband and wife, fair enough, the children can be happy. But I think in the case of divorce and children that's too involved for them."

2. *Local authority social services*

Almost a third of the representative petitioner sample favoured local authority social workers being linked to the family court. Yet comments about them were not generally very complimentary and again suggested a sensitivity to stigma. Of those who did favour them, most did so because they could not think of any other suitable agency. Here are some frequently encountered opinions about local authority social services departments:

> "The local authority I don't like, because you get some of these appalling cases where children are put into care and need protection or are extracted from their homes. I don't think that's the sort of thing one should be thinking about at the time of divorce. It may get to that but not initially."

> "If it was a child care officer I wouldn't go to her, because I'd think 'If I go to her with a problem about my child, perhaps she'd think I wasn't looking after her properly which would be the case if you went to ask for advice.... You think of going to see the child care officer and children being put into care, neglected children....'"

> "Well, I don't think so because they deal with problem families, don't they?"

> "I think child care officers, if they can put children into care, it might put some people off going to see them."

> "I think it depends on the person you get used to. This is in a way sad. You get used to one social worker – I've experienced this – and then after a while, well, it's understandable from their point of view, they're fed up with their job or pick something else – and you get somebody completely different, and you have to adjust to this new person.... I get used to somebody and I find it difficult talking to someone else, explaining the whole thing again."

Many of the parents who expressed reservations about local authority social workers did so without the benefit of direct personal experience. Thus 60 per cent. of the representative petitioner sample and 51 per cent. of the court welfare sample said that they never had dealings with the Social Service Department. But in each sample there was a group (20 per cent. and 26 per cent. respectively) that had had prolonged contact with the department at some point during their lives. All parents who had had any kind of contact with local authority social services were asked their views about them. The following table classifies their replies and shows remarkable similarity for each group.

Table 26

Assessment of Social Workers

	Petitioner Sample n = 102 %	*DCWO Sample n = 82* %
No contact – not applicable	59.8	51.6
Praised social workers	18.6	19.5
Mixed praise	9.8	14.6
Questioned their value, mentioned not receiving help they had sought	7.8	9.8
Generally critical of service received	5.7	4.9

The evidence therefore suggests that of those who had been to the local authority social services about half were pleased with the service and about half critical of it. A number of those who had used the service were critical of the pressures facing social workers, of their limited capacity to provide practical help, and of the rapid turn-over of staff. Many of the workers were often seen as too young and inexperienced to inspire confidence that they understood the problems of stressful marriage even had they the skill to provide positive help.

We had a clear impression that many parents, despite serious social problems and worries concerning family finance, accommodation and the care of children, avoided contact with "the Welfare" if they possibly could.

3. *Health visitors*

The minority of parents who mentioned health visitors generally regarded them favourably. Certainly few parents regarded them stigmatically. Young mothers found them particularly acceptable. One said:

> "I think sometimes all women would like the nurse to call just to say 'Hello.' They like to talk about their children to somebody."

Health visitors were often seen as concerned professional people who knew about infant children and who could be safely confided in. Parents were less sure of their appropriateness where there were older children. Their limitation in the divorce field was that they seemed often to be concerned only with a child's physical health and welfare. As one father said:

> "Health visitors I see as more concerned with the physical welfare of the child. After all it's not so much the physical welfare of a child with divorced parents that is worrying. It's what goes on in the head – their mental welfare."

4. *A new court welfare officer*

Many divorce petitioners felt there was a need for a new specialist social work agency linked with the court. Thirty-one of 102 favoured something of this kind. Some wanted a more appropriate organisation. For example, a mother explained how she felt none of the existing services catered for or understood the needs of divorcing parents:

> "I don't think that for the situation that I'm in at the moment any department exists which caters for it particularly. If you want to do the thing and do it properly, I think a new service would be the best arrangements, if it's going to be tailor made to suit whatever problems arise, and give you most help. I suppose other areas of social service departments *could* be adapted to it, but there again you are making it fit something it wasn't designed to do, aren't you?"

We received many comments suggesting the need for some specialist service for divorcing parents:

> "It should be a completely new person who knows about separation. They should know all about it. A person who meets a lot of broken-up marriages and the children would know more about it than the others."

"Someone specially trained for the whole situation – perhaps special qualifications are less important than that they should be mature people who are fairly happy in their life and had a fairly stable childhood – that sort of thing."

"I think a completely new sort of person – something on the lines of a probation officer, but just for separation and divorce. Because when a child gets to nine or 10 they're more or less independent these days. They ought to be able to go somewhere and be able to talk there about it. My daughter talks to me, but I think there should be someone else as well."

"Yes, it should be a good idea to have a special person, because you usually find with a broken home that the children are still involved with their father or mother which is natural. You can't condemn either parent, and yet in a child's mind I think a break-up condemns one parent. When the parents get married again and perhaps have children, it can't help but cause some kinds of problem and I think the children should be able to speak about it."

One father, when asked what kind of worker attached to the court was needed, replied rather vividly:

"God help me! Well, they should have kids themselves otherwise it's like the Pope telling you about birth control. They should also have powers. Take housing, for example, they should be able to do something about getting you in decent houses if you need it. When it comes to kids from broken homes, they should go to the top of the housing list and the court welfare people or whatever they call them, should have powers to see that they do. They need proper after-care *help* and not just busybodies asking lots of questions."

NOTES

1. The research was planned after consultation with the Law Commission, which under its then Chairman, Sir Leslie Scarman (now Lord Scarman), had established jointly with the Home

Office a working party on family courts. The Finer Committee subsequently had access to the evidence submitted to this Law Commission/Home Office working party, which was suspended when it became apparent that the Finer Report itself would make extensive references to family courts.

2. These questions were asked by the Joint Law Commission/Home Office working party on family courts when requesting evidence.
3. Elston, Fuller and Murch, "Judicial Hearings of Undefended Divorce Petitions" *Modern Law Review*, November 1975, p. 630.
4. See Chapters 5 and 11.
5. See Chapter 9, *ante*.

11 An Appraisal of the Court Welfare Task

In writing this chapter my purpose has been merely to tease out from the research evidence those features of court welfare practice that seem most acceptable to the families concerned and to examine their implication for future practice.

The Nature of the Task

In every instance the overt justification for the officer's intervention was the need for a welfare report.[1] They often also did other more informal and less explicitly authorised tasks which I have classified as cathartic listening, conciliation, child advocacy, family support and welfare rights advice.

(i) *Investigation*

Most parents acknowledged the need for some machinery to safeguard the interests of children. Most had themselves given evidence about their children's circumstances in court, by affidavit, or in the context of the required Statement of Arrangements. They might, therefore, have regarded the officer's intervention as implying the court's mistrust of their evidence. Yet remarkably few parents seemed to object. This can be explained in a number of ways.

First, those in conflict with the other parent seemed the most willing to accept the need for an independent check on the evidence. By contrast, although the numbers were small – 12 cases only, parents in the "satisfaction" cases, where there was no dispute about the children, were more inclined to resent the inquiry. Some of them saw it as paternalistic interference, implying that they were potentially irresponsible and untrustworthy parents.

Secondly, the generally acceptable manner of the officers themselves may have helped to moderate some of the parents' initial reservations about the inquiry. We have evidence to suggest this. It should be remembered that all the parents in this sample were interviewed after the enquiries had been completed so that their recall of how they had felt earlier may have been distorted by later events. My impression was that some parents welcomed the inquiry since it provided them with an acceptable opportunity to have a friendly chat about their own problems. Since the court focus was on the children they did not have to explicitly acknowledge their own personal needs and weaknesses.

Thirdly, most parents saw the inquiries as a child care measure, appropriate to divorce proceedings which in other respects they felt neglected the children. We noticed that many parents assumed that the divorcing population contained a fairly high proportion of irresponsible parents. Their generalisation may be questionable since most excluded their own case. Our evidence was that only a small minority of parents, nearly always those without care or access, in either sample considered their *own* children to be in any way at risk of parental neglect.

Fourthly, most assumed that the welfare report was likely to determine the outcome of the case. This assumption, which is also questionable, is frequently shared and reinforced by welfare officers, solicitors and judges alike. The preparation of the report was seen, not as a mere routine, but as a realistic and necessary response to a genuine quandary facing the court.

Yet evidence suggests that at least where the care of children is disputed, it is rare for the courts to alter the existing status quo whether or not there is a welfare report. Of the 27 disputed custody cases studied by the Oxford research[2] in which welfare reports were sought, only 2 involved a child changing residence as a result of the court's decision. In one of these the judge ignored the welfare officer's recommendation. Similarly, of the 24 custody disputed cases in the Bristol court welfare sample there was only one in which the court ordered that the care be changed. There were four others where change of care occurred but only as a result of a settlement between the parents (which may in part have been due to the welfare officer's intervention). It is also questionable how far welfare reports influence access decisions, particularly since the evidence suggests that in the long-term parents and children work out their own arrangements in most cases. At the same time it should be remembered that court orders may act as a useful short-term restraint on impetuous parents who may be inclined to chop and change their minds about the appropriate arrangements for the children.

(ii) *Cathartic listening*

More than half the parents interviewed experienced their meeting with the court welfare officer as helpful, most usually because of the opportunity it afforded to talk freely and informally about the worries of being a parent in the throes of divorce. Most parents wanted to have continuing involvement with their children and to find ways of making an appropriate contribution as parents to their children's future upbringing. Yet many faced formidable obstacles to the fulfilment of this ambition. These obstacles were both practical and emotional. They were different for those with care of children and those without. For all, probably the most serious difficulty was how to go on being an adequate parent in their own and their children's eyes while at the same time trying to extricate themselves from the ruins of a collapsed marital relationship. Having lost their marital role they faced uncertainty about their future as effective parents. This is probably the key issue at the heart of most disputes about children in divorce proceedings. Loss, threat of further loss and anxiety about their own and their children's future was the dominant concern of almost all those interviewed.[3]

According to many accounts that we were given, officers often re-established a communication channel between the parents. Sometimes this became the means whereby active conciliation was attempted. At other times it served to reduce the element of mistrustful phantasy so that the parents themselves could move once again into closer coalition in relation to their children, thereby reducing the tendency to divide their children's loyalty. For most parents it was vital that it was the same welfare officer who was in touch with the other parent. Some of them were relieved by the knowledge that an independent welfare officer, who had listened to their anxieties and whom they trusted, would test the reality of their fears in an interview with the other parent.

Meeting with the officer enabled some parents to relieve bottled-up feelings of resentment towards the other parent. In Chapter 1 I have argued that the partisan stance of many solicitors often offers divorcing parents emotional support, leaving them with a sense that their own perspective in the conflict has been taken into account. The meeting with the welfare officer may have a similar effect, but because he is cast in the role of neutral intermediary, he may more easily be a moderating influence. In so far as both solicitors and welfare officers are part of the legal machinery of divorce, it can be argued that through their agency the response of the law to parents in conflict is emotionally appropriate. Legal machinery has within it powerful symbolic authority – particularly in the form of an independent judge and court, imposing their presence on the psychological background. It often seems to help people contain, yet not deny, powerful and aggressive feelings. In some of the most conflict ridden cases our research evidence supports the view of Woodhouse that:

> "... the symbol of law and the idea of its capacity for containing or halting violent and destructive expressions of instinctual behaviour frequently proves a positive factor."[4]

(iii) *Conciliation*

The welfare officer's neutral position, backed by the authority of the court, is a powerful one from which to reduce destructive emotions by conciliation. In this context it is important to differentiate between reconciliation and conciliation. The definitions I use are those given in the Finer Committee's report:

> "By reconciliation we mean the re-uniting of the spouses. By conciliation we mean assisting the parties to deal with the consequences of the established breakdown of their marriage, whether resulting in divorce or separation, by giving

> agreements or giving consents, or reducing the area of conflict upon custody, support, access to and education of children, financial provision, the disposition of the matrimonial home, lawyers' fees and every other matter arising from the breakdown which calls for a decision on future arrangements."[5]

The two processes of conciliation and reconciliation are not contradictory nor mutually exclusive. Conciliation by exploring the common ground between the parties may sometimes open up the possibilities of reconciliation.

A few parents had expectations that the welfare officer would attempt conciliation.[6] In about a quarter of the sample the officer had evidently offered to do so. When it was attempted with the approval and consent of the parents, a number of successes were reported – sometimes much to the surprise of the parents concerned. Although it was not possible to say exactly how many times informal conciliation was attempted, it seemed to be more acceptable, and perhaps feasible, in disputes about access than where the care of children was in question. Even so, one of the cases in which conciliation seemed to have been most successful led to a child moving from one parent to the other. In some ways one could say that in the majority of cases an element of conciliation seemed to creep in, even though it may not have been specifically recognised as such by either the officer or the parents.

Where a welfare officer is used to further conciliation, *i.e.* to help the parents and children deal realistically with the consequences of the broken marriage, there is a strong case for earlier intervention. Three-quarters of the parents spoken to urged this, and not just because they felt their cases had been delayed by the welfare enquiry. They often took a more positive view. Because they had experienced the officer as helpful, they would have appreciated his influence in the case at a time when they may well have been facing greater difficulties and uncertainties. The Finer Committee endorsed the view expressed in both the Denning Report and in the report of the Royal Commission on Marriage and Divorce in 1956 that early referral to a conciliation agency was likely to increase the chances of a successful outcome, while long drawn-out conflicts often encourage parties to take up entrenched positions from which negotiated settlement of disputed matters becomes progressively more difficult. The evidence from this research suggests that the vast majority of parents would strongly agree.

(iv) *Child advocacy*

One of the paradoxes of modern English divorce law is that while the interests of children and young persons are in principle regarded as paramount, in practice there is seldom any direct attempt to ascertain how the children themselves view their interests. There are many reasons for this. Adults have nearly always thought they've known what is best for children, and paternalism has characterised a great deal of our child care law and practice. Also the traditional adversary model of justice makes it structurally difficult to sound the views of children in divorce cases. The role of the judge was essentially passive and neutral. As in other litigation the judge was seen as an arbiter between two parties.[7] Although it was possible for children to be separately represented, in practice it was extremely rare. Most solicitors see the children's interests through the eyes of the parents they represent. Yet, as the Justice report observed in 1975:

> "In any custody suit, whether parents are battling against each other or the state, the interests of the children cannot be presumed to coincide with those of either disputant."[8]

In recent years it has been increasingly realised that traditional practices and procedures tend to exclude and hence neglect the views and interests of children. As has been mentioned, this view has been given legislative recognition by sections 3 and 59 of the Children Act 1975.[9]

Partly because of changes in the substantive law, since the late 1950s the divorce courts have slowly and cautiously been evolving ways of consulting children directly when their future well-being is in issue. Nowadays where custody or access is disputed children are quite often interviewed by the judge in his chambers. Even so, according to the Law Commission, judges in the Family Division are reported to exercise this power sparingly.[10] Cases are sometimes adjourned for welfare reports because the judge wants someone to interview the children informally in the familiar surroundings of their own home. It is not possible to tell how often this happens. When a judge asks for a welfare report the welfare officer is not usually present, and the judge's reason is not normally recorded. Even so, welfare officers nearly always do see the children, often individually without the parents being present.

The evidence from this research suggests that most parents give a qualified approval to this practice. My impression is that parents realise it is a delicate and complex task and many of them view it apprehensively. The question that concerns them is not whether it should be done, but rather how it is done. I suspect that this holds good for the children too. In 1974 I conducted a small pilot interviewing programme with 15 children of divorced parents, all over the age of eight. Most indicated that they wouldn't mind being interviewed by a welfare officer provided it was someone they trusted, who would respect their feelings. The dangers of doing otherwise are obvious. For example, to ask children directly which parent they wish to live with (as evidently sometimes happens) may force children to commit themselves to one parent and be disloyal to the other. One 11 year-old girl who had experienced just such a question remarked:

> "I don't think they should ask you *which* parent you want to live with. They should just go round it. After all you love both parents, don't you?"

Yet for a welfare officer to dodge the issue which parent the child would be happiest to live with, when everyone concerned knows it is in question, can be seen by parents and children alike as unrealistic evasion. For my own part, I think this particular question can be safely approached once the officer has established trust with both the parents and the children, and has shown that he wishes to participate in the task of working out *with* them what is best for the children. But when insufficient time has been devoted to establishing the family's initial trust an interview with the children can create great anxiety. As we have seen, some parents were astonished that some welfare officers spent such little time seeing the children or getting to know them – sometimes no more than 10 or 15 minutes. Children that I have spoken to have told me that brief token interviews with the court welfare officer merely made them feel either that they were not being taken seriously or had left them feeling uneasy.

Parents, lawyers, judges and welfare officers alike often become anxious when trying to understand and take account of a child's view of the parents' marriage breakdown. Instead of trying to find out what the child really thinks, they often avoid the issue altogether or only approach it superficially. For example, I have spoken to welfare officers and lawyers about individual cases where there is more than one child, and have been disturbed by the degree of assumed consensus of view attributed to the children. Parents do likewise. Yet in families of which I have close knowledge, the reality is often more complex. Children may have differing allegiances and views amongst themselves, and these may shift quite rapidly over a comparatively short time. Some may pass through periods of ambivalent feelings while their brothers or sisters may seem to hold very clear views. I showed previously how children may have confused and inadequate knowledge of the events that have occurred in their family and which may have dramatically altered the pattern of relationships.[11] Older children may know more than younger ones and have a greater understanding of their parents' differences. Parents vary in how far they are able to talk to their children about the marital problems or answer their questions. Sometimes both parents talk together to the children. In other cases each parent may talk separately to the children, sometimes telling one child more than another, and giving them conflicting and confusing accounts of events and reasons for the breakdown. Understandably enough, perceptions and recall of events can be distorted by emotional stress. All this places heavy demands on a child's capacity to distinguish fact from near fiction. They may be left not knowing who or what to believe. Some children may want to know why the parents don't live together, others appear not to do so. Some may pick up clues from parents and relatives which may be interpreted as meaning that the whole subject is too anxiety-provoking to be talked about openly. In the absence of realistic knowledge, phantasies and misunderstandings may abound and may have no opportunity to be tested.

We undoubtedly met a number of cases, usually those referred by specialist court welfare officers rather than probation officers, where the officer had spent a great deal of time winning the confidence of the parents and children. In a number of these cases it seemed clear that the officer had been able not only to talk with children to obtain their views about their future, but also to help some of them understand more about the realities of their parents' divorce, to help them more to come to terms with it, and to appreciate the way the legal machinery was trying to take account of their interests. In such cases I gathered the clear impression that the officers were providing a positive and direct source of support to the children. In this sense they may well have been doing a lot to break down the sense of isolation which I suspect many children of separated and divorced parents feel. Apart from the court welfare officer and occasionally the judge, there is really no-one within the legal machinery of divorce with specific responsibility to listen to and understand the child's point of view.

(v) *Family support*

(a) *Passage agency.* Divorce regulates the exit from marriage, allowing the former partners to remarry. About 75 per cent. of divorced people do so within four years of the decree absolute. Divorce is concerned with changing people's status. Many parents remembered how, after they had separated, they entered a disturbingly ambiguous phase in their lives when they regarded themselves as neither married nor single. In our representative sample of 102 divorce petitioners, although 47 reported that they had not experienced any significant change in people's attitude towards them because they were separated or divorced. 24 said that they found people treated them with suspicion and caution. 10 that former friends and acquaintances did not seem to know how to regard them. A further eight reported difficulties in this respect when they were first separated which had improved once they divorced. Only two felt that they were treated with greater respect because they had opted out of marriage. Some felt that the terms "separated," "cohabitee," "divorcee" as applied to them carried stigmatic associations, implying a deterioration in social status. They often considered that their roles as parents had also altered. Many mothers with care of children said that they felt that they had somehow to combine the roles of both mother and father. Non-custodial parents often said they felt as if they had suddenly become like uncles or aunts to their own children. Some felt their children treated them almost like strangers and other parents regarded themselves as more like older siblings in relation to their children,[12] implying that they felt they had lost the sense of being a parent altogether. We know much less about how children perceive the alterations in their parents' roles or how they can regard the consequent changes in their own status. Certainly some are confused and some suddenly feel different from other children. All kinds of new patterns of relationships occur particularly when parents start to form new sexual attachments which have implications for the children in the family. How do children see themselves in relation to these new "boyfriends" or "girlfriends" who may be referred to as "uncles" or "aunts" on the way to becoming "step-parents" or "half-parents"? How do their new attachments affect the way they perceive their relationship with their natural parents, particularly the non-custodial parent? Do they feel that in some way their social status amongst their peers at school, in the eyes of their teachers, and elsewhere has deteriorated? In the absence of reliable evidence obtained from children themselves it is impossible to give firm answers to such questions, but the clear impression from the research interviews with parents and from some with children is that some at least do get perplexed by such matters, and may feel themselves to be stigmatised or different from children of intact marriages.

The intervention of the court welfare officer sometimes enabled family members to discuss with a concerned, neutral and understanding outsider the significance of these status changes for themselves and the other members of the family and to gain a sense of support while the processes of emotional change and adaptation were taking place. We met a number of families where parents, some of their new partners, and occasionally the children had come to view the welfare officer as some kind of guide as they passed through new and for them uncharted phases of their lives. This was particularly true of one or two specialist and experienced court welfare officers who were often assumed to be familiar with the complexities of reconstituting the family in these circumstances. In this context, the welfare officer seems to have taken on the role of an agent assisting members of the family as they change their social status. Michael King uses the concept social status to depict a resting place for individuals within the social structure. He writes:

> "Statuses are positions reached by members of society which reflect their self image as well as the opinions of others as to their social value. The time each person may hold a particular status may vary considerably, but each status is of limited duration.... A status passage occurs whenever there is movement on the part of the individual to a different part of the social structure involving a loss or gain of privilege, or power, and a changed identity or sense of self. The concept of status passage covers a wide variety of transitions, from illness to promotion, from marriage to dying."[13]

Glasser and Straus suggest that the task of assisting people in their change of status is one which many professions perform. They postulate that the clients of passage agents are often dependent on the agent for successful navigation of the passage from one status to another.

> "Doctors, lawyers, social workers, counsellors and others see sections of the passage as rough and conceive of themselves as experts who are alert to unknown contingencies with consequences that can be softened. Passage agents make a profession of managing transitions to get passagees through without any bruises."[14]

In the context of marriage breakdown and divorce the solicitor is perhaps the most important passage agent, at least for the divorcing couple.[15] For most of those in our samples the solicitor was the one central and constant figure in the drama of their divorce. By training and experience he was assumed to be familiar with the steps that had to be taken to change status and obtain the divorce, and was often an important source of information, general reassurance and support for the petitioner over the months and even years that it had taken to settle the legal issues arising from the marriage breakdown. It is worth noting that respondents who did not consult solicitors may have been disadvantaged in this respect.

But important though the solicitor usually was, it seemed from what parents told us that welfare officers too could have played a similar role, particularly had they become involved with the family earlier. Welfare officers may have the advantage over solicitors that they have greater understanding of the social and emotional as opposed to legal aspects of the status changes from marriage through divorce to remarriage. More importantly, they are accessible to the children as well as the parents and so can address themselves to the whole family unit as it reconstitutes itself.

The concept of status passage applies not only to individuals but to family units. Families are ascribed corporate identities and may have a collective sense of their place in the social structure. An important part of a court welfare officer's task should be to help the "split family," "reconstituted family" or "one-parent family" find an acceptable accommodation in the community's social structure so that the family members do not experience an unnecessary loss of social status.

Most parents in our samples thought the period immediately before and after separation was the most stressful. Almost a third of the mothers in the representative petitioner sample had experienced violence, which had often increased in severity as the marriage deteriorated. For many of them the final separation was often a relief, even though it may have been accompanied by serious practical problems about accommodation, reduced income and the need to shoulder the complete responsibility for the children. Many of the mothers and more than half the fathers said the period immediately after separation was the worst. For some the emotional shock of separation necessitated psychiatric and medical help. Forty-six per cent. of the women reported prolonged depression which they associated with the marriage break-up. Seventeen per cent. of the women and 45 per cent. of the men reacted with a short period of depression (not more than three months). Sudden weight loss, sleeplessness, psychosomatic skin and stomach complaints were other reported symptoms. Only 26 per cent. of the fathers and 14 per cent. of the mothers said that their health had been unaffected. Seventy-five per cent. of the parents reported increased health and behaviour problems in their children the most common being periods of general emotional upset and distress, *i.e.* increased crying, periods of grief (35 per cent.), periods of bad temper and stubbornness (14 per cent.), flare-ups of headaches, stomach pains, skin complaints (14 per cent.), withdrawal and depression (7 per cent.), increased bedwetting (6 per cent.), delinquency and truancy (4 per cent.).

All this evidence suggests that the period immediately before and after separation is often experienced as a crisis, similar in some respects to a bereavement or sudden illness, during which the emotional equilibrium of the family members is temporarily but seriously upset. Many other studies have also produced overwhelming evidence that parental separation arising from breakdown of marriage often precipitates an emotional crisis in both parents and children. For example, Marsden reported that over a quarter of the mothers in his sample had suffered "nervous breakdowns" and one in nine had made suicide attempts.[16] George and Wilding reported that 66 per cent. of the separated and divorced fathers in their study reported themselves to have been deeply shocked and upset by the break-up of the marriage, often reporting an accompanying state of intense emotional confusion.[17] A small study I conducted several years ago found likewise.[18]

(b) *Crisis intervention.* Marriage breakdown and parental separation often plunge both adults and children into a state of emotional turmoil. The question thus arises whether court welfare officers could be used more often to offer support and help at such times. There is strong theoretical justification for it. Particularly relevant is a method of short-term social work intervention, based on what is sometimes referred to as the crisis model of mental health. It should perhaps be noted that the idea of status passage complements the crisis model and in many respects is grounded in the same empirical observations of behaviour.

This model was first postulated by the American psychiatrist, Lindemann, who noticed an association of depressive disorders in patients who had lost close relatives in a major fire disaster at a local nightclub.[19] The hypothesis, which has since been developed and tested in a variety of circumstances, is that when people are faced with a serious threat or sudden loss which cannot be dealt with by normal coping mechanisms, it is normal for their emotional equilibrium to become temporarily upset. They enter a period of intense emotional stress during which they learn new ways of adapting to the loss. If their adaptation is realistic their overall capacity to cope with similar events and stresses in the future will be improved. But if something interferes with the normal adaptive processes there is increased risk of problems in coping with normal life tasks and an increased chance of an eventual lapse into psychiatric disorder, usually of a serious depressive nature. Normally the various stages of a crisis resolution follow a predictable pattern: initial feeling of shock or bewilderment followed by a slump in morale, preoccupation with the stress-provoking event and accompanying increased difficulty in performing every-day tasks and a sense of emotional exhaustion or depression. Gradually this state gives way to a stage in which emotional defences are established and the person explores new ways of coping. Recovery occurs when a sense of equilibrium is re-established and new patterns of coping became an accepted part of the person's life.

Caplan and others have argued that many crises are predictable, and that community services ought to be so deployed as to ensure sufficient support to those who are not able to call on the resources of their immediate social network.[20] He argues that if social and medical services were deployed in this fashion a great deal of later, more serious psycho-social disorder would be prevented.

In my view this hypothesis is highly relevant to marriage breakdown and could have far reaching implications for the future work of the divorce court welfare service. If the main value of the service lies in the help it can offer families as they struggle to adapt to parental separation then it follows that the time when families are most likely to need and respond to support is during the critical period immediately following separation. Many parents who related well to the officer said that they wished they had met earlier. They appreciated the officer as a person who could look realistically with them at some of the practical and emotional problems that faced members of the family. The difficulty was that in most instances many of the critical decisions had already been taken – for example, decisions about where the children should live, whether the parent with care should go out to work, the arrangements about access, when and how the children should be told about the marriage breakdown. Frequently the welfare officer only came into the case because the earlier decisions taken by the parents had proved in some way unworkable or unacceptable to one of them. This may well have been because they were essentially unrealistic in the first place, the result of maladaptive crisis resolution.

(vi) *Welfare rights advice*

We have already seen that it was unusual for divorcing parents to seek help with practical problems from the court welfare officer and evidently such help is seldom offered. Even so, some officers seemed to make a point of checking that single parents with care of children were receiving their full welfare entitlements. We encountered several cases where this type of help was much appreciated. Of course divorcing parents often most need help in coping with problems of reduced income and finding new accommodation at the point of separation and in the weeks immediately following. These problems are often difficult enough to deal with at the best of times but when they coincide with the emotional crisis that accompanies separation, their solutions frequently seem impossible. At such times comparatively simple tasks such as claiming social security from the Supplementary Benefit Commission can be daunting, particularly when one has never done it before. Many parents had difficulty in discovering what their welfare rights entitlements were. Sometimes the advice they received from social workers was inaccurate. Some social security officials did not inform them about the possibility of extra discretionary benefits. After hearing many depressing accounts of fruitless encounters with welfare officials and bureaucrats, I formed the firm impression that many of these parents had needed someone to act as a guide to the social services and an expediter to enable them to mobilise the social and welfare provisions that many had been entitled to but either missed by default or had received too late.

A substantial minority had passed through a period after separation when it had been a real struggle to survive. Out of ignorance or in panic some had taken decisions which had increased their difficulties. For example, several parents, worried about their reduced income, had given up council house tenancies for a much worse standard of accommodation.

At this point it may be appropriate to refer briefly to some of the practical problems of survival that many parents in our samples encountered on separation. Of 62 petitioner parents who left home, 39 (30 of whom were mothers mostly with children) had experienced at least two moves by the time they divorced. A third of the sample, nearly always mothers, reported difficulties in finding accommodation. Some mothers left children in the care of fathers expecting to find rented accommodation only to encounter difficulties in finding a landlord who would take children. Erin Pizzey[21] and the report of the Parliamentary Select Committee on Marital Violence[22] have given graphic accounts of the plight of the battered wife driven to seek refuge from a violent husband. Our first representative sample contained 22 mothers who had been the victims of marital violence, some of it severe enough to necessitate hospital treatment. Some described how when they finally left they were in a state resembling shell shock – no condition to start the dreary trudge to look for poor quality rented accommodation or to seek minimal social security payments.

Sixty-two of the 102 petitioners in our representative sample said they had to turn to the Supplementary Benefit Commission for help. The majority were mothers or fathers with care of the children. Forty-one had had contact with the Supplementary Benefits Commission lasting more than three months. Although a minority of these parents (21) reported having been received with courtesy, kindness and efficiency, most (39) found it a degrading and unpleasant experience. Some considered the questioning when being means-tested invaded their privacy, a few even found it offensive. Several women said they had been questioned in detail about their sexual relationships because the Supplementary Benefits Commission official evidently suspected them of cohabiting. Some of the fathers who were looking after children on their own had given up work to do so. Several of them reported pressures by Supplementary

Benefits Commission officials to return to work and to get relatives or the local authority to look after the children. We met a number of parents (both fathers and mothers) looking after young children who also worked late hours to maintain their family rather than turn to social security. One of these fathers went out to work at night leaving his five-year-old child asleep at home unattended. Several mothers, preferring to be at home with small children, were low paid out-workers making things like cosmetic bags. They had to work long hours to make an adequate living. A number of them did not know about benefits such as Family Income Supplement.

The problems of poverty and inadequate accommodation have been fully documented and examined by the Finer Committee and described in the studies of Wynn, Marsden, George and Wilding. Our research confirmed all their findings.

In arguing that court welfare officers, if they were able to meet families earlier, could do much more to ensure that they received their full entitlement I am not suggesting that officers should provide practical service themselves. Their role could be limited to giving information, referring parents to the appropriate services, and perhaps acting as lay advocates to help parents press their claims for discretionary benefits. Their task would be to see that parents and children were not unnecessarily deprived of entitlement, and were made aware of other community services both statutory and voluntary which might be able to meet more fully the family's needs. At the very least it would be a step in the right direction if court welfare officers always checked their families were receiving the full welfare entitlements.

The Character of the Welfare Officer's Approach

Parents often attempt to assess an officer's competence by his manner and certain common themes emerge from their comments, now considered under four headings, namely impartiality, family mindedness, avoidance of stigma, and openness.

(i) *Impartiality*

Welfare officers, like judges but unlike solicitors, are clearly expected to remain impartial in any conflict between the divorcing couple.

Curiously, even parents involved in the most acrimonious conflict seemed to retain a sense of an elusive middle ground between them which, with skill and understanding, could be identified by someone who was fair and impartial. It seems as if many people in conflict realise that their perceptions of each other have become in some way distorted, and often welcome the agency of concerned outsiders in their attempts to correct that distortion. How people acquire and retain their sense of fairness is a subject that seems to have been neglected by psychological theory and is certainly beyond the scope of this book. All I can say is that in the population under study, largely struggling with interpersonal conflict, it was observed as a prevalent and powerful underlying force which influenced people's assessment of the system of family justice through which they had passed.

The risk of bias towards one side or another ought to be considered in the selection and training of court welfare officers as I suggested in examining the cases illustrated in Chapter 6. Individual differences between welfare officers undoubtedly influence the conduct and the outcome of cases in which reports are prepared. Their experience, personal values, and emotional disposition condition some to be accepting, others to be controlling, some to be emotionally involved, others to be detached, some to be non-judgmental peacemakers, others to be self-righteous warriors. It may be inevitable that any welfare officer will sympathise with some parents more than others. The best that can be hoped for is that welfare officers are sufficiently self aware to appreciate this.

(ii) *Family mindedness*

Concern for the family as a whole was another feature of a welfare officer's approach much appreciated by divorcing parents. As we have seen, if the welfare officers were themselves parents, a closer and more immediate identification often seemed to be established and increased the parents' sense of confidence in the officers. Parents seemed to expect the officers to have both a personal and theoretical knowledge of the complexities of family relationships.

This implies that welfare officers should be familiar with the main conceptual frameworks for studying the family as a social institution. Traditional probation training and practice is unfortunately often weak in this respect for at least two reasons: first, many social work courses even now emphasise the study of individual personality development to the neglect of the family approach to human growth and development. Secondly, probation practice with, particularly in the past, its emphasis on the treatment and rehabilitation of the individual offender tends to predispose probation officers to work with individual clients, sometimes to the almost total exclusion of their families and other close social networks. The result is that many probation officers, unless they have taken a specialised course in marital and family therapy, have little experience of focusing on the whole family unit, as opposed to the individuals within it. Experience and training of this kind is desirable if they are to appreciate fully their own role in a legal system which regulates social relationships within families. Some welfare officers have told me that they have found the change of orientation from individual work to family work difficult to achieve, without a theoretical base to work from and without being permitted a degree of specialisation.

(iii) *Avoidance of stigma*

The third characteristic expected of welfare officers was that their approach should be non-stigmatic. There are two aspects of this which call for comment. First, the strength of the stigma associated with those social services which address themselves primarily to the poor, underprivileged or deviant members of society. The Supplementary Benefits Commission, the probation service, local authority social services and some of the charitable voluntary social services[23] fall notably into this category. By contrast the legal profession, courts of civil jurisdiction and general medical services are generally excluded. This research validates the Finer Committee's suggestion that the legal machinery should be regarded as treating people in the last resort as the subject of rights and "Not as patients for whom the legal process is just another kind of treatment."[24] Without doubt, many people consider that to be regarded as a patient in need of quasi-psychiatric or social help is tantamount to admitting personal failure to manage one's own life according to the prevailing social standards of the day. Solicitors were often seen as providing a particularly acceptable form of informal emotional support to divorcing couples. This was partly because an approach to them for legal service, while valid in its own terms, often seemed to act as a face-saving mechanism allowing people to receive covert emotional support without loss of self respect. Similarly acceptable was informal psychosocial help given by general practitioners to patients who had gone ostensibly for medical attention. Where the divorce court welfare service is concerned, the evidence suggests that it is generally regarded as non-stigmatic largely because of its association with the High Court. However, once its ambiguous links with the probation service are made known, people tend to have reservations.

There is a second aspect to be considered. Individual welfare officers as representatives of society can themselves become the agents through which stigma and moral disapproval are transmitted. It is true that in this research most parents felt accepted and encouraged by their welfare officers. Even so, there were some who felt that their officers regarded them as in some way socially inferior or morally irresponsible for having divorced, particularly while they had dependent children. The minority of parents who felt their welfare officers regarded them in this light often seemed to experience it as sharply demoralising and even socially alienating, no doubt partly because of the authority that such parents generally ascribed to the welfare officers' position. As has been mentioned in one case, the officer was reported as saying that in his view it was contrary to biblical rules for a mother to go out to work and for the father to tend the children.[25] Similarly, several of the mothers who had left to live with another man, leaving children temporarily in the care of their father, reported welfare officers who had expressed disapproval of their sexual morality.[26] Again, single and working parents on a number of occasions mentioned to us that going to work seemed to have aroused the welfare officers' disapproval, even though the parents themselves considered it was the best way to provide an adequate standard of living for the family and helped to avoid them becoming members of what some regarded as the socially stigmatised claimant class. Some parents remarked that they felt that their welfare officers approached them with the implicit assumption that all divorce was morally wrong, symptomatic of poorly adjusted or immature personalities, and inevitably emotionally damaging to children. Several parents commented that they felt that such an attitude on the part of a court welfare officer was inconsistent with the spirit of a reformed divorce law that had abandoned the fault principle for the notion of irretrievable breakdown of marriage. They argued that, if they had a legal right to divorce, it was not for the welfare officer to make moral strictures upon them when they exercised that right.

It may be argued that guilt on the part of parents may have led them to read condemnation into the officers' stance when it was not in fact there. As a research team we had of course to accept what parents told us and had no way of objectively validating their reported experiences.

The imposition of practitioners' own moral values on citizens who have taken their family problems to the courts of law, although to some extent inevitable, raises a number of difficult practice and policy questions. The cases reported in Chapter 6 illustrate the nature of the difficulties. Even though it can be argued that any degree of discretion allowed to welfare officers inevitably gives them licence to communicate their own moral and social values to litigants, the important questions arise what sorts of social morality are welfare officers likely to transmit and equally importantly should they transmit? How is it fair to citizens who take their problems to court, if welfare officers differ widely both in the values that they hold and in the extent to which they seek to impose them on litigants and their children? Such questions apply equally to judges, solicitors and barristers. Unlike the criminal law, there are many areas in the practice of family law where the standards of private morality or the criteria for adequate child rearing are by no means easily determined. In family matters there is the added problem of differing cultural standards. Different social groups, classes and individuals may often reach quite different judgements about a given set of circumstances. In many instances we are here in a no-man's land where law as the yardstick against which behaviour is measured no longer gives any useful guidance. Where there is a clash of opinion between a parent and a welfare officer about the exercise of the parent's responsibilities, the question arises whose social standards will the court uphold? The balance of power to enforce social and moral values lies with the welfare officer and the judge and in exceptional cases may lead to situations in which parents' rights are restricted, children placed under supervision or even deprived of liberty by being committed to care. Even so, such decisions at least have the safeguard of having to be publicly justified in a court of law where litigants usually have rights of representation and appeal.[27] Perhaps most worrying is the subtle and probably largely unconscious imposition on litigants of the welfare officers' personal values during the time when the investigation is taking place when many parents feel particularly vulnerable emotionally. Then, implied or actual criticism of their values and behaviour may serve only to weaken their morale, render them less able to adapt realistically to what may be a rapidly changing and emotionally fraught situation, or may even alienate them from the system of law which is trying to find solutions to their problems. At the very point when they may need encouragement and a degree of personal validation they may have to face disapproval, the harder to deal with if not acknowledged by the officer concerned. Welfare officers may need to remember that we are not talking about people who have broken the law, but about citizens whose private morality may merely differ from their own. Yet the problem is that the welfare officer may consider quite sincerely that the parents are behaving in ways which cause unnecessary suffering to their children. The welfare officer may take the view that that is worse than minor crime.

The welfare officer is only one of a number of potential labellers in the machinery of divorce. In this small exploratory study this kind of stigmatisation seemed to affect only a minority of parents, although it was noticed that the great majority seemed particularly sensitive and vulnerable to being so regarded. To date, to the best of my knowledge, no systematic study has been made of this aspect of divorce and of its effect on members of families where divorce occurs. I suspect that the focus of stigma in divorce is changing, away from concern with marriage failure *per se* towards its assumed adverse consequences for children. In these days the ascribed social disgrace is not so much for failing in marriage as for failing as a parent (the implied message for the children being that they have parents who have failed them). Stigma is one of the social processes by which, through deterrence, conformity to social rules of marriage and parenthood are enforced. Howard Becker suggests that the notion of deviance is not something that is inherent in the behaviour of certain individuals (as descriptions like "immature," "irresponsible," "neurotic," "feckless" tend to assume), but is an ascriptive label conferred upon actors in particular social situations. He writes:

> "Social groups create deviance by making the rules whose infraction constitutes deviance and by applying these rules to particular people and labelling them as outsiders. From this point of view, deviance is not a quality of the act a person commits, but rather a consequence of the application by others of rules and sanctions to an "offender." The deviant is one to whom that label has successfully been applied: deviant behaviour is behaviour that people so label. . . . We must see deviance and the outsiders who personify this abstract conception, as a consequence of a process of interaction between people, some of whom in the service of their own interests make and enforce rules which catch others who, in the service of their own interests, have committed acts which are labelled deviant."[28]

The Divorce Reform Act 1969 formally abandoned the notion of the Matrimonial Offence, but its shadow lingers on in the more subtle informal practices and processes of family law. People want a system which respects them as equal citizens able to manage their own lives responsibly, regardless of the degree of personal suffering and distress they may have experienced privately when the marriage collapsed. Benign paternalism which labels them as deviant tends to relegate them to a lower social order, and to damage their morale. It is not surprising if some react adversely to legal and welfare practices which keep them largely ignorant of the decision making process or exclude them from it on the implied assumption that somehow they are too irresponsible to make a positive contribution.

(iv) *Openness*

There was no doubt that the parents in the survey responded best to welfare officers who had an accepting open approach. Straightforwardness coupled with sensibility increased parents' trust in the officer, made it easier for them to share their more personal concerns, and in several cases seemed to make more acceptable those parts of the officer's findings which ran counter to the parent's individual aspirations and interests. By contrast a detached, sceptical, evasive or even secretive manner aroused mistrust, anxiety and sometimes outright hostility. In so far as openness is a feature of the legal process these parents can be said to have endorsed it and expected it to characterise the court welfare officers' approach.

In the earlier discussion about whether divorcing parents should see the welfare reports,[29] I suggested that there was a clash of principle and approach between those who believed in open justice and those with a more paternalistic philosophy who considered that welfare officers should have wide discretion to decide what was in their clients' best interests, a discretion which included the power to withhold from clients information that directly concerned them. Davis, critical of professional discretion of this kind, observed:

> "The seven instruments that are most useful in the structuring of discretionary power are open plans, open policy statements, open rules, open findings, open reasons, open precedents and fair and informal procedures. The reason for repeating the word open is a powerful one: openness is the natural enemy of arbitrariness and a natural enemy in the fight against injustice."[30]

He and others suggest that there is a divergence of principle between what can be termed the justice approach, characterised by clear rules which limit the exercise of discretionary power and make it publicly accountable, and the welfare approach, relying on discretion to further treatment and rehabilitative ideas.

When social work is practised in a voluntary setting, clients have a power of patronage over the social worker which is absent in social work for statutory authorities.[31] Client patronage tends to balance the professional's power which is derived from expertise and specialisation. It enables the client to authorise the worker and determines the extent and limit of that authority. Above all, patronage makes the professional accountable to his client. It is, for example, an important feature of the relationship between a solicitor and his client, as is implied for instance when solicitors refer to "taking instructions from their clients." Clients of statutory social workers have no such power and far less control over the relationship, though the social worker may have considerable statutory power to control and regulate the client's life.

The two approaches of justice and welfare reflect the legal and social work professions' different sets of occupational values. Practitioners tend to internalise the dominant values of their own professions and to combine them with their own personal values. The resulting amalgam is reflected in the approach and attitude the practitioners take towards their clients. Parsloe, writing of the differences between lawyers and social workers, points out that

> "... because of the essential ambivalence of human nature, few except thorough fanatics are likely to hold only one set of attitudes, although one approach will usually predominate over others. Institutions have developed to express ... the justice approach and the welfare approach, but many lawyers whose profession institutionalises the justice approach hold some ideas drawn from the welfare approach. Equally many social workers who as a group stand for a welfare approach, act at times as if they were agents of justice."[32]

My argument is that as far as the bulk of the divorcing population is concerned agents of justice are precisely what divorce court welfare officers are supposed to be. In that respect, they may be distinguished from other kinds of social worker, particularly those in the statutory social services with a social control function, regulating "deviant" social minorities. By contrast the "open justice" approach implies a respect for divorcing parents and their children as citizens with equal rights and responsibilities before the law, citizens who are expected to participate jointly in working at the common task of resolving the family's conflicting interests with lawyers, court welfare officers and judges. Viewed in this way, all the actors in the process need to be open and frank with each other about the fundamental issues and how they see them.

The practice of "participant" justice (which I discuss in Chapter 14) though still evolving, has become a feature of much civil, one might almost say "middle-class" litigation, particularly that which is finally resolved by settlement. The divorce court welfare officer's role within such a model of justice would have to be characterised by impartiality and openness. It would have to be seen as family minded and as non-stigmatic. This is an ideal capable of achievement as I will argue later.

NOTES

1. Although exceptionally welfare officers undertake the supervision of children in divorce proceedings, this aspect of their work was not studied in this investigation and so is not considered.
2. Eekelaar, Clive, Clarke and Raikes, *Custody after Divorce* (Centre for Socio-legal Studies, Oxford, 1977).
3. See *post.*
4. Douglas Woodhouse, Director of the Institute of Marital Studies, Tavistock Clinic, London, in an unpublished paper to the Home Office Working Party on Marriage Guidance.
5. Finer Committee Report.
6. Chapter 2, Table 10.
7. See Chapter 13, *post.*
8. *Parental Rights and Duties and Custody Suits* (Justice Report, Sweet and Maxwell, 1975).
9. Chapter 1, p. 47.
10. Law Commission Report on Matrimonial Proceedings in Magistrates Courts, Law. Com. No. 77 (HMSO, 1976), p. 127.

    The President of the Family Division, Sir George Baker, has ruled in the case of *Re T.* (1974) 118 S.J. 78 that magistrates have no authority to interview children in custody cases in their private rooms.
11. Chapter 5.

12. Marsden also reports the phenomenon of mothers having sole care of children regarding their daughters and sons more like sisters and brothers following the separation from the father. See Dennis Marsden, *Mothers Alone* (Allen Lane, 1969), p. 127.
13. *Warwick Law Working Papers*, No. 3 (1977). A status passage analysis of the defendant's progress through the magistrates court, p. 8.
14. B. G. Glasser, A. C. Straus, *Status Passage* (Routledge & Kegan Paul, 1971), p. 51.
15. See Chapter 1.
16. D. Marsden, *Mothers Alone* (Allen Lane, 1969), p. 119.
17. V. George and P. Wilding, *Motherless Families* (Routledge & Kegan Paul, 1972), p. 112.
18. M. Murch, "Motherless Families Project" *British Journal of Social Work*, Vol. 3, No. 3, p. 365.
19. Erick Lindemann, "Symptomatology and Management of acute grief" *American Journal of Psychiatry*, Vol. 101, September 1944.
20. Caplan, See also Parad 4, *Crisis Intervention* (Family Service Association of America, 1965), pp. 193–284.
21. Erin Pizzey, *Scream Quietly or the Neighbours Will Hear* (Penguin, 1974).
22. Report from the Select Committee on Violence in Marriage, M.C.553 (1974–75) (HMSO, 1975).
23. From a policy point of view the deterrent of stigma can serve a useful function in reducing demand for services and controlling their deployment, a reason perhaps why stigmatic associations are tolerated and sometimes even encouraged by policy makers.
24. Finer Committee Report, p. 175.
25. See case reported on p. 111.
26. See pp. 112–117, *ante*.
27. The case of *R.* v. *Welwyn Justices ex P.S. (1978) 123 S.J. 17* shows that in certain care proceedings parents may not be regarded as party to the case and may not be able to be represented. Legal aid is not available.
28. Howard S. Becker, *Outsiders: Studies in the Sociology of Deviance* (New York – Free Press, 1966), pp. 9, 163.
29. See Chapter 7.
30. Davis, K. C., *Discretionary Justice* (University of Louisiana Press, 1969).
31. Terrance Johnstone, *Professions and Power* (Macmillan, 1972), pp. 65, 80–81.
32. Phyllida Parsloe, "Social Work and the Justice Model" *British Journal of Social Work*, Vol. 6.1, April 1976.

Part 3

Policy Considerations

In the next three chapters I propose to examine various policy approaches to the socio-legal problems of families affected by divorce. I term these the welfare approach, the judicial approach and the participant approach. The third is partly a synthesis of the other two but rejects some of the assumptions underlying both of them. Each approach is considered in the light of the research findings already presented. The final chapters suggest a new system of family tribunals and family courts using the participant mode.

12 The Welfare Approach to Divorce – from Marriage Saving to Child Saving

No evaluation of welfare provisions in the administration of divorce law can be made without some reference to its historical context. I can only briefly indicate certain themes and issues which seem most relevant to the contemporary debate about the role of welfare officers in divorce proceedings.

Matrimonial Proceedings Before Magistrates – Marriage Guidance for the Poor

Social work in courts with matrimonial jurisdiction began in the magistrates' courts at the end of the nineteenth century. These courts have long been regarded as "pre-eminently the poor man's court." Women first obtained the right to go to summary courts to secure partial relief on the ground that their husbands had been convicted of aggravated assault upon them by the Matrimonial Causes Act 1878. Thereafter, until 1950, although there were further measures which increased the power of magistrates' courts to grant maintenance and separation orders, the jurisdiction was used almost exclusively by working class women who, in the absence of legal aid, could not afford divorce.

Court social work in magistrates courts developed under the impetus of evangelical and philanthropic philosophies current at the time. The courts' primary objective was to enforce the working man's obligation to maintain his wife and children so that they should not become a burden on the state. Under the provisions of the Summary Jurisdiction (Married Women) Act of 1895, the courts turned to the police court missionary or probation officer to encourage reconciliation. "Moral rectitude and community self interest went hand in glove."

The period of growth

Courts soon began to evolve a sifting mechanism to deal with applications for partial relief. Thus, by 1936 a departmental committee reported:

> "There is reason to believe that many persons go to a court with the intention of making an application who are seen by the Clerks, probation officers and other officials of the court. Some of these are found to have no legal grounds for an application. A large number decide not to proceed with their applications because a reconciliation has been effected or because they are led rightly or wrongly to believe that an application will be fruitless."[1]

This sifting mechanism, or application court as it was sometimes known, was an almost inevitable consequence of courts having to deal with people who could not afford legal advice or representation. Police court missionaries or probation officers who became involved in this practice often found themselves giving informal legal advice and sometimes arranging for the applicant to obtain access to charitable funds for legal representation.

The departmental committee gave detailed consideration to this aspect of the probation officers' work. They carried out a nation-wide survey which showed remarkable variations between courts in how applications for matrimonial relief were dealt with. In some areas many applicants were never seen by the courts at all:

> "In the Metropolitan Courts the great majority of persons addressed themselves in the first place to the probation officer; the remainder went to the court itself through the Warrant Officer. Outside London the commonest practice is for the applicant to go to the Clerk's office, though in several towns and in some of the rural courts the general rule is a direct access to the courts or individual magistrate."

Many of the probation officers at that time held deep religious convictions and were motivated by missionary zeal. These officers viewed marriage in the traditional Christian way, as a sacred and life-long institution. Indeed some were also local priests or ministers. Not surprisingly, such officers would see it as their moral duty to effect reconciliation whenever possible. No-one would deny the value of helping couples who sought help with their personal relationship problems. Yet the zealousness of certain probation officers to save marriages created problems: for example, the 1936 committee report comments:

> "We cannot help feeling that under the present system there is a real risk that conciliation may be carried too far. The practice adopted in so many courts of allowing the probation officer to see all persons who come to them in matrimonial difficulties may well tend to lead to some denial of justice. It is not his function to determine whether on legal grounds the case should properly proceed to a hearing. There is a strong temptation to the zealous officer to settle as many cases as he can out of court and he may even be actuated by personal convictions as to the sanctity of the marriage tie."[2]

The report was here highlighting the clash of interests between legal principle and welfare discretion; a problematic issue for the practice of Family Law to this day.[3]

The 1936 report contains some remarkable figures to show the effectiveness of the filter mechanisms operating in the courts at that time. Out of 6,222 applications studied in their sample in 1935, only 1,776 reached a hearing in the courts. It was almost exclusively working class women with marital problems who were encouraged by these procedures to enter the probation office. In the divorce court, with its predominantly middle class clientele, there were no such procedures.

The use of probation officers in application courts continued well into the 1950s. Their role continued to be to offer informal quasi-legal advice and to deflect people from legal proceedings if they could be persuaded to attempt reconciliation. Between 1950 and 1972 the numbers of applicants to the magistrates courts remained remarkably stable, "the yearly average ranging round 32,000 to 33,000 over the entire period."[4] Had it not been for the practice of the National Assistance Board (later the Supplementary Benefit Commission) of refusing benefit to deserted or unsupported wives unless they had applied for a court order to enforce their husband's obligation to maintain, the numbers of women applying to magistrates courts would probably have fallen substantially during this period.

The period of decline

Once legal aid was extended to domestic proceedings before magistrates' courts by the Legal Aid Act 1960, the amount of this kind of work undertaken by probation officers decreased steadily. It became apparent that both applicants and court officials considered lawyers a more suitable source of information and help. Moreover, the Probation Department of the Home Office was unenthusiastic about the probation service doing matrimonial conciliation work when there were alternative voluntary agencies available. Several chief probation officers have told me that in their view the decline in referrals since 1960 was not due to lack of success in the former years but rather to lack of training in marital work. In the early Home Office courses for probation officers, some of the best marital therapists and lecturers on the subject were employed to teach it. Nowadays there is virtually no special training given. Thus, new probation officers enter their appointments with little idea how to approach marital work and, not unnaturally, they show it. The chief probation officers to whom I have spoken consider that there might still be a strong demand for marital help with a view to effecting reconciliation. In their view, legal aid merely allows couples to by-pass help that might have been offered and accepted.

The decline in the probation service's reconciliation work derived from the court has been dramatic. Manchester and Whetton have shown that while in 1960 there were 9,569 referrals by magistrates to probation officers, by 1970 the corresponding figure was only 5,448 and by 1976 had dropped to a mere 1,450.[5] Referrals from the divorce court have always been few: in 1974, only 637 and in 1976, 549.[6]

The number of direct referrals to the probation service has also dropped steadily; during the period from 1960 to 1970 from 33,274 to 22,280.[7] Between 1974 and 1976, the figure was down from 7,966 to 4,702.[8] This rapid decline occurred during a period when the numbers of divorce petitions rose from approximately 26,000 to 143,698.[9]

It is hard to avoid the view that when citizens involved in matrimonial proceedings are left to decide, without encouragement or pressure, whether to seek reconciliation through the agency of a third party linked to the court, only a small number do. In 1974 the Finer Committee reviewing the English experience of reconciliation through the courts, and similar experience overseas came to the conclusion that such measures had had very little success in actually preventing marriage breakdown though they may have helped "in civilizing the consequences of the breakdown."[10]

During the 1960s, the work of the National Marriage Guidance Council, the other major organisation concerned with marital conciliation and guidance, showed only a small increase, and indeed remained at a fairly static level at around 20,000 new cases a year from 1966 to 1970. By 1975, after a lot of publicity, the figure had risen to about 30,000. Yet, when their performance is compared with the decline in the probation service's share of this work, it becomes quite clear that the number of people taking their marital problems to both agencies for help with reconciliation is comparatively not large. One can only speculate why this is so. It is possible that both have acquired a public image that acts as a deterrent to those who might otherwise seek help. Many people may feel that a direct approach to an agency for help with a marital problem would involve too much loss of face. Whatever the reasons, the available evidence suggests that the marriage-saving movement that had such strong philanthropic and religious origins had by 1970 largely failed to achieve its purpose. The poor, who had been the original target of this movement, had largely slipped the net. From 1950 onwards they obviously preferred to avail themselves of the hitherto predominantly middle class institution of divorce. Yet in the divorce court social work was to develop not so much with a marriage-saving as a child-saving rationale. This was to raise a number of social policy problems.

Social Work in the Divorce Court

The system of divorce had from its inceptions in 1857 provided the middle class with a remedy not just to mitigate a broken marriage but to terminate it. This meant that in the nineteenth century English matrimonial law developed a schism which amounted to segregation by social class. On the one hand, there were courts for the poor who, although they could not afford divorce, had the benefit of social work help aimed at repairing marriages. On the other hand, there were divorce courts, which made virtually no use of social workers, but which allowed the well-to-do to end marriage. As the Finer Committee remarked "long acquaintance with this duality may blunt the power to recognise its peculiarity."

Some consider that the question of social class can be over-emphasised in evaluating our modern system of family law and the part that welfare officers now have within it. Yet it would be wrong to ignore it when the divided jurisdictions within the system seem so obviously to reflect class differences. Contrary to what one might expect, one of the distinctive features of the divorce court welfare practice which has developed in the last decade is that its focus has not been noticeably directed towards poorer families. This may be because judges, rather than welfare officers, have up to now selected cases for report. Even so, there are now signs that divorce court welfare work might develop in ways which will concentrate on the families of the poor, in ways reminiscent of earlier practice in magistrates' domestic proceedings.

The idea of social work in the divorce court, as opposed to the Magistrates Court, was first seriously proposed by the Denning Committee set up in 1946. It arose from an increased concern for the marital problems of servicemen separated from their families by the war. The Committee envisaged such a service serving two major purposes; first, to promote reconciliation; secondly, as a preventive child care measure. The two tasks were related:

> "Children are the innocent sufferers from any estrangement of their parents, and it is in their interests that every possible attempt at reconciliation should be made. We realise that an unhappy home may be worse for the children than a home with one parent only; but true reconciliation means a happy home with both parents which it is desirable for every child to have.... It should be open to the court in every case where there are children under 16 years of age, at any time after the

petition is filed, to refer the case to the Court Welfare Officer for enquiry and report as to the welfare of the children whether the petition contains a claim for their custody or not."[11]

If one looks at the Denning Report's proposals, one can see that broadly speaking it took an egalitarian, non-authoritarian view. The committee saw it as important that the proposed court welfare officers should

"Be able to obtain the confidence of persons in all sections of the community."

Litigants should be persuaded rather than compelled to use the service. They considered that "the Welfare Officer should have access to every petition ... and in such cases as he thinks suitable should write to the parties or their representatives offering his services" so that they would know "to whom he or she should go for advice if desired." Even though the final choice to whom the approach should be made was the welfare officer's, the committee placed the responsibility for deciding to use the service squarely on the litigant. In this respect, their underlying philosophy seems to have been participant, where possible inviting but not forcing litigants to take part in a process of conciliation.

The Denning Committee's report and recommendations did not receive much attention. It may be that there appeared to be more important issues confronting the nation at the time. The idea of a special court welfare officer to provide social work help for what was, at the time, a predominantly middle class clientele may have seemed strange to those more used to the notion of social work being traditionally for the poor and disadvantaged. It is true that the Marriage Guidance Council as we know it today, although started before the war, received a certain endorsement as a result of the Committee's recommendations and subsequent committees of enquiry, notably the Royal Commission on Marriage and Divorce (1956) and the Finer Report (1974), have given the Denning Report acknowledgement; but at the time many of its proposals were ignored.[12]

The Development of the Child-saving Philosophy

Only when the Denning Committee turned its attention to children of divorcing parents did its general egalitarian philosophy give way to a more authoritarian approach. Thus they remarked:

> "No subject has caused us greater concern than that of the welfare of children whose parents are or have been involved in divorce proceedings.... We have had to consider whether the present machine is the best that can be devised for their welfare. We are of the opinion that it is but poorly fitted for the purpose. The principal defect is that the children are rarely, if ever, separately represented before the court and the judge is never in possession of the report of an independent person as to their welfare unless it is obtained by one of the parents. The result is that the welfare of children is subordinated to the interests of their parents."

The committee considered that provision for children in divorce was much less effective than it was in wardship proceedings in Chancery or guardianship proceedings before magistrates or in the county court. The committee saw the children as "the innocent sufferers from any estrangement of their parents." Accordingly they stressed the value of reconciliation provisions, and suggested that the court welfare officer "had access to every petition" so that he was "able to investigate every case and make application to the court at any time for directions as to the custody, education and maintenance of the children whether the courts make application or not."

The Royal Commission's Report in 1956 endorsed this child-saving approach, seeing marriage breakdown and divorce as inevitably a traumatic affair for the children that could have dire social consequences. They were impressed by a good deal of professional clinical opinion that supported it. They wrote:

> "There is a wealth of testimony as to the effects on children of the breakdown of normal family relationships. Where family life breaks down, there is always risk of a failure to meet fully

the child's need for security and affection. If in fact there is such a failure, the child may become so emotionally disturbed as to reject the influences of the family and this may result in anti-social behaviour.... Where divorce takes place it is therefore essential that everything which is possible in the circumstances should be done to mitigate the effects upon the children of the disruption of family life."

This kind of thinking led them to recommend traditional child-welfare policies based on investigation followed by supervision or taking children into care. In the process they took an unmistakably moralistic and authoritarian approach to divorcing parents who they considered should be "made to realise at the outset their obligations to their children" in the hope that some would decide to abandon the idea of divorce. They refer elsewhere to the "desirability of bringing home to parties in the divorce suit their continuing parental responsibility."

They clearly considered that there was a morally irresponsible minority of divorcing parents who neglect their children. The court welfare officer was to be the agent by which the court could identify and deal with them. This was essentially an authoritarian preventive, and in relation to those parents, almost punitive line of thought.

The tone of the Royal Commission's discussion was authoritarian. It recommended selectively interventionist policies. Gone were the Denning Committee's compassionate proposals of the offer of help and advice to all families; gone was the requirement of the service to provide all divorcing parents with opportunities to consult a knowledgeable mature adult. Instead certain parents were to be singled out for investigation and possible surveillance. The service was to be used sparingly. They rejected the idea of investigation in every case on the ground that:

"the impression might be created in the minds of some parents that the decision about the future of their children was largely being taken out of their hands, and that their views counted for less than the Court Welfare Officer's report. Their sense of parental responsibility would be diminished not strengthened. Where the parents were genuinely concerned to do the best for their children (and we believe the majority are) investigation by officials might only cause resentment and frustration and would be counter to what is most desirable, namely that the parents should themselves be encouraged to fulfil their responsibilities."

It seems to me that the Royal Commission was here worried about the response of middle class parents. Investigation in every case would have meant that many families who belonged to the professional and managerial classes, whose children are often sent to independent boarding schools when marital problems occur would have become subject to investigation. Of course it can be argued that such parents are making responsible provision for their children. Even so I think there is little doubt that such official intervention in family life would have offended their middle class values of privacy and freedom from state interference in the conduct of their family affairs. Such an argument is difficult to make explicit. Yet once you take the view that all children from broken homes are potentially at risk the logical conclusion is that the court should investigate every case or find some other means to determine who are at risk. Thus Lord Scarman, when Chairman of the Law Commission in 1968 told a conference of court welfare officers:

> "... if we can move towards a family court structure supported by a Welfare Service responsible to the court, then I should think that it would be possible where there are children for a Welfare Officer in every case to make a routine call to see them and report back to the court."

Similarly Mortlock has written:

> "If we are really concerned about the wellbeing of the children of broken marriages, then a Welfare report is not too much to ask in every case."[13]

The usual argument used against the idea of investigation in every case is that there are insufficient welfare officers to do it. This was a view taken by the Denning Committee in 1947, by John Hall in 1968 and by the Law Commission as recently as 1976 in their report on matrimonial proceedings in magistrates courts when they said:

"For our part we have no doubt that ideally there should be a statutory provision for seeing that a Welfare report is before the court in every case (whatever the nature of the proceedings) in which the court has to consider making a custody order in respect of a child. We accept that the ideal is impossible of attainment at present, because the demand for the services of social workers and probation officers has grown so rapidly that for the time being it would not be practicable for any major additional burden to be placed upon them."[14]

As long as there are insufficient welfare officers to investigate every case some kind of rationing becomes necessary. The problem is that there are as yet no formally agreed criteria for selection, a point that concerns a number of welfare officers. They consider that the selection process as exercised by judges and registrars is too random and haphazard. The 1976 Report of the Family Law Sub-Committee of the Chief Probation Officers Conference comments:

"We maintain that there is ample evidence of too many families receiving too little help, of too many children being passed by with little more than random selection for investigation. This social epidemic of divorce may well lead to a bitter harvest of troubles if it attracts so little concern in terms of remedial resources. The outcome often leads to delinquency in the children and/or further marital breakdowns in the marriages of those from broken homes."[15]

The shortage of available welfare officers, which it is claimed prevents their use in every divorce case involving independent children, has led to attempts to decide those cases most deserving of the court welfare officers' intervention. Although there is no official policy, and judges differ widely in the use they make of reports, there is a certain amount of evidence to suggest that reports are more likely to be sought when children are being looked after by fathers, when there is dispute between the parents about the children's future care (more likely to occur when the children are of school age) and when the children are in the care of the local authority or third parties.[16]

Until recently, social class does not appear to have been significant in determining selection as exercised by judges and registrars. As far as could be deduced from the small court welfare sample in our research the social class composition of the families did not differ significantly from the rest of the divorcing population or from the general social class distribution of the still married population.[17] There are signs that this may change now that welfare officers wish to assume responsibility for selection. They are dissatisfied with what they consider to be the vague selection criteria used by courts.[18]

In 1976 the Family Law Sub-Committee of the Chief Probation Officers Conference proposed that all divorce cases involving dependent children

> "... should be referred by the registrar to the DCWO for scrutiny when the petition together with the statements of arrangements about the children is filed in the court.... The Welfare Officer should go through every case involving children and all cases suggested by him should be put back for full investigation. The judge could, of course, add to the list but not subtract from it. The kind of issues that prompt the Welfare Officer to require a report are a matter for him and his expertise.... It might assist if in addition to the petitions and statements filed, a document were introduced for completion by one or both parties that would state the parents' views and intentions with regard to the children."

As Judge Jean Graham Hall has rightly pointed out, this proposal

> "... amounts to a change of roles by Welfare Officers from that of providing reports when called upon by the court, to becoming the initiating authority with prior right to decide whether reports should be made."[19]

Noting that the chief probation officers' report contained nothing to indicate the criteria that welfare officers themselves would use, she was critical of this proposed extension of the welfare officers' power and influence over the conduct of proceedings. Yet what the chief probation officers seem to intend is that their selection should be in line with traditional child welfare thinking which concerns itself primarily with the children of the poor. This can be seen if one examines the background to their controversial proposal.

In 1975 and 1976 the probation service conducted two enquiries designed to find out how many divorcing couples and their families had had previous contact with either the local authority Social Services Department or the local probation service. This enquiry was pursued because it was thought that petitioners' statements of arrangements often did not disclose such information. It was considered that this would be relevant to the decision whether or not the court should ask for a welfare officer's report. The first investigation was conducted in the North of England. It showed that in a representative sample of divorce petitions, involving children drawn from two large district registries, the proportion of families already known to these two social services were 39 per cent. and 43 per cent. respectively. A similar study of 500 divorce cases with dependent children drawn from courts in the South-west region revealed a figure of 180 or 36 per cent. already known to the two services.

The results of these two investigations have been used to justify the establishment of procedures in certain areas whereby the names and addresses of all cases involving children are sent to the Social Services Department and probation office covering the area in which the children are residing or have been residing. If the family is already known, the chances are that a welfare report will be sought. One chief probation officer explaining the introduction of this procedure in his area put it this way:

> "We know that a significant number of children in divorce cases are known to these services, some are in care and some have been thought to be in considerable jeopardy, but they have not been subject to investigation by the divorce court because the facts were not disclosed by the parents when completing their form for the arrangements for the children."

This officer clearly saw the proposed scheme as primarily a preventive child care measure, remarking that the

> "... field of divorce is about the only element of preventative work left to our service. It is an area where we feel we have considerable experience and can achieve some real benefit to

> a group of people at a critical and vulnerable point in their lives."

At the same time he indicated unease about possible interference into the privacy of family life remarking:

> "I am sensitive of the fact that any so called improvement can be interpreted as an intrusion and as thrusting ourselves into areas which some may say are not strictly our concern."

He later added:

> "In fairness to the parents, perhaps they should be told that inquiries of the two services will be made?"

He expressed the personal view that they should. In fact, in this particular area parents are only informed if a welfare report is to be prepared. Such cases are only put back for reports if the services approached express concern about the outcome of the divorce. This kind of screening and preliminary investigation is undertaken by divorce court welfare officers under the general aegis of the county court registrars. At the time of writing, I know of several schemes operating in this way and there may well be more, set up following the general administrative upheaval that resulted from the extension of the special procedure to all undefended divorce cases and the restrictions on civil legal aid which became operative in April 1977.

The practice of making enquiries of other agencies will lead to one obvious consequence: the families chosen for welfare reports will be drawn predominantly from poor working class families (social classes IV and V) because the clientele of the local authority social services and the probation service come predominantly from these social groups. Middle class families, not previously known to these organisations, will largely avoid being scrutinised.

The Case Against a Preventive Approach to Divorce Court Welfare Practice

The case against the traditional preventive child welfare approach to broken homes can be argued in a number of ways. My own view is that while each argument is not by itself conclusive, taken overall the case is sufficiently strong to give us pause before framing policies on these lines. For this reason it is worth looking at the arguments.

On the face of it, there is evidence to establish a link between broken homes and delinquency in children. The best known study is that of Douglas[20] which showed that when the family break up was caused by separation or divorce occurring before the child was six in families of *non-manual* classes there was a three-times greater risk of delinquency than where the child came from an intact home. In the educational field, there is evidence to suggest that children from broken homes have lower educational attainment, but no more so than those for children from intact families drawn from semi-skilled and unskilled working class homes.[21] Emotional disturbance, stress reactions and unduly anti-social behaviour in children from broken homes have been found by all kinds of clinical studies, for example in studies of the populations of schools for maladjusted children,[22] approved schools,[23] detention centres[24] and Borstals. Yet the Finer Report concluded that the difficulty raised by all these studies was that it was impossible to tell whether it was the existence of other factors such as the atmosphere of disruption, tension and conflict that may have preceded or even followed the final break-up. Having reviewed the researches on the subject the Finer Committee concluded:

> "One very common feature appears in the background of one-parent family children who demonstrate relatively poor standards of attainment and behaviour, namely the poor socio-economic circumstances of the families."

Poverty, especially if combined with conflict-ridden family relationships, may produce disturbed behaviour as indeed it does in the case of many children in intact homes who suffer from family insecurity and emotional deprivation "while many children from broken homes lead a normal happy life."[25]

It is probable that the stresses engendered by financial insecurity aggravate the tensions in the family relationships. It may even be that other stresses may be more damaging than poverty by itself. Yet such is the state of current knowledge that there is no known and proven way of indicating which particular children from which particular families run the greatest risk of manifesting later emotionally disturbed behaviour, and poor educational attainment.

Advocates of the preventive model of welfare often argue their case by analogy from preventive medicine. Social work intervention is justified as a kind of innoculation against various kinds of later social disease. The analogy is a poor one. It assumes a direct causal connection between the particular social fact of marriage breakdown (see in similar terms to a disease-producing bacterium), and later social malfunction. The difficulty is that so far no direct causal link between marriage breakdown and later malfunction has been established. Available evidence merely indicates that factors such as delinquency and poor educational performance are associated with, but not necessarily caused by, poverty, overcrowding, and other adverse social circumstances as well as with broken homes.

Rutter and Madge have observed:

> "To an important extent these associations probably represent causal processes which account for some kinds of continuities in disadvantage. However there is vigorous dispute concerning the size of the effects, the setting in which the effects are mediated (the home, school or community) and the mechanisms by which mediation occurs. Unfortunately most theorists have sought only to support their own positions and have either not looked for ways of testing alternative hypotheses or have not regarded this a worthwhile activity. Nevertheless it is important to determine the mechanisms which are operative as each carries rather different implications for social policy."[26]

This raises another major limitation of the medical analogy; namely that we do not know how behaviour is affected by particular social circumstances even though there may be causal connections. We do not know therefore how to break the causal chain if such it is. Moreover the analogy overlooks the possibility that marriage breakdown, juvenile delinquency and poor educational attainment may have a common cause, merely producing different effects on different members of the family. Thus it may not be the behaviour of the parents that leads to delinquent or disturbed behaviour in children, but common social circumstances which influence both the behaviour of the parents and of their children. If there is a common social cause for delinquency and other childhood disturbances, and marriage breakdown, then poverty, low income and poor social conditions may be the most obvious. Yet it should not be forgotten that the middle classes seem to be almost as vulnerable as the working class in the area of marriage breakdown. In short the analogy of preventive medicine is inapplicable at present because when applied to social malfunction in children it lacks precision.

Even so, I acknowledge that this argument by itself is not as strong as it might be. One can take the view that if there is an association between marriage breakdown and children's malfunction and if social work intervention can prevent the said malfunction then there may be a case for it regardless of causal chains and statistical precision.

Yet there is an even more serious argument against the preventive approach, namely that it may contribute to the very behaviour it seeks to prevent. The whole notion of labelling theory as advanced by modern sociologists is that once children are identified and publicly labelled "delinquent," "disturbed," "at risk," etc., their behaviour alters and they may well tend to act out the ascribed role. This may work in various ways – for example, once social agencies such as the school, the police, the probation service know that particular children come from "broken homes" which are considered likely to produce delinquency, they are singled out for particular attention, and behaviour that would otherwise go unnoticed is more likely to be given public attention. Also as Rutter and Madge have suggested, stigmatic labelling may even directly cause disadvantage. Children of broken homes may be considered "bad risks" for positions of responsibility. They therefore become disadvantaged by the very fact of their parents' marriage breakdown and public identification. This is no mere academic point. It is particularly applicable to children who are placed under supervision of probation officers or of the local authority as a result of matrimonial proceedings. They can very easily be considered in some ways "on probation." The evidence of this research suggest strongly that divorcing parents are well aware of this danger to their children. Some judges also seem to be aware of the potential stigma attached to being subject to a welfare report and try to reassure parents about it.[27] This may also be one of the reasons why so many parents objected to the idea of investigation by probation officers who are associated with the control of and treatment of delinquency. Even so, it should be remembered that this research suggested that once parents were in contact with probation officers their reaction to the label tended to be less strong.

Another criticism of the preventive approach is that there is no proof that it works. Because the "pathogens" are neither clearly identifiable nor removable, welfare officers are not able to demonstrate how they can prevent later delinquency, improve a child's school attainment or ensure that when children subsequently marry they will be happy. The preventive concept of welfare places a high value on state intervention and the supervision of families considered to be at risk. It assumes that benevolent, vigilant authority can forestall a whole range of misfortunes as long as it has the discretionary power to control the situations that may arise. Yet when preventive social work policies are examined to see whether they produce the intended results the facts suggest that they do not. In the child care field the preventive measures of the Children and Young Persons Acts of 1963 and 1969 were designed to prevent children coming before the juvenile court or being received into care, yet the absolute numbers of both groups of children are as high now as they have ever been. Likewise the 1959 Mental Health Act was designed to prevent admission to mental hospital by providing for greater community care – yet almost 20 years later admissions to hospitals are higher than ever. It has so far not been possible to demonstrate that the use of probation has halted or reduced the reconviction rate of offenders.[28] There are other illustrations one could use which show that "preventive" measures of social work intervention are not justified by obvious beneficial consequences or the attainment of their stated purpose. As Jordan says:

> "... prevention of disasters by social work intervention is at best a fairly unverifiable business; we can seldom produce hard and fast evidence of its occurrence."[29]

A further criticism of the preventive approach is that it encourages state paternalism. This tends to imply a lack of confidence in parents, may weaken their sense of responsibility and encourage a misplaced sense of superiority in the practitioners. Many judges are critical of the paternalistic approach to court welfare work. Lord Scarman, when Chairman of the Law Commission, discussed the Hall report and put it this way:

> "There are some judges who feel the whole thing is too paternalistic. We are treating parents who have had the misfortune to break down as though they were not adult. . . . One distinguished judge has said to me 'this is nonsense: you are failing to treat people as adults. I am all for respecting the individuality and adulthood of independent men and women.'"[30]

One of the most rigorous critics of paternalism is Jordan who puts the case against it in the following way:

> "the great weakness of paternalistic provision has been its failure to recognise the dangers of excessive interventions with other groups and how well-meaning assistance, especially in the name of the state, may crush or distort the lives of those who receive it. It tends to over-estimate the value of supervision, and underestimate the frustrations of interference. It has little idea of the previousness of freedom to marginal members of society, or the resentment that can be engendered by dispensing advice and assistance from a position of superiority. It has no clear concept of citizens' rights. It assumes that people value help more than equality, so it gives them help at the expense of equal status. It distrusts the decision-making powers of all but the benevolent, ruling elite, and is anxious to control and keep a watchful eye on all, and especially on the deprived. It has an inflated opinion of its ability to solve people's problems for them, and to avert potential dangers and catastrophes in their lives. In trying to overprotect, it infuriates many, ruins others.
>
> Paternalism prescribes multiple interventions on grounds of generalised welfare investigation and assistance. It advocates the wholesale referral of people to social workers and

> other professionals and experts, on the sole ground of the apparent possibility of their getting in some kinds of difficulties. Such a policy is dangerous and destructive in many ways.
>
> Paternalism tends to obscure the differences between liberty and loss of liberty in its dealings with deviant behaviour and social problems by providing a range of supervisions, treatments, controls, checks and intermediate facilities. Once they become clients, people pass imperceptibly from one to another, ending up in restrictively punitive conditions without knowing how they got there. Because decisions are often taken for them, on the basis of their unreadiness for responsibility for their own lives, they lose the sense of controlling their own destinies. They literally forget how to be free. Freedom only exists if we are free to lose it. Preventive welfare interventions can take away people's liberty to lose their liberty in any other way, except by the slow process of being welfare cases. Whether in crime, debt or any other form of deviance, people need to know what the consequences of their actions are, and to experience these as their own, rather than as a result of decisions made by experts about them. They need to know what they can do for themselves to keep their freedom, not to lose it by degrees in a process they cannot understand."[31]

This research into the practice and policies of divorce court welfare has revealed instances of a paternalistic approach which effectively limit parents' rights.[32] The most obvious example is the practice of not showing them the welfare officer's report even when they are legally entitled to see it. But another more recent example is the practice in some areas of finding out whether families are already known to other social services, whether they are "on the books." It is more than likely that not only will many families be kept in ignorance of these enquiries, they will be unable to prevent them or to ensure that the information that is passed to the court welfare office is factually correct and does not contain biased subjective value judgments. Almost certainly parents who have dealings with the probation service or the local authority social services will not be told that in future, should they divorce, information about them will be passed without their consent to the divorce court welfare service. Of course it may be relevant to a welfare officer to know that a family may have sought help of a local authority over a child care problem. A non-paternalistic, participant approach to this matter would be first to ask the parents themselves and then to ask them if an approach could be made to the agency. The paternalistic approach on the other hand would decide that to consult the parents is either not necessary, since it's justified in the child's interests, or even likely to produce an evasive or dishonest response.

The case therefore against the development of a preventive child-welfare approach to divorce court welfare work is a strong one. There is risk that its vigorous pursuit may do more harm than good. Yet against these objections must be weighed the possibility that children may be suffering while their parents wrangle. This reseach has clearly demonstrated that most divorcing parents, when questioned, replied that they thought it right that the court should investigate their children's circumstances and those of other divorcees. But it has also shown that they were glad to have had the opportunity to discuss their various difficulties and plans for the future. They did not object to intervention save in a few cases. What was important was the style and manner in which it was done. What they clearly wanted was an open, even-handed approach which defined the limits of the welfare officer's intervention and did not infringe their basic legal rights if things went wrong. They valued most those welfare officers who helped the family as a whole adapt to the consequences of marriage breakdown. This was so whether the officer merely provided a sympathetic neutral ear or mediated when matters such as custody or access were in dispute. The divorce court welfare officer and the system he represents may be understood as facilitating the family's reorganisation. The weight of this research evidence suggests that this point should be acknowledged as the welfare officer's primary task. Such a task would seek to meet the main social and emotional needs of the families concerned and would be in line with much informal court welfare practice, if the testimony of the parents interviewed is to be believed. It also accords with the social casework axiom of "starting where the clients are" by considering their interests first. By contrast, as

Platt and others have argued, the preventive child-welfare approach has at its root the need to protect community interest whether this be by preventing delinquency or other forms of deviant behaviour considered to disrupt the workings of society.[33] One of the problems of paternalism claiming to act in other people's best interests is that it may arouse suspicion that it is not what it seems. Instead, other interests, including those of the practitioner, may be given preference. The mistrust and alienation that this may lead to may contribute to the very problems the preventive approach seeks to forestall. On the other hand, a participant approach to divorce court welfare practice, aimed at getting alongside families and working *with* them as they reorganise themselves after divorce would not only have more specific and realistically obtainable goals, it would help avoid the risk of consumer alienation and mistrust that sadly seems to have become a consequence of some of the most well-intentioned preventive social work. Paradoxically, this might well prove the correct way to be efficiently preventive.

NOTES

1. Report of the Departmental Committee on Social Services in Courts of Summary Jurisdiction, Cmnd. 5122 (HMSO, 1936).
2. *Ibid.* p. 12.
3. An attempt to safeguard the applicant's legal rights was made by the Magistrates Courts Act 1952 which provided that a conciliator should only be called in by the court after both spouses had appeared before it.
4. A. H. Manchester and J. M. Whetton, "Marital Conciliation in England and Wales" (1974) 23 *International and Comparative Law Quarterly* 349.
5. Home Office, Report on the Work of the Probation and After-care Department 1972–75 (HMSO, 1976), para. 118.
6. Report on the Probation and After Care Statistics 1975 and 1976 (Home Office, November 1977), Table 18.
7. Manchester and Whetton, *op. cit.*
8. Report on the Probation and After Care Statistics 1975 and 1976 (Home Office, November 1977), Table 18.
9. Judicial Statistics Annual Report 1976 (HMSO, July 1977), Table G.6.
10. Finer Report, para. 4.310.

11. Final Report of the Committee on Procedure in Matrimonial Causes, Cmnd. 7024 (HMSO, 1947).
12. The Denning Committee's report did not fall on entirely deaf ears. In the early 1950s certain commissioners for divorce and judges began to request probation officers to make enquiries in cases where divorcing parents were in dispute about their children. It is not entirely clear why these enquiries were undertaken by the probation service rather than by the Official Solicitor except that in the provinces it might have been considered cheaper to use local probation officers. Similarly, in London from 1950 onwards an experimental scheme attaching a welfare officer to the Divorce Division of the High Court was set up. In certain areas, notably the South-west, some of the principal probation officers had established close working relationships with their local judges and personally undertook occasional enquiries for the High Court. Some of these principal officers acquired in the process a strong commitment for this work, recognising its social and emotional complexity and the heavy responsibilities for deciding children's future wellbeing which lay in the judges' hands. Probably for these reasons, there seems to have been a marked reluctance on the part of these principal probation officers to delegate this work to younger and less experienced staff. Judges varied a great deal, as they still do, in the use they made of this service. Even so, by 1954 several well established schemes were operating such as those in Cornwall and Plymouth. This arose as a result of co-operation between Judge P. C. Rawlins and the respective chief probation officers, Mr. F. Terry and the late Mr. H. Greville. Similar schemes, modest in scope, soon developed in other counties. One aspect of these developments must be noted – namely that they came about as a result of initiatives taken by certain judges and probation officers. Central government, particularly in the form of the Home Office, gave little or no encouragement.
13. Mortlock, B., *New Law Journal*, May 28, 1970.
14. The shortage of social workers did not prevent the remarkable expansion of local authority welfare services during the 1950s and 1960s nor their being given increased statutory responsibilities under the Children and Young Persons Acts of 1963 and 1969. On the other hand, it is only fair to say that it was only in the 1970s that the public began to realise that the quality of these services often left much to be desired.
15. Chief Probation Officers Conference, Report of Family Law Sub-Committee: "Divorce Court Welfare," September 1976.
16. Practice direction.

17. See Appendix 1, page 291, *post.*
18. G. Davis and M. Murch, 'The Implications of the Special Procedure in Divorce'' *Family Law* (1977), Vol. 7, No. 3, pp. 71–78.
19. Judge Jean Graham Hall, "The Future of the Divorce Court Welfare Service" (1977) *Family Law*, Vol. 7, No. 4, pp. 101–104.
20. J. W. B. Douglas, J. M. Ross and H. R. Simpson, *All Our Future* (Peter Davies, 1968).
21. R. Davis, N. Butler and H. Goldstein, *From Birth to Seven* (National Children's Bureau, 1972).
22. M. S. McNair, *Survey of Children in Residential Schools for the Maladjusted in Scotland* (Oliver Boyd, 1968).
23. J. D. Uytman, J. F. McMary, "A psychiatric survey of Approved School Admissions" B. J. of Criminology, January 7, 1967.
24. Charlotte Banks, "Boys: detention centres" in C. Banks and P. C. Broadhurst, *Studies in Psychology* (University of London Press, 1965).
25. Finer Report, Appendix 2, p. 385.
26. Michael Rutter, Nicola Madge, *Cycles of Disadvantage* (Heinemann Educational Books Paperback, 1976).
27. E. Elston, J. Fuller, M. Murch, "Judicial Hearings of Undefended Divorce Petitions" *Modern Law Review*, November 1975, p. 630.
28. Philip Bean, *Rehabilitation and Deviance* (Routledge and Kegan Paul, 1976), pp. 65, 89.
29. Bill Jordan, *Freedom and the Welfare State* (Routledge and Kegan Paul, 1976).
30. Conference of Principal Probation Officers, Divorce Court Welfare (Discussion Paper No. 2), p. 13.
31. Jordan, *op. cit.*, pp. 214–215.
32. See Chapters 7 and 8, *ante.*
33. Anthony Platt, "The Child Savers" from *The Invention of Delinquency* (Chicago Press, 1969). See also Joel Handler, *The Coercive Social Worker* (Markham, 1973).

13 The Judicial Approach to Divorce – Recent Trends and Their Implications for Court Welfare Practice

In the previous chapter I examined what was essentially a welfare approach to families involved in divorce proceedings. I suggested that it was largely influenced by a preventive child-saving ethic. In this chapter I look at the judicial approach to divorce, arguing that fundamental changes in its character are taking place as a result of changes in substantive and procedural family law. This in turn has implications for the future role of the court welfare office.

In 1964, Friedmann pointed out that family law was moving away from a preoccupation with the doctrine of the matrimonial offence and an exclusive concern with the relationship of husband and wife. He argued that one important corollary of the greater consideration given to the needs of children and their place within the family unit as a whole

> "... would be a shift from the adversary to the inquisitorial function of the public authority dealing with divorce – be this in an ordinary court, a special family or domestic relations court or an administrative board which would take the place of a litigation procedure altogether. No longer can it be maintained that divorce proceedings are analagous to an action for breach of contract, damages in tort, or the recovery of property. A judge, a conciliation board, or any other public official entrusted with an equitable arrangement for the care of children cannot possibly rest content with the allegations – contested or uncontested – of the parties in regard to the conduct of the other spouse."[1]

Friedmann, in many respects was prophetic. Developments in divorce law since 1958 have certainly prompted a move from adversarial to a more inquisitorial procedure. Even so, the adversary model still forms the basis of procedure where there are conflicts about the so-called "ancillary" matters concerning financial provision and the care and custody of the children. In my opinion both models of adjudication have serious weaknesses where the conduct of family litigation is concerned.

The main problem with the adversary model is that it overemphasises the elements of conflict between the parties. It assumes there is a clear justiciable issue. The efficiency of adversarial procedure is based on the assumption

> ". . . that if each adversary is motivated to get in the record all the evidence most favourable to his own case the chances are maximised of getting all relevant considerations before the court."[2]

This kind of procedure does not permit a general search for truth but restricts evidence to what is relevant to the issue in dispute.

> "As a procedural matter, the adversary system may be viewed as resting upon an assumption of genuine conflict."[3]

Yet in modern divorce there is often no dispute between the parties. For example, since the 1969 Divorce Reform Act, which virtually abolished the fault principle, more than 98 per cent. of all petitions are undefended. Before the introduction of the special procedure the adversarial procedure as applied to the hearing of the petition itself had become completely ritualised.[4] Even where there is dispute between the parties, for example over custody of children, there is a strong argument that as the parties are likely to be involved in continuing relationships with each other after the legal issues of the case have been dealt with, procedures should seek to minimise and limit the areas of conflict, not expose and aggravate them.[5]

The adversarial approach does not easily allow the judge to carry out his duties in regard to the welfare of children. Traditionally his role is essentially passive and neutral, acting as an umpire between the parties in order to see that the rules of the game are observed. While he may ask questions of a witness he must not interfere too much.[6] The judge does not usually "insert himself into the substantive questioning during the trial."[7] In normal litigation then, the judge is an independent arbiter between the parties in a system that "sets the parties fighting."[8]

Yet in cases where there is dispute about children and the court is faced with conflicting evidence from both parties, or at least the likelihood of it, judges have increasingly turned to the welfare officer as an independent source of information. When this happens it represents an inquisitorial graft onto the basic adversary model of justice. As we have seen, many parents believe that in such circumstances the welfare officer's findings are crucial to the outcome of the case. Yet, remarkably, the evidence from this study and that of Eekelaar *et alia*[9] suggests that this is seldom the case, at least where the care of children is in dispute. Only a very small minority of children actually get transferred from one parent to another as a result of a decision by a judge assisted with a welfare report.

When in 1958 the court was given the duty to satisfy itself that the proposed arrangements for the children were satisfactory or the best that could be devised in the circumstances, it became even more difficult for judges to adopt their traditional passive stance, since they had a duty themselves to test the evidence relating to children. Judges either had to accept at face value the petitioners' statement of arrangements or challenge and test the evidence themselves. The report of our court observation study conducted in 1973 showed clearly that when satisfaction was dealt with at the hearing of the petition, judges, if they asked any questions at all about the children, did so in fairly formal and perfunctory ways.[10] Hall, in his report for the Law Commission in 1968, had commented that the greatest weakness of the system was that it gave the impression of superficiality. As the Lord Chancellor recognised when announcing the extension of the special procedure to all undefended divorce cases:

> "Inevitably it is very difficult for the judge to do more than approve whatever arrangements the petitioner proposes."[11]

The Introduction of the Special Procedure – a Step Towards an Inquisitorial System of Justice

First introduced in 1973 for childless couples divorcing by consent after a two-year separation, the "special procedure" enables courts to grant divorces on the basis of affidavit evidence alone without a hearing in open court. The previous elaborate adversarial procedure had become ritualised and petitioners often found even a brief appearance in the witness box of an open court to be an unpleasant experience. After several intermediary stages the "special procedure" was extended to all undefended divorce cases on 1st April 1977.[12] It has radically altered the whole character of the judiciary's involvement in divorce proceedings. The staff of the county court under the aegis of the registrar now have responsibility for scrutinising the documentary evidence supporting the petition. The role of the judge is reserved primarily for the conduct of appointments in chambers with parents, usually the petitioners, the purpose of which is to consider the circumstances of the children and what is proposed for their future. After the statement of arrangements has been filed, and the respondent parent given the chance to state his wishes, the rules now state:

> "Unless in the circumstances of the particular case, the court thinks it inappropriate to do so, the registrar shall fix an appointment for consideration by a Judge in Chambers of the arrangements for the children and send notice of the appointment to the petitioner and respondent."[13]

This new system of private appointments for parents, many of whom are not accompanied by solicitors because of the restrictions in legal aid, raises two important questions; how do judges interpret the above rule? and how do they conduct the appointments? A preliminary investigation of these questions suggests that most judges see their new task as to enquire further about the children and to test the parents' evidence, albeit in more informal ways than previously. The children appointment has become another part of what seems to be evolving into an essentially inquisitorial system which enables the court itself to seek the facts. Further evidence for this proposition can be found in increased use of the court welfare service itself and in the burgeoning of a number of different schemes set up by local registrars to test the adequacy of information filed with the petition. In some courts, special questionnaires are now sent to divorcing couples before the judicial appointment to augment the information contained in the petition, the statement of arrangements and in the prayer for relief. Other courts are experimenting with the greater use of pre-trial directions hearings. All these measures amount to an inquisitorial approach, the purpose of which is to collect, scrutinise and test the information coming into the court machinery. The introduction of the special procedure has provided the opportunity for such developments.

The Weaknesses of the Inquisitorial Approach

The special procedure seems to give courts and judges much wider discretion to decide what to investigate, how to investigate and even what to do as a result of investigation. To some extent this was inevitable, the more family law sought to regulate close interpersonal relationships. As Ormrod L.J. has pointed out, one consequence of this is that the judges' own personal value judgments will find greater expression. This process alters the traditional role of the judge and raises problems about the exercise of judicial discretion and authority. Ormrod L.J. commented:

> "Sound knowledge of the law and the ability to evaluate evidence and reach accurate and impartial conclusions on the facts of a situation are not enough. Something else is being demanded of courts and Judges which is in fact that old unfashioned and often forgotten quality which used to be called 'wisdom.' This is quite a lot to ask, particularly in a society in which conventional moral values are no longer acceptable as 'guide lines' and the conclusions of the social sciences are at best unstable."[14]

Under the special procedure if judges are to engage in informal discussions of child welfare matters with parents there is a very real risk that some at least will find it difficult to restrain themselves from expressing, justifying and even imposing with the weight of judicial authority their own subjective value judgments. This problem may be compounded by the private nature of the encounter, particularly in the case of unrepresented parents, so that apart from court staff nobody else may know what goes on. All kinds of hobby-horses may be ridden by judges with absolutely no check.

At the moment there are no principles determining either the scope or the limits of these developing informal inquisitorial practices. It is certainly not clear whether parents can object to the judge's conduct of the appointment. There are no rules to ensure that a record is kept of what happened. As we have seen, even where the use of welfare reports is concerned, and where rules provide for parents to have sight of the report, in practice ambiguity and inconsistency flourishes. The law has traditionally valued certainty and consistency and viewed the exercise of discretionary power on the part of authorities with caution. The principles upon which inquisitorial judicial activity is to be based should be enunciated clearly so that they may be understood both by the legal profession and by the public.

Inquisitorial measures allowing wide measures of judicial discretion, if combined with a preventive child welfare approach, could make a powerful authoritarian paternalistic force, posing a real threat to the rights and liberties of ordinary citizens and their families. The problem arises because of the lack of accountability of both welfare and judicial authorities. One of the advantages of our traditional legalistic judicial attitude is that judges are likely to want to check and curb any misuse or abuse of welfare powers. Yet it can be argued that under the special procedure the judges themselves have effectively become welfare authorities. Yet as Street has pointed out, in times when the state's executive power to control and regulate the lives of its citizens has increased and is increasing, the courts should be the bulwark of civil liberties.[15] This constitutional function may be jeopardised once the courts abdicate their traditional role and attempt to perform child welfare tasks. Informal alliances between judicial and executive welfare authorities, who already have extensive powers, could weaken the impartiality of the courts. If this happened all the objections to a preventive child-saving movement that I have outlined in the previous chapter would apply with equal, if not greater, force to the judges themselves. In my view, nothing would shake the public's confidence in the courts more, if the constitutional check against welfare excess was weakened or removed.

The introduction of the special procedure has already served to confuse the roles of judges, welfare officers, and court ancillary staff. The distinction between their tasks becomes less clear as old procedures based on the adversary model give way to more inquisitorial methods.[16] For example, it has led to the strange spectacle of judges announcing to empty courts the names and addresses of those granted decrees, on the face of it a clear case of administrative rubber stamping. Not only are judges sometimes performing a preventive child welfare task in their private appointments with divorcing parents, in some cases welfare officers are coming near to assuming a judicial role since there are courts that almost invariably follow their recommendations. In part this role confusion has been caused by the advent of the divorce court welfare service. Wherever they have established a role for themselves in a host institution, for example penal establishments, hospitals and clinics, social workers have prompted reappraisal and redefinition of other more established roles and interests. This is no less true of the divorce court. The arrival of divorce court welfare officers in some respects represents a challenge to what was hitherto an almost exclusively legal domain where middle class social values predominated. They have introduced a new element of competitive professional rivalry for the power to influence the policy, practice and decision making process of the court. Although lawyers and welfare officers often co-operate in the pursuit of common goals, a potential conflict of interest between them remains. Each has differing occupational value systems, different ways of understanding, different tasks and priorities, and so they must redefine their roles in relation to each other.

Thus some stark questions concerning the whole nature and purpose of court proceedings in relation to family matters arise as a result of the introduction and development of a court welfare service. Should the welfare officers' task to investigate and report on the circumstances of children with divorcing parents be understood primarily in terms of an adjunct to the courts' traditional role of adjudication, as many lawyers would understand it? Or should adjudication merely provide a setting for court welfare officers to initiate preventive social work measures, as some welfare officers themselves would argue? In other words, how far should the traditional role of the civil courts, as a forum within which family disputes are adjudicated, be adapted to advance preventive child welfare measures? Indeed, ought uncontested divorce and related family matters be regarded as matters for a process of adjudication at all? No clear policy decisions have yet been taken about these sort of questions. Instead, piecemeal rules have been framed which have allowed judges and welfare officers wide discretion to work out their own individual answers. Thus where the special procedure is concerned, it is already clear that there is a wide variety of approach both in terms of the conduct of judicial appointments and in the use made of the divorce court welfare service. We are in danger of producing "a system of rampant discretions." As Philip Bean has argued, in relation to criminal jurisdiction, the welfare experts in the last 30 years have steadily asked for more and more professional discretion.[17] The balance between discretion and justice is in danger of shifting in such a way that it no longer accords with basic notions of fairness. Davis remarks:

> "Where law ends, discretion begins, and the exercise of discretion may mean either beneficence or tyranny, either justice or injustice, either reasonableness or arbitrariness."[18]

Another problem is that of determining the point at which judicial inquisition should finish and standard adversarial procedures begin. Take for example a case where a judge has been actively enquiring at the children's appointment into the way a child is being provided for, and difficulties subsequently arise over custody or access. If that judge has already expressed opinions to one party about the child's circumstances and future welfare, can either parent be assured that the judge will remain impartial? Of course, there was risk of this even before the introduction of the special procedure, but it may be aggravated now that everything is heard in private and most parents are unrepresented. Even if that objection can be met, some judges may still have a problem in changing role from investigator to traditional adjudicator. Unless a wholescale revolution in modes of trial in family law is to be undertaken, some confusion and uncertainty is bound to arise from efforts to combine two such fundamentally different methods of adjudication. The time may have come to stop tinkering with the system and to think out the conduct of family litigation afresh. Ad hoc development of procedural law merely risks perpetuating ambiguity and uncertainty of purpose.

In my view, a firm distinction between adjudication and welfare must be maintained, and the responsibilities of judge and welfare officer clearly delineated. Then, as Parsloe has argued, the exercise of welfare and judicial discretion must be controlled, recognising "that to confine, structure and check discretion is not to end it, but to prevent it becoming arbitrary."[19] There must also be a clear system of open accountability. As Latey J. said in the case of *Re B*, reported in the *Guardian* on January 27, 1977:

> "If justice is administered in secret behind closed doors, who can know what is happening? Who can know whether what may in the past have been a good law has become a bad one in need of change? How can criticism and discussion happen on an informed basis? Without this [openness] there is danger of bad laws and bad justice – of injustices perpetuating themselves."

Traditionally the welfare officer has been accountable to the judge, and judges in their turn through the system of appeals have been accountable to superior courts. The rules concerning divorce procedures should be drawn to preserve these principles.

NOTES

1. W. Friedman, *Law in a Changing Society* (Pelican, 1964), p. 189.
2. Harry Bredemeier, "Law as an integrative mechanism" in *Sociology of Law* (Ed. Vilholm Aubert, Penguin), p. 56.
3. Jerome Skolnick, "Social Control in the Adversary System" *Journal of Conflict Resolution* Vol. XI, 1967, p. 52.
4. E. Elston, J. Fuller, M. Murch, "Judicial Hearings of Unde-

fended Divorce Petitions" *Modern Law Review*, November 1975, p. 630.

5. See Chapter 1.
6. R. M. Jackson, *Enforcing the Law* (Penguin), p. 155.
7. H. Abraham, *The Judicial Process* (Oxford, 1962).
8. Ibid.
9. J. Eekelaar, E. Clive, K. Clarke and S. Raikes, *Custody after Divorce* (Centre for Socio-legal Studies, Oxford, 1977).
10. E. Elston, J. Fuller, M. Murch, *op. cit.*
11. *Hansard* (Lords) June 15, 1976. Debate: *Legal Aid and Legal Services*, p. 1218.
12. The Matrimonial Causes (Amendment No. 2) Rules 1976. (S.I. 1976. No. 2166 (L 39).)
13. Matrimonial Causes Rules 1977, r. 48 (4).
14. Sir Roger Ormrod, *Sixth Hilda Lewis Memorial Lecture*, October 1973.
15. H. Street, *Justice in the Welfare State* (Stevens, 1968), p. 129.
16. G. Davis and M. Murch, "The implications of the Special Procedure in Divorce" *Family Law*, Vol. 7, No. 3, 1977, p. 71.
17. Philip Bean, *Rehabilitation and Deviance* (Routledge & Kegan Paul, 1976), p. 144.
18. K. Davis, *Discretionary Justice* (Baton Rouge, 1967), p. 3.
19. Phillida Parsloe, "Social Work and the Justice Model" *British Journal of Social Work*, Vol. 6.1, April 1976.

14 Participant Justice

From 1958 onwards the divorce court has struggled to synthesise or find an appropriate accommodation between the requirements of justice and the interests of welfare. In the last two chapters I have attempted to show that a paternalistic philosophy committed to preventive social policies has been an important influence on welfare practice in courts with matrimonial jurisdiction; that the judicial approach has traditionally rested on the adversary model of justice whereby the role of the judge is essentially passive and neutral rather than interventive; and that the requirement that courts should place the welfare of children above all else has inevitably imposed limitations on the adversary model and fostered a move towards a more inquisitorial approach.

Divergent social philosophies arouse confusion in those required to administer a system so split. Thus in 1976 a study group of Surrey Divorce Court Welfare wrote in the preface to their report:

> "The need for this report arose from an uncertainty experienced by officers as to the precise task when reporting on the welfare of children."[1]

Whereas in the 1960s, as we have seen, many welfare officers interpreted their task in predominantly preventive child-saving terms, the signs are that a new approach is struggling to emerge. During the 1970s the writings of welfare officers contain more and more references to taking advantage of the formal enquiry to attempt conciliation and to reach informal decisions by a process of settlement. The model many of them have in mind is clearly "participant" in character in the sense that it involves working in collaboration with families and depends on receiving their authority to do so. For example Buttle, a practising welfare officer, has written:

> "The task of both the judge and the Welfare Officer assisting him, is generally to bring about a situation where parties to

the dispute and their children can end an impossible situation with the least damage to all concerned."[2]

Dudley, a senior divorce court liaison officer, who carried out an investigation of court welfare work in the county of Devon, wrote in his report:

> "One of the prime tasks of our enquiring officer is seen as frequently to re-establish, or even establish for the first time, a meaningful communicaton between the parents either directly or indirectly through the medium of the officer. An enquiring officer would not have done his job properly if he confined himself merely to ascertaining and reporting facts.... The enquiry situation was seen as offering many opportunities for short-term casework and officers asserted that these must be grasped."[3]

Such comment implies a recognition that parents and children may have active roles to play within a process that is seen as settling family disputes and creating a more accepting atmosphere in which family relationships can continue after divorce. This view accords with that of the majority of parents interviewed in this research. It suggests that a more participant model of family justice is already sometimes being practised informally and perhaps largely intuitively. It seems less authoritarian and paternalistic than either the welfare or traditional judicial approach to proceedings.

In the 1960s, as Kathleen Bell has pointed out, participation became something of a "hurrah" word[4] in social policy and administration. In the planning field the Skeffington Report explored the idea of greater community involvement, and the Seebohm Report which led to reorganisation of local authority services also thought the principle of consumer participation in the provision of social services should receive greater acknowledgement. The problem was that "participation" lacked precise definition. It could range from merely consulting consumers or potential users of services, not necessarily even on a representative basis, to giving users of services power to control policy. Bell is probably right in suggesting that there is a movement towards making "the boundaries separating providers and receivers of social services less rigid" but there are formidable problems involved in finding ways of doing this, problems which "participation rhetoric tends to obscure."

Settlement as the Key to a Participant Approach to Justice

Sir Roger (now Lord Justice) Ormrod's lecture is a good point to start from. He remarked:

> "The structure and machinery of courts was designed essentially for *deciding* disputes. We have, in some instances, adapted them for *settling* disputes, as Sir John Donaldson said recently of the Industrial Relations Court. This process of 'settling' rather than 'deciding' is certainly developing in the Family Division. It turns the advocate into the negotiator and the judge into a problem-solver or honest broker, and enables the parties to adjust themselves better to the situation as it is. This is all to the good. Imposed solutions are sometimes unavoidable but they are better avoided. But this is as far as courts can go. They cannot function as welfare authorities. They sometimes think that they can play a supervisory role and try to, but the structure prevents it. They are wholly dependent on what they are told by the parents or social worker; they are incapable of initiating any action themselves; and incapable of carrying out any action except in the last resort to make orders and enforce them. As settlers they keep their essentially authoritarian character discreetly, but not too discreetly, veiled, because it helps to effect settlements. As deciders, they reveal it as plainly as possible because in the last resort they are enforcers too. But this essential characteristic of courts effectually precludes them from adopting the roles of conciliator, or supervisor. No system of Family Law can do without courts as a last resort, but if they are to serve their purpose they must function as courts, efficiently, sensitively and humanely, and avoiding legal technicalities, as far as possible, but retaining their essential characteristics of a court. Their role begins when the parties and their advisers and the welfare authorities have failed to resolve the difficulties. They require all the

assistance that social workers can give them but they should not be regarded as a part of the social services."[5]

There are many points here that need elaboration; the most important concerns the shift of emphasis from deciding disputes to fostering settlement. Both the traditional adversary judicial model and the paternalistic welfare approach involve a decision making process in which judicial authority itself takes the decision and "hands it down" to the litigant or client. This casts the decision maker in an elevated or superior position and the recipient in a dependent submissive role. There is no doubt that some people find such a process entirely satisfactory – it hands responsibility for the resolving of conflict or uncertainty to the authorities. Yet it means that they lose a measure of authority or control over their own lives. In psychodynamic terms, one can argue that such an approach encourages authorities to collude unrealistically with clients or litigants in the process of relieving them of responsibility, and that may have a demoralising effect. On the other hand in marriage breakdown interpersonal conflict and stress sometimes reach the point when parties feel so estranged from each other, so wounded and threatened, that the only way conflict can be contained or resolved is to appeal to an external neutral superordinate authority.[6] I have argued that the whole working of law is basically appropriate as a specialist social institution that has evolved, over centuries, techniques of conflict resolution. Through the agency of solicitors it provides people with partisan support which may also restrain them when emotion may temporarily defeat logic. Yet the need for this sort of thing may only be temporary. Judges and lawyers have long recognised the value of decisions reached by negotiation and consent. It is remarkable how often warring litigants quite suddenly see reason and show a willingness to compromise when they reach the door of the court. Decisions reached by mutual consent have a greater chance of being kept and acted upon in an atmosphere of good will, than those imposed on parties where one feels the winner and the other the loser. This is especially important in family matters concerning custody and access to the children, or over maintenance. The parties will have a continuing relationship of some kind and share a measure of responsibility as parents towards their children. If each party to the conflict can share a commitment to its resolution, the chances of later breakdown will be minimised. The great advantage of settlement, as a process of decision making, is that it mobilises the commitment of all parties to a common goal.

Features of the Participant Approach

(i) *Primary task*

The participant model defines the primary task of legal and welfare processes in a new way. It starts from the assumption that there is a common objective about which all parties could reach agreement, even though they may differ as to the means of reaching that objective. This common objective is that of arriving at a fair and reasonable basis upon which the family can reconstitute itself following divorce, paying due regard to the interests of the children. In other words, the primary task of divorce machinery is to find a way of providing for the interests and welfare of family members after divorce. I doubt very much whether more than a small minority of divorcing parents would not subscribe to this objective, likewise few lawyers or welfare officers would dissent fundamentally.

(ii) *Membership of the conflict-resolving system*

Once it is accepted that there is a common objective, all the actors within the machinery of justice – judges, members of the Bar, solicitors, welfare officers and the family members themselves, who have temporarily become part of the system – can be perceived as being bound together in a common pursuit of an agreed objective. This becomes the task, and each actor within the system has a responsibility to work towards the common goal. To a large extent therefore the task of working towards the common goal becomes itself an authority from which the actors derive their responsibility and by which their roles are defined and differentiated.

This way of thinking perceives the court, its welfare officers and the legal representatives combining together with family members to form a group or small organisation with the purpose of changing the divorcing couple's status, resolving conflict, and safeguarding according to law the welfare of the children.

The work of Bion,[7] Miller[8] and Rice,[9] Richardson[10] *et alia* has contributed much to our understanding of formal organisations and social groups. Their approach assumes that every group comes together for a purpose, and in many instances members of the group, organisation or institution may have a conscious awareness of what that purpose is, although this is not always so since the purpose can be assumed implicitly. Group activity nevertheless will be intended to further it.

Bion, the originator of this conceptual model, used the term 'leadership' to indicate each individual's capacity to take and share responsibility for the performance of the group's rational task. In the divorce context this would include the couple themselves, their children as far as they were able, the lawyers, court welfare officers and the court's judicial officers. Each takes a different role in relation to the task, yet each actor has a valid contribution to make to it.

But Bion suggested that there are at the same time aspects of group or organisational behaviour that do not always further the stated rational purpose, but which nevertheless seem to satisfy the emotional needs of its members in ways that are often largely unacknowledged by the individual members of the group. These aspects of interpersonal behaviour which sometimes assist, but often hinder, individuals in their attempts to take responsibility for their share of the group's rational task Bion terms "basic assumption" activity.

This kind of behaviour is often obscure and puzzling, but Bion suggests it can be comprehended on the basis that members had come together and made a tacit assumption about what the group had met for, an assumed purpose that was sometimes quite different from the consciously avowed one. Miller and Rice remark of this "basic assumption" behaviour:

> "In so far as group members develop attitudes and beliefs about each other and about the group that transcend the

purpose for which they have met, they are making assumptions about themselves as individuals and about the group as a group. These assumptions, together with their attitudes towards their purpose, provides the emotional climate in which they meet."

Three kinds of basic assumption behaviour have been identified:

(1) that in which one member of the system is ascribed dominant power and authority, relieving the others of their share of responsibility to work at the task. This could for example occur when it is assumed that the whole future of the case depends on what the judge or the welfare officer decides;
(2) that when it is assumed that the outcome of the case depends almost entirely on a dominant, paired, "partnership" within the system. In the divorce court context this may be the parties, their two legal representatives, or for example a dominant combination of welfare officer and one parent;
(3) that when the system's energies are concentrated on the conduct of emotional conflict or fight to the extent that the nature of the system's task is lost sight of. In its most obvious form the conduct of adversarial litigation channels people's energies into emotional dispute to such an extent that the interests of children for example can be entirely overlooked. In short, the drama of the fight can encourage the system to ignore the realities of its primary task. Similarly this kind of task avoidance can occur if its members go into emotional flight which may manifest itself by delay, by getting bogged down in largely irrelevant procedural matters, by excessive and diversionary prevarication of one kind or another.

This is not the appropriate place to elaborate what is a much more complex and sophisticated behavioural analysis than I have suggested. Each case generates its own individual dynamic within which any one or all of these basic-assumption themes may interfere with the performance of the primary task. Here I want only to indicate that a conceptual framework already exists which would help explain what is a new, yet realistic, approach to family justice; an approach which in many respects is already being practised even though it may not be fully acknowledged.

Two points must be kept in mind; first the notion that all the actors in the drama of divorce proceedings may be perceived as forming a temporary social system. By including the family members themselves within the boundary of the system, instead of seeing them as external to it, it becomes possible to see them as having an important contribution to make to the decision-making process itself. This is realistic because their perceptions and circumstances must be taken into full account. By their control of information which they may give or withhold to their solicitors, to the welfare officer, or to the judicial officers, they influence the decisions which the court can make. The participant model thus becomes a system which is dependent for its effective function on the collaboration of all its members. Their collaboration depends on trust. That is fostered by procedures based on openness, and by the frank recognition of the value of each member of the system.

Once the actors recognise that they are members of a system they more easily recognise their relatedness to each other. By contrast, more authoritarian approaches, particularly those based on the inquisitorial justice model or a preventive child welfare approach, start from the presumption that the family is to be regarded only as a social system distinct from the decision-making system. In a sense the family becomes an object to be processed. We have essentially two systems, the family and the legal machinery, confronting each other. This results in the reinforcement of all the attitudes that go with confrontation – mistrust, secret procedures, reluctant communication and so on.

The second point concerns the notion of a common primary task, and the assumption that members of the participant system can share a sense of commitment to a common purpose however elusive it may appear to them at times. But this means that the definition of the task by the actors within the system becomes a crucially important issue, since in order to pursue it they have to agree what it is. At present it seems the actors are frequently at cross-purposes. Judges, welfare officers and solicitors individually often define their tasks in different ways. Is it any wonder that parents and their children may feel confused and helpless? Such confusion arises from the interaction of competing philosophies, value systems and perceptions at work within a system that has developed pragmatically and rapidly within the last quarter century, in the absence of a clear policy.

The realities of divorce as they affect modern families are forcing the actors, whatever the nature of their assumptions, to acknowledge the most important issues – namely that a large and growing number of children are now affected every year by their parents' marriage breakdown; that the State cannot possibly assume more than a brief responsibility for their future welfare without enormous expense; that most parents wish to do the best they can in the circumstances for their children, and that it therefore makes sense to try to mobilise their resources and strengths in the pursuit of that objective; that when marriages break up some division of responsibility in relation to the future care of children and the family property has to be made.[11] Decisions about all these matters must in the last resort be reasonably acceptable to the family members themselves if they are to stick and be made to work, and if the risks of future emotional conflict and litigation are to be minimised. Today no-one dissents from the Law Commission's view that one of the purposes of a good divorce law should be that:

> "... when regrettably a marriage has irretrievably broken down (the law should) enable the empty legal shell to be destroyed with the maximum fairness and the minimum bitterness, distress and humiliation."[12]

Mortlock has written:

> "It is, I think, now fairly generally accepted that our adversary procedure tends to increase the distance between husbands and wives. But a rational divorce system, whose objective was sensible family reorganisation would surely be aiming to achieve exactly the opposite. It would seek the containment of hostility, the reconciliation of divisions between the parties, the introduction of whatever level of

understanding of the marital interaction were possible so that the element of personal betrayal, responsible for so much unhappiness, might be eliminated or reduced as a continuing factor. In this way, communication of some kind might become possible between those formerly married. At the very least, the pressures splitting their children's loyalties could be diminished."[13]

Given the increasing acceptance by practitioners of objectives such as these, one must ask which strategies and tactics are most likely to contribute to a fair and civilised reorganisation of the family after divorce and what kind of machinery is needed to give effect to them. As I have already argued, the basic choice of strategies is between seeking to do things *to* and *for* families, or, by encouraging their participation, seeking to work *with* them towards agreed objectives.

In the remaining chapters of this book I want to examine the influence of these different approaches on the policy debate about the kind of judicial and welfare machinery needed to administer family law in the future.

NOTES

1. Surrey Probation and After-care Service, *Report on Divorce Court Welfare*, 1976.
2. C. Buttle, "Divorce – a consideration of work of the Divorce Court Welfare Officers" *Social Work Today*, 1975, Vol. 6, No. 11.
3. H. R. Dudley, *Report of an investigation in the field of Court Welfare Work* (Devon Probation and After-Care Service, September 1973).
4. Kathleen Bell, *Disequilibrium in Welfare* (Octave, University of Newcastle, 1973), p. 8.
5. *Sixth Hilda Lewis Memorial Lecture*, October 1973.
6. M. Murch, *The Role of the Solicitor in Divorce Proceedings*, *op. cit.*
7. W. R. Bion, *Experience in Groups* (Tavistock, 1961).
8. E. J. Miller, *Task and Organisation* (Wiley, 1976).
9. E. J. Miller and A. R. Rice, *Systems of Organisation* (Tavistock, 1967).
10. E. Richardson, *The Teacher, the School and the Task of Management* (Macmillan, 1975).

11. Indeed some solicitors have told me that they are finding that property is becoming an increasingly bitter area for dispute; just as upsetting in its own way for the parties, and sometimes for their children, as direct dispute about them.
12. Law Commission, *The Field of Choice*, para. 15.
13. Mortlock, *The Inside of Divorce* (Constable, 1972).

15 The Advance of Family Courts – Reality or Mirage?

The development of divorce court welfare work during the last decade has been overshadowed by one dominant issue; the possibility of unifying family jurisdiction within a single system of family courts. This raises the question of the relationship between the courts and the welfare authorities, in particular whether the court should control its ancillary welfare services.

During the late 1950s and early 1960s, before the startling increase in divorce petitions began, the social and behavioural sciences began to focus on the nuclear family, seen as a crucially important social unit. As a result, many social institutions which had hitherto focused their attention on individuals or on dyadic relationships within families (mother/child, husband/wife, etc.) began also to consider how they might address themselves to the family as a whole. Thus in the social work field, children's departments, as they then were, began appointing specialist family caseworkers following the approach started during the war by the family service units. There was a move to establish family advice centres.[1] There was a general spate of discussion papers, books, and conferences all taking as their theme working with whole families. Social workers began to flirt with the idea of family therapy which was gaining ground in psychiatric medicine, particularly in the United States. There was increasing debate about how to reorganise social services so as to provide comprehensively for the needs of all family members. This debate culminated in the establishment of the Seebohm Committee whose recommendations led to the creation of local authority social services departments. The Probation Service wished to retain its separate identity linked with the courts and fought hard and successfully to avoid inclusion in the reorganised social services of the local authority even though its stance created ambiguities.[2] A basic question facing the Probation Service was whether it was appropriate for it to retain its non-penal responsibilities, particularly its voluntary matrimonial work and its work in courts with matrimonial jurisdiction.[3]

Lawyers, too, at this period were increasingly accepting the notion of family law as a substantive body of law in its own right. The redefinition of matrimonial law, and children's legislation within the wider compass of family law gave currency to the view that a complete reorganisation of the machinery of justice was necessary to administer it. By the end of the 1960s English family law had become a jungle of ad hoc rules, procedures and remedies exercisable or obtainable in a wide variety of courts with different jurisdictions. The unsatisfactory state of this branch of civil law led to pressure for reform, pressure which had been reinforced by the steadily rising divorce rate throughout the decade. This was placing the existing machinery under strain and forcing a fundamental reappraisal of its purpose, its methods, and the use of its resources. Some thought what was needed was a tidying up operation. Others saw the need for a major rethinking of the law's whole approach to the family. Both sets of reformers pinned their hopes on the idea of a family court.

In 1965 the White Paper *The Child, the Family and the Young Offender* foresaw family courts developing out of the juvenile courts and in the first instance dealing primarily with delinquency. This could be described as a "social work" proposal for family courts, heavily influenced as it was by a child-saving social control philosophy which sought to widen and extend social workers' professional discretion to intervene in and regulate the family. A very different, lawyer's view of family courts was advanced the following year by the newly appointed chairman of the Law Commission, Sir Leslie Scarman.[4] He suggested the creation of the Family Division of the Supreme Court with a supervisory and appellate jurisdiction over regional family courts, which would deal with all kinds of family disputes many of which had nothing to do with the criminal law. Such a conception had a lot in common with the kinds of Family Courts already in existence in certain parts of the United States.

The advance of socio-legal research also increased the pressure for root and branch reform, exposing for the layman the inefficiencies and anomalies of the magistrates' domestic jurisdiction.[5] It was increasingly recognised that because the two systems of family law as administered by the magistrates' court and the divorce court had developed separately, they often operated in different and even contradictory ways. When the Divorce Reform Act 1969 removed the concept of the matrimonial offence from divorce, the principles upon which the magistrates' court granted relief short of divorce became even more anomalous.[6]

The arguments advanced at this period in favour of procedural and structural reform of the administration of family law within a single, unified system of family courts were largely pragmatic, aimed merely at achieving consistency. In the usual English way, underlying and conflicting philosophical issues, for example whether or not the system should develop on paternalistic lines, were seldom made explicit. I shall argue later that because in many respects these philosophies were fundamentally incompatible, the ambiguity of purpose that they fuelled was largely responsible for the later stagnation of the family court movement. Nevertheless, in the late 1960s and early 1970s the notion of the family court appeared to be gaining momentum.

It gained a certain amount of currency from the divorce law reform debate. For example in 1966 a proposal for family courts was put forward by Mr. Quinton Edwards in *Putting Asunder*, the report on Divorce Law Reform prepared by the group appointed by the Archbishop of Canterbury.[7] In the following year, 1967, the Latey Committee's report strongly favoured the idea although it made no suggestion about the court's structure or jurisdiction.[8]

In December 1969, Parliament debated a bill to create a Family Division of the High Court which was subsequently established by the Administration of Justice Act 1970. In the House of Lords debate, Lord Gardiner remarked:

> "It is most important that all family matters, whether they involve the parties to a matrimonial dispute or the care, adoption or guardianship of children should be dealt with in the most sympathetic atmosphere and by Judges and Officials who really understand family problems and how to

> grapple with them. More and more emphasis is now laid on the importance of welfare; the welfare of every member of the family who may be concerned in any domestic case that comes before the courts."[9]

Lord Gardiner's remarks are typical of those made by many well meaning humane judges and lawyers appreciative of the shortcomings of the traditional adversarial model of justice when applied to family matters, but naïve in their understanding of the complex nature of the policies and practices of statutory welfare authorities. As Mortlock remarked:

> "No one could disagree with the wish to have family matters dealt with sympathetically by people who really understand them. But how is this to be dealt with by calling the Divorce Division the Family Division and transferring to it some of the functions of the Chancery Division? The well-meaning lawyers without specialist training in anything other than the legal aspects of family matters who administered the process in the one will continue to administer the same process in the other. Where is the advance except in nomenclature? The system will remain precisely the same. And it is a system which needs so badly to be altered."

Judge Jean Graham Hall in her pamphlet *Proposal for a Family Court* accepted Lord Gardiner's reasoning for a reorganisation of courts and suggested that it was equally applicable to the creation of family courts at a local level.[10] Yet, as Mortlock has pointed out, what Judge Graham Hall proposed was little more than a tidying up process whereby the jurisdiction of the county court and magistrates courts would merely be combined. It endorsed a continuation of adversarial procedure and the continued involvement of lay magistrates and county court judges.[11] Even so, her pamphlet may have helped stimulate the Law Commission to set up jointly with the Home Office a Family Courts Working Party in August 1971.

This working party deliberated for four years. It started optimistically but eventually suspended its operations, ostensibly because the Finer Committee set up in 1969 was traversing the same ground and produced its report first.[12] Nevertheless, the Working Party did initiate some useful discussion about the family court and particularly about its relationship to welfare authorities. Apart from anything else, by canvassing the views of social workers they prompted them to consider the possibility of family courts, and the role that social workers might play within them. One of the questions the Working Party asked specifically was "what welfare services should the court have in its own control?"; a question subsequently discussed in some detail by the Finer Report, and a matter of vital importance to the future of the divorce court welfare service.

The Social Work Services of the Family Court

When the Finer Committee reported in July 1974 it strongly advocated family courts,[13] as had a number of other official reports produced over the preceding decade.[14] It went further than the others both in the strength of its endorsement of the principle and in its detailed examination of feasibility. It saw local family courts as providing accessible and inexpensive facilities for the settlement of a wide range of family legal issues. There would be no duplication of remedies, and no possibility of choosing between different courts of first instance. The Committee was determined that family courts should exercise nothing but a civil jurisdiction and have no association with criminal matters. To confuse these two jurisdictions when dealing with family disputes was to show "a manifest disrespect for the needs and feelings of the parties concerned."[15] The Committee emphasised that the family court must be an impartial, fully judicial institution and not a quasi-administrative tribunal. It saw no argument for disassociating the court from the rest of the judicial system by severing its connection with the Family Division of the High Court.

Considerations of this kind led the Committee to the view that the family court must have "a professional staff serving the court and answerable to it" to help the court to reach sound decisions on welfare issues. The Committee proposed that social workers should be attached to the court to carry out investigations and to produce expert impartial evidence. The court welfare officer, with the authority of the court, should assist parties by means of conciliation to deal with the consequences of marriage breakdown. The aim of these proposals was that the court, with the help of its welfare agency, should be both judicial and conciliatory, trying to help families "make the best decisions and reach the best solutions over a wide range of problems which the fact of marital breakdown produces." In effect this was to develop the kind of service that as we have seen is already performed in a limited fashion by divorce court welfare officers. The crucial point was that this work was seen by the Committee as an integral part of the judicial machinery for the determination of family legal disputes. The committee members were concerned to draw a sharp distinction between this kind of work and traditional social work practice. In their view:

> "... the court must not see the men, women and children with whom it is concerned as 'clients' and still less as 'patients' for whom the court process is just another kind of 'treatment'.... The individual in the family court must, in the last resort, remain the subject of rights and not the object of assistance."

In all these respects the Finer Committee's proposals can be said to accord fully with the main findings of this research reported in Part II.

Family Courts – the Obstacles to Change

The Finer Report did not propose a detailed blueprint for a system of family courts. It confined itself to arguing the case for reform and to outlining some of the principles and objectives of a reorganised system. In many respects, their recommendations were modest. They envisaged a reconstruction of the existing system:

> "In seeking to bring structural order out of confusion there can be no question of starting afresh with brand new materials. There has to be a model court, but it can be established by using the components that are, or are likely to come to hand."

While they could see no case for continuing with a reconstructed matrimonial jurisdiction of the magistrates courts, it was clear that they saw the new family court being developed within the county court system. Mostyn has argued that this would in effect do little more than "reform only the existing hierarchical disorder, change a few names, and leave the substance as it is."[16]

It might be said the Finer Committee concentrated their attention rather too narrowly on the court structure itself, thus ignoring for example the important role of lawyers in the pre-litigation phase. On the other hand Finer was probably trying to be politically realistic, believing that the institutions of the law would not accept radical change. Indeed it can be argued that the Committee's report fell between two stools. Had it been bolder, proposed root and branch reform and worked out the cost, something might have happened.

By 1975 it had become quite clear that no ministerial action would be taken to implement the Finer Committee's proposals for a family court. The government's initial response was to postpone detailed consideration until the 1975 Children Act had been passed and the report of the Law Commission's working party on matrimonial proceedings in magistrates courts had been received. When the Finer Report was debated in the House of Commons, the then Secretary of State for the Social Services, Barbara Castle, concluded by saying that "the government could see no prospect for accepting the recommendation for Family Courts."

This was said even though the Labour Party manifesto contained a commitment to the principle. The following year the Law Commission's Working Party report acknowledged that consideration of family courts was not part of their brief, but remarked that they thought "formidable economic, administrative, and practical difficulties" stood in the path of reform. The Royal Commission on Legal Services also considered the issue lay outside their scope.

Thus by the late 1970s the concept of a Family Court seemed to have run out of steam. An impasse had been reached. The harsher economic climate of recession and its restriction on public spending seemed to have blighted the chances of substantial change. Yet the tide of divorce rose relentlessly, and with it the cost of civil legal aid. The Rules Committee, through such stop-gap measures as the extension of the special procedure, did its best to bring procedural coherence into the system. The Supplementary Benefits Commission stopped its policy of encouraging deserted wives to seek orders in the magistrates courts before granting them assistance. This helped to reduce the load of work on that discredited system. Even so, by the end of 1977 no less an authority than the then President of the Family Division, Sir George Baker, was testifying that the system was near breaking point, at least where the High Court was concerned. He told the Law Society's National Conference:

> "The number of ancillary proceedings has risen sharply and of late alarmingly. We are now at saturation point, not only because of the increase in divorce but because some matters – especially wardship, never end until death or until the younger child is 18. . . . Even if I had more judges, there is no spare accommodation for more courts in London and in some other places. One attempt at alleviation has been to increase the number of judges in the long vacation. They too have been swamped. . . ."[17]

Given that there was no prospect of family courts the President envisaged as the only alternative a policy of darn and mend. By making further changes in both substantive and procedural law the pressure on the system would be relieved somewhat. Thus he remarked: "We cannot have Family Courts, but there is much that can and must be done." He indicated the likelihood for example of undefended divorce simply on the basis of 12 months separation, and the introduction of a Domestic Proceedings and Magistrates Courts Bill to remove the major anomalies arising from the divided jurisdictions of the magistrates and divorce courts following the recommendations of the Law Commission's working party. Yet further simplifications of divorce procedure will do little to deal with the continuing problem of children and property disputes. Since about 60 per cent. of married people now own their own homes, when marriages break down there is more often than not a substantial equity in the matrimonial home. The result is an increasing number of financial disputes pursued in the courts.

Thus a position had been reached where all authorities seemed to agree in principle that the system had to change, yet there was no agreement about what the nature of that change should be. As Mostyn put it:

> "Is a system set up in 1858 to deal with the then grave social crime of adultery (until 1937 the only ground for divorce) but affecting only a small group of affluent people, tinkered with from time to time, now capable of administering on an almost universal basis an instrument of social change and family reorganisation which is what divorce has become? The answer is not in doubt, what is in doubt is the succession."[18]

I would like therefore to examine more closely the obstacles to change. I suggest that these are as much to do with the nature of institutional behaviour as with more practical problems of social policy. In my view unless a careful analysis of the forces that oppose change is made, no reform is likely. I consider first the so-called "formidable economic, administrative and practical difficulties" referred to by the Law Commission's working party and examine how formidable these considerations are likely to be.

Finance

The mid 1970s was a period of severe economic restraint. In the public sector the general assumption made by policy makers tended to be that anything new would cost more. In the case of family courts this has been stated in a number of parliamentary debates, the most recent being that in the Domestic Proceedings and Magistrates Courts Bill.[19] Yet, that assumption has never been examined, simply because the idea has not advanced to a point where its financial implications can be estimated. Indeed it has been suggested that new schemes might well be cheaper than the existing system with its cumbersome procedures and divided jurisdictions.[20] No one has attempted, as far as I know, to estimate the cost effectiveness of even the existing machinery. There is a strong prima facie case that savings could be made: for example, the new procedure for undefended divorce removed barristers from such proceedings. The restriction on legal aid meant that more litigants were preparing their own petitions. These two changes were claimed to have saved about £6,500,000 in the first year.[21] Until recently the system could scarcely be regarded as rigorously cost conscious. There are many more areas where savings could be made by altering procedures. The procedure for dealing with undefended divorce remains appallingly fragmented; each part being dealt with separately on different occasions. The Registrar scrutinises the evidence supporting the petition and later deals with financial provision, while the judge pronounces the decree and looks into the arrangements proposed for the children. Substantial savings would almost certainly result if all uncontested matters were reviewed at a single consolidated trial as the Family Law Sub-Committee of the Law Society have recently suggested.[22] The true cost of the existing machinery is unknown. It makes little sense to claim that a new system would cost more, as the Law Commission's working party did in 1976. The economic argument is not yet proven. Its introduction at an early stage in the policy debate about family courts suggests that it was being used as a cover for more substantial, less rational objections. Anyone familiar with the workings of the higher bureaucracy in this country will recognise the approach: you state a desirable end, announcing that we must pay more attention to the needs of our children, then make token piecemeal reform to give credence to the idea that something is being done, the Divorce Division of the High Court becomes the Family Division. But you resist any major attempt to examine the reality of the problem in detail, notwithstanding the existence of reports from Royal Commissions or Committees of one kind or another. Instead, you announce that major change would be too expensive, despite the damage we are doing to children which might be avoidable in another context. We then settle back to our familiar tasks.

Administrative Considerations

The administrative objections looked more substantial. The argument was that the legal machinery, particularly the county courts, was not ready in the late 1970s to accommodate fundamental change, since it was still re-establishing itself after the major reorganisation which set up the crown court. By this the county courts lost a number of their more experienced administrative staff who transferred to the new courts. The 1970s also placed many new responsibilities on county court staff following changes in the substantive law, for example, the system of pre-trial review introduced by the Administration of Justice Act 1973, and the extra work that arose from the Consumer Credit Act 1974 and the Rent Act 1974. Above all they were also having to respond to the big increase in matrimonial work and adapt to the introduction and extension of the special procedure and the restrictions on legal aid which had the effect of forcing court administrative staff into a more active relationship with the public, particularly in providing informal advice. All the pressures on the county court probably made them both less enthusiastic about further change, and dissatisfied with their increased load of responsibilities. Thus whilst the county courts superficially looked a likely venue within which to construct the family court, in practice the time and climate were not right in the 1970s.

Administratively, many other interests would potentially be affected by the establishment of family courts. Not only would magistrates lose their domestic jurisdiction, but juvenile courts too, in the long term, might lose their involvement in care proceedings. In the absence of a clear proposal for family courts no one can say quite what the overall effect on the system of magistrates courts would be. As it is, the magistrates' domestic jurisdiction has been decreasing by contrast with the increase in the work of divorce courts, so that there might not be much opposition from that quarter. On the other hand attempts to alter the composition and jurisdiction of juvenile courts is likely to provoke a very vigorous debate, as it did after the 1965 White Paper. Following this in the late 1960s it seemed to be generally assumed that this problem could be circumvented by establishing family courts with only matrimonial jurisdiction in the first instance. Nevertheless the long-term threat to juvenile courts remains.

At central government level, the advent of family courts would certainly mean that the responsibilities in the family law field of the Home Office, Department of Health and Social Security, and the Lord Chancellor's Office would need to be reconsidered and rearranged. In the absence of a superordinate authority this could well be the most difficult task, though this may be an area where there is big scope for cost-saving. The Judiciary too is likely to be concerned to see that any new system harmonises with the Family Division of the High Court. Very reasonably they might want it to provide new High Court judges with valuable experience of family matters.

As there is no clear, reasoned and detailed proposal for a system of family courts, none of these interests has had publicly to declare its hand. As a result it is impossible to gauge the real strength of opposition. When faced with a detailed blueprint opposition may either wilt or gain momentum.

In my view, at present, because the notion of a family court is still relatively ill-defined, the arguments against it on the basis of cost and administrative inconvenience have not been properly advanced nor are they the main stumbling blocks. One has to look into the workings of the existing system itself to understand why major reform has seemed so elusive. There may be two main reasons. First, because the system contains many deep philosophical contradictions. Its ambiguity and confusion allows all kinds of conflicting interests to be served – at the cost of consumer satisfaction. Secondly, the system by its traditional caution offers practitioners within it, and also in a sense the parties, and officials, for example, registrars and judges, a high degree of emotional security. Practitioners seem to need this in order to deal with the problems arising from matrimonial and family conflicts which may provoke within them deep anxiety. In short, the existing system functions as a kind of institutional defence against anxiety, and attempts to change the system are perceived as threats to this emotional defence mechanism. This may to some extent account for the inertia which seems such a powerful force in resisting change.

Defensive Ambiguity

"Flawed as it is by its own internal contradictions" some have seen the system as weak and vulnerable. But one can also take an opposite view, namely that it derives its strength from being able to accommodate conflicting interests and philosophies. Indeed my purpose in reviewing the history of matrimonial jurisdiction and the place of welfare services has been to highlight the way differing notions of justice and concepts of welfare find expression within the system. Ambiguity about such things as what constitutes the welfare of children, or the principles upon which welfare services are employed in the divorce court, allow professional discretion to flourish unchecked in ways which sometimes, as we have seen, do not equate with normal standards of fairness and may not serve the overall interests of families. Any attempt to structure and limit discretion would carry with it the need to define more clearly the values and attitudes associated with its exercise. In part, of course, this would not allow for the pragmatic way we do things in this country. Thus structuring discretion risks exposing potential differences of approach between lawyers and welfare officers. Once made explicit, such differences might have to be resolved in some way. Ambiguity on the other hand allows these difficult issues to be avoided. Thus welfare officers are not often rigorously examined about their reports, judges are not challenged about their assumptions when they make "welfare" pronouncements, attempts to control and regulate the behaviour of parents who are considered unreliable or irresponsible are wrapped up in terms of benign offers of help. The existing system seems to hold deep philosophical incompatibilities in a state of suspension. This may not be altogether a bad thing because it does at least keep open a lot of options, yet it can present a picture of confusion to users of the system. It seems to me that an uneasy balance between the interests of justice and welfare is maintained; state authoritarianism often finds expression at a formal level, but is counterbalanced by more democratic practices in informal exchanges between families, solicitors and welfare officers, especially when settlements are being sought; legalism can espouse the cause of egalitarianism while paternalistic welfare considerations and practices can foster selectivity and social segregation.

Emotional Resistance to Change

Isabel Menzies, in her classic study of nursing in hospitals, has postulated that avoidance of change by organisations can be understood as an institutionalised defence mechanism to help its members cope with anxiety. Since we are considering a system of family law that shows every sign of resisting fundamental structural change, it is worth considering more closely what Menzies has to say on the subject:

> "Change is inevitably to some extent an excursion into the unknown. It implies a commitment to future events that are not entirely predictable and to their consequences and inevitably provokes doubt and anxiety. Any significant change within a social system implies changes in existing social relationships and in social structure. It follows that any significant social change implies a change in the operation of the social system as a defence system. While this change is proceeding, that is while social defences are being restructured, anxiety is likely to be more open and intense."[23]

Jaques' work in 1955 had shown that resistance to social change can be better understood if it is seen as the resistance of groups of people unconsciously clinging to existing institutions because changes threaten existing social defences against deep and intense anxieties.[24]

Menzies' work was distinctive for advancing the view that resistance to change was just one of a number of institutionalised defence mechanisms which the hospital she studied had evolved to help its members cope with the performance of a very stressful task, namely the continuous care of the sick and the dying. Menzies postulated that the hospital itself had developed practices and procedures which helped nurses deal with the anxiety that such work provoked:

> "Much of the institution's cultural structure, and mode of functioning are determined by the psychological needs of its members."

Amongst many such mechanisms that she identified were procedures which made it difficult for nurses to establish relationships with patients; which encouraged the nurses to deny feelings and to assume an air of impersonal detachment; which restricted their responsibility for decision making in patient care but substituted ritual tasks instead so that nurses would not experience the anxiety associated with making choices, and procedures which obscured the formal distribution of responsibility within the hospital hence removing or limiting the element of accountability. Above all, as we have seen, she pointed to the way resistance to change was used defensively by the institution.

A similar analysis can be made of the practice of family law. Family conflict and marriage breakdown generates considerable anxiety not only in the family members concerned but in practitioners like doctors, lawyers, judges and social workers who are called on to deal with the consequences. Marriage breakdown and the whole process of family reorganisation that follows in certain respects challenge firmly held traditional beliefs in the value of marriage and the integrity of the nuclear family unit. Most people have phantasies[25] built up since early childhood both about the nature of "good secure happy relationships" and "bad aggressive" forces which can damage and destroy individual relationships and family integrity. The breakdown and stress in other people's family relationships can easily, through a process of projective identification, activate the practitioner's own inner fantasy world and arouse stress and anxiety. Most adults will have experienced rejection and the powerful grief and depression that follows broken emotional attachments. The need therefore to differentiate their inner fantasies and feelings from the objective reality of the case being dealt with, can make heavy demands on the maturity and experience of the practitioner. It is only too easy for a practitioner to project his own fantasies into his current work so that he becomes uneasy and anxious because he experiences external situations and events as a mixture of objective reality and fantasy. I think this goes some way to explaining the frequently observed phenomenon of practitioners who make powerful identification with, and assumptions about, the position of the children of a breaking marriage. The more sensitive the practitioner the greater the risk of his being overwhelmed by intense and unmanageable anxiety. It is perhaps not surprising therefore that individual practitioners, their organisations and the wider social systems within which they work, develop techniques, practices and procedures which help the individual contain and modify that anxiety. Nor is it surprising that they should seek to preserve these defences when change is threatened.

Menzies' hypothesis and its application to the practice of family law may help explain many of the practices that consumers of the system complain of, such as procedures which depersonalise,[26] create delays and which fragment the handling of their affairs by parcelling them up so that different parts are dealt with by different people in different places, at different times. The hypothesis also probably goes some way to explain the manifest resistance to major reform. When the rational case for reform of the system is so strong, obstruction tends to take the form of inertia, or prevarication. It is only to be expected, therefore, that a failing social system contains many members who cling to the familiar even when the familiar has obviously ceased to be appropriate or relevant.

There is thus paradox in the debate about family courts: the greater the external pressure to reform the system, the more tenaciously will those seek to preserve it who draw comfort from protective but inappropriate procedures and practices. The opposition to change will be stronger if the likelihood of change increases. Anxiety and uncertainty about the nature of the possible change and its consequences is, in my view, inhibiting constructive discussion and planning and may explain why the chances of structural reform seem to be receding at the very moment when the President of the Family Division himself warns that the system is approaching breakdown. It seems only a matter of time before a major crisis will occur, or the public at large will lose faith in the institutions that are supposed to serve them.

NOTES

1. A. Leissner. *Family Advice Centres* (Longmans, 1964).
2. Robert Needham, "Probation Politics" B. J. Crim., January 1967. See also M. Murch, "Seebohm a Painful Dilemma for Probation" *Probation*, April 1969, Vol. 15, No. 1 and W. Jordan, "The Probation Service in the 1960s" *Social and Economic Planning*, April 1971, Vol. 5.
3. David Haxby, *Probation, a Changing Service* (Constable, 1978), pp.

74–121. Haxby provides a most comprehensive and critical examination of this issue, concluding that the service has become in effect a community correctional service and should relinquish its matrimonial duties.

4. The Honourable Mr Justice Scarman, *Family Law and Law Reform* (Public Lecture, University of Bristol, March 1966).
5. L. Blom-Cooper, O. R. McGregor, C. Gibson, *Separated Spouses* (Duckworth, 1970).
6. It took almost another decade before legislative steps were taken to remedy this state of affairs by the provisions of the Matrimonial Proceedings Act 1978. Some have seen this as a measure which will serve to perpetuate a discredited system of adjudication. Others regard consistency of the substantive law as a necessary precondition before the establishment of a unified system.
7. *Putting Asunder* (S.P.C.K. 1967).
8. *Report of the Committee on the Age of Majority.* Cmnd. July 1967 (HMSO, 1967).
9. *Hansard*, Vol. 308, No. 18, col.198, December 4, 1969. Quoted in J. Graham Hall, *Proposal for a Family Court*, and in B. Mortlock, *The Inside of Divorce.*
10. Judge Jean Graham Hall, *Proposal for a Family Court* (National Council for One-parent Families, 1970).
11. B. Mortlock, *op. cit.*, pp. 19, 190–191.
12. Law Commission, Ninth Annual Report, Law Com. 64, para. 31 (HMSO, 1974).
13. *Report of the Committee on One-Parent Families,* Vol. 1, Chap. 4, Sect. 13 (Cmnd. 5629, HMSO, 1974).
14. *Report of the Committee on the Age of Majority (The Latey Report)* Cmnd. 3342 (HMSO, 1967), p. 68. See also *Report of the Departmental Committee on the Adoption of Children* (The Houghton Report) Cmnd. 5107 (HMSO, 1972).
15. Finer Report, *op. cit.*, Vol. 1, p. 200.
16. F. E. Mostyn, *Has Divorce a Future?* (LAG Bulletin, p. 285, November, 1975).
17. Address given to the Law Society's Annual Conference, October 7, 1977. *Guardian and Gazette,* Vol. 74, No. 37, November 1977.
18. F. E. Mostyn, *op. cit.*
19. *Hansard,* January 30, 1978, col. 598.
20. F. E. Mostyn, *op. cit.*
21. Sir George Baker, O.B.E., President of the Family Division of the Supreme Court, *Some Results of Reform.* Public address reported in the *Law Guardian and Gazette*, Vol. 34, No. 37, October 26, 1977.
22. "Family Law Sub-Committee of the Law Society: A Better Way Out," *Law Society*, January 1979.

23. Isabel Menzies, *The Functioning of Social Systems as a defence Against Anxiety* (Tavistock), pamphlet No. 3.
24. E. Jaques, "Social Systems as a Defence Against Persecutory and Depressive Anxiety," *New Directions in Psychoanalysis* (Tavistock, 1955).
25. I use the term "phantasy" in the psychoanalytic sense to denote something that is unconscious.
26. E. Elston, J. Fuller, M. Murch, "Judicial Hearings of Undefended Divorce Petitions" *Modern Law Review*, November 1975, p. 630. See also p. 18.

Part 4

The Future

16 A Scheme for Participant Justice

In the remaining chapters of this book I outline a participant model of justice for dealing with family matters. In thinking of the future I have tried to identify what seem to be the good informal practices that lie within the confusions and contradictions of the present system. I have tried to use them as the general framework around which a reorganised system might be built. It is necessary first to summarise briefly the findings of the research.

There seemed to be a remarkable consensus about the kind of legal machinery that the majority of divorcing parents interviewed felt to be necessary. They did not appear to think that the individual constituent elements of the machinery were wrong or inappropriate. Most were satisfied with the services of solicitors whose role was seen to provide protection of their clients' legal interests and to offer a degree of partisan emotional support. Most parents considered that it was essential to have an independent and impartial court machinery. We encountered no serious desire to have marriage breakdown and divorce treated by psycho-therapeutic or social work processes rather than by the law. Even so, the court's adjudicative role was seen as beginning only when the family, its legal advisers and related conciliation agencies had failed to resolve disputes and difficulties. Most parents were agreed that the state, through the court, should exercise a limited residual responsibility for children of divorcing parents; but most also thought that in the first instance the main responsibility for working out arrangements for the children's future care should lie with the parents, and that the state should encourage parents and offer consultative facilities to help them before intervening to impose solutions and regulations.

There was general approval of the divorce court welfare service. Most appreciated were the various informal services that many officers seemed to offer families during the enquiry process. These included impartial, sympathetic listening, mediating in disputes, talking with children, providing welfare rights advice and generally offering support to family members as they adjusted to the consequences of the parents' marriage breakdown. The welfare officers' formal task of investigating the children's circumstances was assumed to be necessary and indeed often thought to be vital to the outcome of disputed cases involving children even though this may not be true.[1]

Parents were also generally agreed about the principles which should characterise divorce procedures generally and the approach of court welfare officers in particular, namely that families should be treated in a fair, open manner; that they should not be regarded stigmatically, and that there should be no association with criminality; and that the official approach should be family-minded rather than solely partisan or litigious. Reasonable informality enabling easy, straightforward communication between the family and the system of divorce was appreciated. All parents seemed to respond well to approaches which respected their rights and views as citizens and did not treat them with paternalistic condescension.

Most parents thought a court-based social work service should be on hand to offer informal advice and assistance in the early phases of marriage break-up and to be available to conciliate. This was often done informally by court welfare officers in the few cases they encountered. Many parents felt that conciliation should be acknowledged as the primary task of the court welfare service, and should be offered as a service to all involved in divorce as early as possible in proceedings. At the same time social enquiry should continue to be reserved for cases of particular difficulty. This conclusion is supported by research into court records carried out at the Centre for Socio-legal Studies, Oxford.[2]

Parents identified weaknesses and deficiencies in the system: it was too slow in dealing with issues concerning the children and the division of matrimonial property, and the wide unstructured discretion of welfare officers was on occasion seriously called into question.

It seems then that the existing system has many of the essential components required of a system of family law but that they are assembled within an outmoded structure. Attempts to make the present system responsive to modern values and family needs result in confusion of role and inconsistent, even contradictory practices. The structure needs to be recast, and its valuable components reassembled in a more appropriate way. Concealed within the present confusion lie the growth points for the future.

The new structure must facilitate practices which enable parents to work with practitioners towards the common goal of arriving at a fair settlement which takes account of the children's interests and the wellbeing of all family members. The objective is more likely to be advanced if it is appreciated that marriage breakdown involves all family members in a task of reorganising their family relationships, adapting to separation and loss, redefining old relationships, discovering and framing new ones. People affected by marriage breakdown have to discover a new and appropriate emotional, social and economic equilibrium. Sometimes family members work it out for themselves or with the informal help of friends and relatives. But they often require the help of outsiders. Many, but not all, will turn to the legal system, as they must if they are formally to change their marital status by divorce. Then the shape of their lives will in part be fashioned by the skills, specialist knowledge, understanding and attitudes of lawyers, court welfare officers, and judicial officers who engage with family members in the search for the fair settlement upon which they can base their future. Authoritarian approaches and imposed solutions used insensitively can do more harm than good and are often dreadfully expensive. In my view they should be used sparingly and held in reserve for use only when more participant approaches fail. Even then, they should only be exercised within a clear structure which defines and limits professional discretion and makes it openly accountable.

The Shape of Things to Come?

The scheme I propose views the legal machinery of divorce as a whole system, the essential components of which are the family, their solicitors, court welfare staff, other court officials and judicial officers. All interact with each other. Thus I envisage a unified structure using the skills of a number of different people in the service of families. The structure should facilitate the resolution of conflict through the processes of the law, rather than through treatment or therapy, because that is the approach that the families themselves have chosen.

It is essential to think in terms of this machinery working in stages, each of which would come into operation in a given set of circumstances.

Stage one: The promotion of informal settlement in the pre-litigation phase

When people take their matrimonial problems initially to solicitors the matter is essentially private to themselves and their legal representatives. It is only later, when it reaches court, that it becomes more public. In the pre-litigation phase the task for parties and their lawyers is to identify the issues, explore options, delineate the areas of potential dispute, determine where agreement might be reached, and to prepare litigation where this seems the best course. Where marriage breakdown is imminent or recent the parties often simply need legal and welfare information. Contrary to popular belief my impression, from other investigations I have recently conducted,[3] is that many solicitors, probably the majority, do not adopt an unqualified partisan stance when dealing with family disputes. Many realise that they need to protect their clients' interests without stimulating further family conflict, and to find ways of fostering realistic settlement without making their clients feel that the lawyer's allegiance is weakening. Undoubtedly in many cases lawyers manage to strike an acceptable balance. They often persuade their clients that the wisest course is to negotiate for a settlement. The parties to family disputes, unlike many other kinds of litigation, are likely to be involved in relationships with each other after the legal issues of the case have been dealt with, a point appreciated by many lawyers.

Conciliation in family disputes. We have seen that solicitors are not well placed to attempt conciliation, because they are not seen as impartial. Welfare officers can only attempt it in the small minority of cases chosen for welfare reports. The evidence suggests that there is a demand for conciliation particularly in problem areas like access, and that the existing system fails to meet this demand adequately. Anything that can help reduce the areas of conflict and lead to a more appropriate atmosphere in which families can settle their differences without fuss and bother can only serve the interests of children and reduce the emotional and financial strain on families. What is needed is a family conciliator linked with the court structure who can be on hand to offer immediate help to families in the early stages of proceedings. Such a person would be helpful in almost every case where there are access arrangements to be made – not just where there is dispute. Many arrangements made just by the parents will be coloured by their immediate feelings and may not be workable in the long term. An experienced and objective outsider could see possible future snags such as a solicitor tends to point out in matters of finance and property. The conciliator should be available not just in cases involving issues over children but also where there are disputes over property and finance, since often these have important implications for children. Few people are financially better off after divorce than they were before it. Husbands frequently think they give up too much and wives consider they get too little, both failing to appreciate the economic realities of their altered circumstances. The bitterness this can generate can blight relationships within the family and affect the children. This is a field where a family conciliator may be able to help both come to terms with the reality. Once people recognise the realities they are more likely to see what is a fair compromise.

I see a reconstituted court welfare service as being the vehicle to provide family conciliation. Its main use should be the pre-litigation phase of marriage break-up, though it may also be involved later if the parties or the judicial machinery consider it necessary. The idea is not as revolutionary as it may seem. Divorce court welfare officers are clearly already often performing this kind of task informally. The problem is that at present welfare officers are not given a clear mandate to do so, and generally only enter the case in the later stages which is often too late. New machinery needs to rectify these deficiencies.

Family conciliators should work within the shadow of the

judicial machinery and share its impartiality, but should in no way have a judicial role. In the pre-litigation phase they would be authorised only by the parties themselves or their representatives to whom they would be primarily accountable.

Such a scheme is not unrealistic. Already in Bristol a small pilot scheme similar to this has been set up with the support of the Law Society, the bar, the probation service and the courts. It is funded by various trusts. The primary task of this service is to offer assistance in the pre-litigation phase. Where there is an apparent possibility of reconciliation, this is explored with the couple concerned. Conciliators try to help divorcing couples continue to make the maximum contribution as parents, while at the same time helping them to disengage realistically and with the minimum bitterness from their broken marital relationships. The assumption is that this complex emotional and social readjustment may be eased with the help of a skilled conciliator working collaboratively with the family and their legal representatives.

The emphasis of this scheme is on conciliation in the pre-litigation phase. Solicitors refer clients, with their agreement, to the conciliation service at the earliest opportunity while remaining involved themselves. Families are given an undertaking that no-one else will be informed without the family's authorisation. Conciliators do not offer legal advice. Legal matters continue to be handled by solicitors or the parties themselves if they are unrepresented. One of the advantages of a conciliator working with both parties is that it helps avoid the expensive protracted disputes that can arise when discussion is confined to written communication between solicitors when disputing parties often get drawn into entrenched positions.

At the time of writing this book it is too early to assess the effectiveness of the Bristol scheme although the early results are encouraging. Naturally enough there were teething problems: solicitors took a while to become familiar with the scheme and were cautious about it. Most of the early cases referred, which were successfully resolved, concerned access disputes. The conciliators had to get used to working in a legal setting. The responsibilities of the divorce court welfare officers and the conciliators had to be defined. Initially there were difficulties about funding and accommodation to be overcome.

How might a full-scale family courts conciliation service be staffed? The Finer Committee suggested that suitably qualified married women, unable to work full-time in a professional capacity because of family commitments would be most suitable because of their combination of training and personal experience of bringing up children. The experimental Bristol scheme started with nine such women most of whom were trained social workers, several being former marriage guidance counsellors. Recruitment and selection was not a serious problem. A series of training meetings familiarised conciliators with relevant aspects of family law and legal procedure and advances in social work with families. Because of the distinctive character of the work the service is likely to develop new skills and adapt old ones. The important point to notice is that the task of conciliation is seen as being structurally quite distinct from social investigation for the judicial machinery. This continues to be carried out by a small team of divorce court welfare officers.

Whether or not the small scheme set up in Bristol is a success there is no doubt that it is in line with developments in other countries. Take for example the United States. Probation officers working in the domestic relations divisions of some court services there are now known as divorce counsellors. Daphne Scarr, an English probation officer who visited Minnesota in 1963 and 1977 reported:

> "There has been an interesting change in philosophy and nomenclature. In 1963 I did custody investigations. In 1969 they became custody studies. By 1977 I find the counsellors are doing evaluations. The role has changed from private investigator to mediator.... Clearly there will always be some disputes which can only be resolved by a court and its legal representatives, but there does seem evidence to suggest that much hostility and bitterness could be avoided if we were introduced at the beginning of the divorce process as mediators rather than later as laborious report writers when much more damage has been done...."[4]

John Haynes of the School of Social Welfare, State University, New York, has shown that family court conciliation may be distinguished from other kinds of social work or psychotherapeutic intervention. He uses the term "non-therapeutic divorce mediation," and suggests that although social work skills and understanding are essential, they have to be adapted to the legal context which is concerned with the resolution of conflicting interests. He suggests that the divorce mediator, emerging in many American courts, is rather like a labour mediator assisting management and labour reach settlement in industrial disputes.[5] In the United Kingdom support for increased conciliation in family disputes has come in recent years from a number of quarters, most importantly from the Finer Committee. Since then Judge Jean Graham Hall has advocated a conciliation bureau attached to each local divorce county court, headed by a circuit judge and staffed by specially trained and selected social workers.[6] The Centre for Socio-legal Studies at Oxford in their report on custody disputes have suggested that there should be a shift of emphasis in divorce court welfare work "from the provision of information in uncontested 'satisfaction' cases to that of counsellor." The report suggests that this "might be beneficial to the parties and bring about savings in Judicial time."[7] The Law Society too recommend that a counselling service should be attached to the family court.[8] The research reported in this book shows that such an approach would be supported by the majority of parents interviewed.

Stage two: The family tribunal

Once someone petitions for divorce or seeks ancillary relief, the marriage breakdown ceases to be an essentially private affair. At this point the state acquires a statutory interest. As we have seen, this consists of a responsibility to satisfy itself that the marriage has broken down, that the arrangements for the children are satisfactory or the best that can be devised in the circumstances, and that neither party suffers unnecessary financial hardship. Once these conditions have been met, in the absence of dispute decrees and orders sought by the parties are granted. At present, the necessary sifting and investigation of these matters is carried out by court officials who in the first instance check the petitions and affidavits that are filed, and by court welfare officers, by registrars and by county court judges.

Depending on their nature, disputed matters may be heard and determined by either a registrar or a judge. All these activities take place within the county court, fragmented and beset by role confusion as they are.

Under the scheme I propose, all disputed matters that could not be settled by negotiation or conciliation would be determined by a Family Court presided over by a judge or registrar sitting in a judicial capacity. But the preliminary proceedings would have to be dealt with by a body I refer to as the Family Tribunal. The Family Tribunal and the Family Court would have different primary tasks and powers.

The tasks of the family tribunal. These would be fourfold:

First, to sift the documentary evidence and to evaluate the interests. All family matters arising from matrimonial jurisdiction, adoption, wardship, etc., would be commenced in the offices of the tribunal. It would perform the kinds of administrative tasks carried out at present under the aegis of the county court registrar, and the magistrates clerks office.

Second, to investigate those matters where there was insufficient or unsatisfactory documentary evidence to justify the making of the orders sought. The chairman of the tribunal would have power to invite parties to discuss for example questions of satisfaction concerning children. He could order further evidence or initiate investigations into the circumstances of children or financial means or property, in the same way as county court registrars or judges may do at present.

Third, to grant orders where there is no dispute and where the state's interests are satisfied on the strength of the evidence before the tribunal. It would have to scrutinise and ratify informal agreements about the care of children and the division of property reached by the parties where "by consent" orders were being sought.

Fourth, to promote settlement of family disputes in the first instance by processes of negotiation, and conciliation. Where on the face of the evidence there seemed to be dispute, the parties and their representatives would be invited to the tribunal for a pre-trial review. The object would be to get the parties round a table with the members of the tribunal[9] with the minimum of formality to see how real the dispute was and to explore the possibility of settlement. Where settlement could not be reached at the time, the tribunal hearing could be adjourned with the parties' consent, pending further negotiations or for an agreed attempt at conciliation with the help of a family mediator. If the parties did not agree to this, the case would be set down as a disputed case for hearing at the family court (see Stage III, *post*).

The tribunal would have no power to impose decisions on families. Its orders could only be made with the parties' consent. Its authoritarian powers would be limited to investigation of evidence, and to the enforcement of orders made originally by consent. It would, through its various officers, be seeking to work with the family, to limit dispute and to pursue settlement. In this sense it would become the forum for what I have termed participant justice. Families coming before the tribunal would be told that they could not be compelled to accept the tribunal's findings. If agreements could not be reached the case would have to be considered afresh by the family court which would have full powers of enforcement. Of course the price that would be paid for this would include further delay and greater financial cost.

Something on these lines seems to have been in Mortlock's mind when in 1972 he proposed the establishment of a family tribunal and conciliation service.[10] I would not go quite so far as he would in suggesting a disregard for formal rules of evidence and complete informality. Certainly the atmosphere should be friendly and relaxed. They should encourage all the relevant evidence to be presented, if need be searched for on the initiative of the tribunal itself, and tested. The proceedings should be private but a record should list all the decrees made and the orders granted. The documentation prior to the proceedings and a clear record of the outcome should be kept.

Who should make up the tribunal? The chairman should be a qualified lawyer with experience of dealing with family matters and some training in marital and family interaction (see Chapter 18, *post*). He or she should be regarded as a judicial officer and take responsibility alone for the orders made. Some chairmen might initially be county court registrars provided they possessed adequate qualifications and were selected for their suitability. Others might be experienced family solicitors.

A recent S.S.R.C. report comments that registrars as a professional group are already "accustomed to dealing with ordinary people, listening to them and helping them to solve their problems" and should accordingly play a central role in any future system.[11] The chairman should be able to consult with the specialists who would sit with him to hear the evidence: first there should be a family finance officer, possibly someone seconded from the Supplementary Benefits Commission, who would be trained and knowledgeable about family finance, taxation and social security regulations. The chairman should also be able to consult a court welfare officer from the independent court welfare service which I propose in the next chapter. There may also be a place for a third lay consultant, possibly a J.P. or person appointed for his experience in family matters and with good understanding of the problems experienced by those who divorce. Three consultant, non-judicial members of the tribunal would generally be enough. All members of the tribunal should be appointed for their capacity to remain both sympathetically concerned yet neutral in the face of family affairs which might provoke anxiety in the less aware and experienced.

Kathleen Bell, whose research on tribunals in the social service is well known, and who pioneered investigation of consumer experience of supplementary benefit appeal tribunals and national insurance tribunals, I think understands the modern citizen's increasing dissatisfaction with authoritarian decision-making. She writes:

> "People appear to want more than a rather impersonal system which deals out unblemished judicial decisions. Appealants turning up for the hearing of their case wish to have a full discussion and an airing of their grievance, even if, as far as the Tribunal is concerned, the legal position is not in dispute."[12]

Such sentiments accord with the general tenor of remarks made by divorcing parents when they were asked their views about possible family courts. The danger is of course that the family tribunal that I propose will either tend to become too formal, particularly if the lawyer chairman lacks sensitivity and becomes too dominant, or may lapse into disorderly and unproductive discussion. The skill of the chairman will lie in his/her capacity to achieve that "combination of formal procedure and informal atmosphere"[13] which the Franks Committee regarded as the hall-mark of a well-conducted tribunal.

I believe the existence of a tribunal dedicated to achieving settlement would have far-reaching consequences for the practice of family law. Provided it was backed up by a family conciliation and welfare service it might reduce the number of disputes about both divorce, children and property to a minimum because lawyers would adapt their practice to meet the Tribunal's requirements. Cynical litigious lawyers would encounter the disapproval of the tribunal. This does not happen in existing magistrates courts or many county courts which have largely accepted conduct appropriate to the adversary model. What I am proposing is that all cases would have to pass through a system designed to promote settlement. Only irreconcilable conflicts would proceed to adjudication in the traditional way before the family court.

Recently in Bristol the county court has been experimenting with referring cases set down originally as defended divorce suits to a court welfare officer for conciliation, after a pre-trial directions hearing. This scheme was initiated at the suggestion of the then presiding judge, the Hon. Mr. Justice Dunn, M.C. Of the first 28 cases so dealt with, only four resulted in trials in the family division. Fourteen accepted the offer of the services of the divorce court welfare officer as a conciliator and most of the remainder reached settlement after the appointment. Although this was only a small and limited experiment in one court, it raises the question why the parties and their solicitors had not been able themselves to settle the case earlier. Some may have been slow, some solicitors may have considered that settlement did not come within the terms of their instructions. But it seems as if the appointment before the registrar somehow made many of the parties and their solicitors realise that a settlement was better than an imposed solution. One surprisingly successful feature of this experiment has been the use of the divorce court welfare officer to conciliate in the search for common ground between the parties in disputes not only about children but also about finance and property.

In short, I'm suggesting that family tribunals should function in broadly the same way as this local scheme; namely by getting the parties and their legal representatives around a table with a neutral authority to explore the options for settlement which they may not have been previously willing to consider. Such a procedure by leaving open the option for a full trial, and allowing parties legal representation, does not in any way restrict their legal rights, but it does provide a fresh opportunity for further thought and perhaps wiser counsel to prevail. It also of course would reduce the expenditure by reducing the number of trials of disputed cases, would cut down delays, relieve the pressure on the judges, and most important of all would enable the responsibility for the outcome to be shared between the parties themselves and the tribunal. It is clearly more satisfactory for the parties, their children and society as a whole if both parties emerge in an amicable frame of mind. As was pointed out by the Consumer Council in 1970 when arguing the case for a small claims court:

> "A judgement assigns blame to one party, it presupposes that one party was wrong and the other right and so emphasises the conflict between them. The parties are unlikely subsequently to sustain any friendly relations. Whereas in a freely made settlement neither is put in the wrong."[14]

Stage three: The family court

If no settlement could be reached, then the case should be brought before a judge or registrar, sitting with full judicial powers in the family court. If a state of affairs had come to light in the tribunal stage that caused serious concern, for example children whose interests were being obviously neglected to the extent that *prompt* intervention was warranted, then procedures should exist to allow the family court to hear the case without delay. Unlike the tribunal, the family court would be essentially a conventional judicial body. Having heard the evidence, tested and weighed it, the court would make enforceable decisions. Appeal on matters of law would be to the Family Division of the High Court. In cases where facts alter substantially after the court decision, it would be preferable to have a review in the family court rather than an expensive appeal to the High Court, assuming that no settlement could be reached in the light of the altered circumstances. The proceedings of the court should be properly recorded. The general public should be excluded, and there should be strict restrictions on press reporting. But privacy should not be used as an excuse to limit the public accountability of those who conduct such proceedings. Careful recording and the right of appeal should be adequate safeguards in this respect. It should be a basic rule of the court that citizens coming before it should have the right to know the facts upon which the case is decided, to be given reasons for the decision, and, if requested, an explanation of how it had been arrived at. There is an argument in favour of publishing decisions like conventional law reports. While it is true that an explanation given for a decision may be unacceptable a decision given without explanation can too easily lead to a bitter sense of injustice – a point probably more often ignored by social workers than by judges.

The family court judge should act in the traditional way in hearing disputed civil matters. Judges should specialise or be given special training. Like family tribunal chairmen they should be familiar with the behavioural and social sciences. This might help them appreciate both the strengths and weaknesses of "welfare" arguments that might be advanced in the court, and make them better able to assess the value and limitations of the social services. In cases of special difficulty, judges might be assisted by special consultants, similar to those assisting the tribunal, who would hear the case with him. They would not have the power of decision, but the judge could turn to them if he wanted second opinions before reaching a decision. Such consultants should not be practising social workers employed by the local authority, probation service or voluntary agencies since this might prejudice their opinions, especially if the social services were already in some way involved in the case.

Welfare services for the family tribunal and court. In the system I propose welfare officers would continue to carry out social enquiries for both the family tribunal and the family court. From a professional and administrative point of view, family conciliators and welfare officers should form two branches of a single family court welfare service. Both conciliation and social investigation are supplementary to the main task of resolving family disputes by legal process, whether it be by settlement or adjudication. Conciliators and welfare officers require the same kind of professional knowledge and skill, which has to be adapted and developed for the specialist setting of family law. In my view, it is essential that conciliation should be distinguished from social investigation: the objectives of each are different and so are the methods, a point that clients and their legal representatives should be able to appreciate. A greater degree of professional discretion should be allowed in conciliation since there is also the safeguard of accountability to clients. In social investigation, the potential power of the welfare officer to restrict people's rights and liberties is greater, and there is less direct accountability to the families concerned. Once a court or tribunal orders a welfare officer's report there is little people can do but agree, and submit to the methods employed.

The research evidence presented earlier strongly suggests that the discretion allowed welfare officers in the conduct of the social enquiry needs to be limited. Rules governing welfare investigation should be framed in accordance with principles of open justice. In particular there need to be rules which make it quite clear that social enquiry reports are to be subject to the same rules of evidence and standards of proof that apply in the conduct of other civil proceedings. Rules should also ensure that parents are informed whenever it is proposed to make an enquiry from other authorities. The parties in the case should have the right to see and challenge the report's contents. The family tribunal and court should ensure that the parties always see it as well as any other reports that concern the family, for example those obtained from local authority social services departments, education authorities and from medical services. The tribunal and court should also check that the parties understand the report. I think justice miscarries quite a lot when people don't understand words. There may be temptation for social workers to evade accountability behind ambiguously worded technical jargon. Yet at the same time welfare officers should have the right to make representation that parts of the report should not be shown to the parties if the officer has particular reason to believe that harm to the children might result. In this event the matter ought always to be dealt with in the family court, and the parties and their representatives informed that the welfare officer has made such representations. The judge should cross-examine the officer before deciding whether or not to order disclosure.

The whole matter of the welfare officer's attendance at both tribunal and court should be regulated to ensure some uniformity of practice. In the normal course of events welfare officers should be present to be cross-examined about their enquiries. In the family court which has power to adjudicate and impose solutions welfare officers should always be present. Tribunal chairmen and judges while valuing the reports should retain a professional detachment in relation to them. They should not shirk their responsibility by accepting reports without question. They should also consider all the other evidence and other possible options before accepting welfare officers' recommendations.

Family conciliators and welfare officers should see themselves as agents of justice. Their constitutional position should lie within the structure of the legal system administering the courts. The whole machinery that I have outlined, which for convenience could still be referred to as the family court, should be regarded as an integral part of the system of civil law. Once established, consideration might be given to incorporating within it certain of the responsibilities of supplementary benefit appeal tribunals and national insurance tribunals as they affect families. Even though these tribunals might remain in their present form there is an argument that a right of appeal should lie from them to the family court, rather than to the High Court as Calvert suggests.[15] In due course also I would like to see much of the jurisdiction of the juvenile courts brought within this structure especially where it concerns care and protection proceedings, responsibilities under the Education Acts and adoption. The same kind of issues concerning the care and upbringing of children and the regulation of family life arise in this court as in matrimonial jurisdiction. Nevertheless the new structure should start with matrimonial proceedings, administering the law that is at present haphazardly and illogically divided between the magistrates' domestic jurisdiction and the divorce county court. The Lord Chancellor's Office, as the department of state responsible for administering civil legal services, should have overall responsibility for the new structure including its welfare services. A major difficulty is likely to arise here, since such a move would involve a major administrative reorganisation of social work in the courts and might have serious repercussions at a local level in the probation and after-care service and the local authority social services. At central government level the responsibilities of Home Office and the Department of Health and Social Services would be affected.

NOTES

1. Eekelaar, Clive, Clarke and Raikes, *Custody after Divorce* (Centre for Socio-legal Studies, Oxford, 1977).
2. *Ibid.* pp. 71–75.
3. My conclusion is based on the findings of a recent survey of 50 solicitors interviewed in a study of the response of community agencies to marital violence.
4. Daphne Scarr, "The Divorce Experience" *Probation*, Vol. 25, No. 1, March 1978.
5. John M. Haynes, "Divorce Mediator: A New Role" *Social Work* (Journal of the National Ass. of Social Workers Inc.), January 1978.
6. Jean Graham Hall, "The Case for Conciliation Bureaux" *Family Law*, Vol. 6, No. 8, 1976.
7. Eekelaar, Clive, Clarke and Raikes, *op. cit.*, p. 75.
8. Family Law Sub-Committee of the Law Society, *op. cit.*, pp. 58–60.
9. For details of membership and qualifications see pp. 260–61, *ante*.
10. B. Mortlock, *The Inside of Divorce* (Constable, 1972), p. 195.
11. W. Barrington Baker, J. Eekelaar, C. Gibson and G. Raikes, *The Matrimonial Jurisdiction of Registrars* (SSRC, 1977), p. 86.
12. K. Bell, *op. cit.*, p. 17.
13. Report of the Committee on Administrative Tribunals and Enquiries (HMSO, 1957), p. 15.
14. Consumer Council, *Justice Out of Reach: A Case for Small Claims Courts* (HMSO, 1970), p. 32.
15. H. Calvert, "Appeals structures of the future" in Adler and Bradley, *Justice, Discretion and Poverty* (Professional Books, 1975), pp. 183–206.

17 The Reorganisation of Court Welfare Work

I accept the Finer Committee's view that there are three ways in which a social welfare service for a family court[1] could be provided; by the probation and after-care service, by the local authority social services department, or by a new specialist service. The Committee did not consider the option of social workers from both the probation service and the local authority serving the court as happens as at present in the divorce court and the juvenile court. This was because they valued a system with clear lines of accountability as I do. They also considered that:

> "... there should be no conflicting demands on the time of the welfare workers or on the way in which they carry out their functions. They should be entirely available to serve the courts needs."[2]

The case for probation

(i) The probation service's strongest card is that it has the merit of being the service with the greatest experience of this kind of work. It has pioneered and developed the divorce court welfare service. Probation officers are closely familiar with the requirements of the courts and the legal profession, having built up a special relationship with the judiciary upon which the social work service for the family court could be established. In some people's opinion, probation offers a ready made court welfare service directly accountable to the court and the judiciary. If, as Finer argued, the family court requires a welfare service adapted and responsive to the court's needs, then the welfare officers should be accountable only to the court itself. Some would argue that the probation service already fills this requirement.

(ii) Another argument is that probation has a high proportion of suitably trained and experienced staff, a number of whom have attended specialist, post-professional courses designed to develop their understanding and skill in dealing with the complexities of conflict within marriage and the family. The service can justifiably claim that it has been able to recruit and retain the kind of staff needed for this kind of work more easily than other branches of social work. In particular it has a greater proportion of middle-aged married men than the local authority social services. In the probation service as a whole, men outnumber women by a ratio of approximately two to one.[3] In a sample of 82 officers doing divorce enquiries in the South-western counties, Birks showed that 66 per cent. were married men, a further 12 per cent. married women, and 17 per cent. single women. (Only two officers had themselves been separated or divorced.)[4]

(iii) Probation also has the necessary organisation to allow for flexibility in staff deployment. An administrative support service has been built up to supervise officers' work and to provide a career structure. The service's responsibilities are sufficiently wide and diverse to allow officers to develop their careers in a range of directions.

The case against probation

> "Historically, currently, and in the minds of the public the Probation Service is dominantly associated with the work of the Criminal Courts and with dealing with criminal offenders. Despite the responsibility it discharges in matrimonial jurisdiction the relationship between the Probation Service and criminal business has, if anything, been strengthened in recent years." (Finer Report, para. 4320)

This statement, substantiated by the findings of this research, encapsulates the basic argument against the probation service. It requires some elaboration:

(i) Although the service has pioneered social work in the family law context, it can be argued that interest in its development has become half-hearted, preference being given to work with offenders. In some areas, arrangements have been made to refer matrimonial conciliation to marriage guidance councils. The probation service now does less domestic work in magistrates' courts, partly because litigants do not want it and partly because legal aid is more widely available. Also the message has been put about to magistrates, clerks and judges that probation officers are so heavily burdened dealing with crime that they should only be asked for help in the matrimonial field in exceptional circumstances. Not surprisingly, less than 10 per cent. of the average probation officer's caseload is work from courts with matrimonial jurisdiction.[5] In many areas divorce court welfare work remains undeveloped, as the enormous variation in the volume of this work between authorities shows. Its vigorous pursuit in a minority of places is due largely to the idiosyncratic enthusiasm of a few C.P.O.s, judges and registrars.

(ii) Some would claim that any newly acquired enthusiasm for matrimonial work by the probation service as a whole is now motivated only by an eleventh hour realisation of the full implications if this work were removed to a more specialist court welfare service or to the local authority. This is likely to come about as a result of various measures in penal policy over the last 20 years which have effectively restricted its primary task to the control and treatment of criminality.[6] Haxby presents the most lucid and comprehensive account of these developments. He shows that the Home Office has gradually turned the probation service into a community correctional service for adult offenders. Chief probation officers are now realising that this seriously threatens the comparative independence of their local probation authorities. If the last remnants of their responsibility for matrimonial work were removed, the next step might well be for the Government to combine the probation service with the prison department into a single Department of Corrections under the direct control of the Home Office itself. In 1971 the Parliamentary Public Expenditure Committee having taken evidence from the service about the pressure of work that confronted it commented:

> "In any attempt to reduce the burden on the service, matrimonial work would seem a natural candidate for removal."[7]

Apart from anything else such a development would further identify the service in the public's mind with criminality, thus reinforcing the stigmatic association which deters many couples from taking their marital problems to it.

(iii) As it is, the Home Office connection with the probation service already creates problems for the service's participation in courts with family jurisdiction. Local probation committees are not masters of their own destiny. Home Office penal policy largely determines the extent of the Service's resources and how they should be deployed. The Home Office has little interest in the administration of civil courts or the development of family policy. These matters are the responsibility of the Lord Chancellor's Office and the D.H.S.S., neither of which has a direct interest in the probation service. Probation authorities enthusiastic about family court work are likely to experience an uneasy tension between the Home Office and themselves over the direction in which resources should be deployed. Since crime is the Home Office's primary concern, crime will always have to take priority. He who pays the piper will call the tune. The Finer Committee was well aware of this:

> "Some 97 per cent. of the entire criminal business of the country is dealt with by the Magistrates, and the Probation Service is liable to be concerned with all of it. We have no doubt – indeed on a balance of national priorities it must be right for it to be so – that Magistrates and Probation Officers will continue to be principally devoted to this business. But it would be indefensible, in our view, to set up a Family Court, and then to provide it with a welfare arm whose main energies must be concentrated to purposes which would fix the new court with the ancient criminal taint."

(iv) The probation service might not always be seen by the families as impartial. As an agency of social control it may well be supervising one of the parties to a family law dispute – for example a prisoner on parole. In such cases it may be difficult for the parents to see how a probation officer working in the family court is bringing to their case a fresh and unprejudiced mind. People who have been before the criminal courts may need to be particularly reassured in this aspect.

The case for the local authority

The Finer Committee thought that, on the whole, the local authority could make a stronger claim than probation since its services are not tainted with the stigma of criminality. There are four main arguments in its favour.

(i) It would avoid a duplication of social services. The family court will deal with a significant proportion of people who will have been clients of the local authority social services department. This already provides a wide range of services for families, including the provision of discretionary material benefits for family support under section 1 of the Children and Young Persons Act 1963, child guidance clinics, and residential child care services of various kinds. It has developed a considerable body of expertise in the treatment and care of deprived, disturbed and delinquent children. By providing the welfare staff of the family court it would ensure that the court had maximum knowledge of the local services available. Such an arrangement might ensure the maximum liaison between the court and the local authority, and make good sense administratively. As the Finer Committee pointed out:

> "All this argues strongly for having the Court served by a specialist group of Welfare Officers drawn from among local authority social workers and maintaining their attachment to the local authority. In this way overlapping services, administratively uneconomical and confusing for the public, would be kept to a minimum."[8]

(ii) Local authority social services are able to offer good career prospects including the provision of in-service training. The scale of its services enables staff to experience a wide range of jobs contributing to job satisfaction and allowing for good chances of promotion. Therefore social services ought to be able to attract and retain good staff.

(iii) The provision of court welfare officers by the local authority would prevent the family court becoming too closed a system. Since the welfare officers would be accountable to the local authority and not to the court, the welfare officers would enjoy a measure of professional independence from the court.

In this way judicial values and formal "legalism" would be less likely to supersede welfare values.

The case against the local authority

But there are strong objections to their providing the welfare service of the family court:

(i) It would infringe the constitutional principle of the separation of powers which seeks to maintain the distinction between the judiciary and the executive. This rests on the view that the community will respect and trust its judicial authorities only if they are seen to be impartial and independent of sectional interests. Such a principle protects the family against the abuse or misuse of power by the executive agencies of the state. Local authorities do *not* share the essential impartiality and independence of the judiciary. As their extensive powers to intervene and regulate family life increase, they will become more involved in legal disputes with their own clientele. For example, under the 1969 Children and Young Persons Act they are responsible for instituting court proceedings and are thus parties to legal disputes between families and the state. This is likewise the case where parents appeal against the assumption by the local authority of parental rights in child care cases,[9] or against the making of contribution orders. The local authority also have powers of prosecution under the Education Acts. Because of such functions they cannot be considered capable of providing impartial social investigation for the court, the very court that will be dealing with the dispute. Indeed sections 64, 65 and 103 of the 1975 Children Act which provide for the separate representation of children in care cases and the appointment of panels of independent social workers recognises this very point.[10]

The arguments for a fresh and independent view apply particularly to the social enquiry functions of the family court. These should be seen as distinct from the executive function of the local authority. In times of growing unemployment and economic stagnation the number of families relying on state welfare provision for their survival has grown and shows signs of increasing further. Handler,[11] Jordan[12] and others have shown how since section 1 of the Children and Young Persons

Act 1963 came into force social policy has been developed to encourage families to turn to the local authority for help, sometimes as an alternative to supplementary benefit, often as a supplement to it. Ironically this can make them worse off. For example Jordan writes:

> "People referred to social services very often do not get the benefit of what are supposed to be universal services. The existence of a local authority department ... actually deprives many of those referred to it of what they should be getting from the major services, and gives them an alternative and in many ways inferior service in its place. To take the example of social security: the closing of small supplementary benefits offices, the running down of visiting services and the increasing inability of the enlarged service (Supplementary Benefit Commission) to deal with urgent and exceptional need have all resulted in a tendency to redirect very deprived claimants towards Social Services Departments even if their needs are purely financial. The BASW Poverty Group's research found that in London boroughs, about half of all payments under Section 1 of the 1963 Act were to people who were on supplementary benefits, and almost all such payments were for items like food, rent, bed and breakfast, furniture, fuel and clothing for which they could have claimed from the Supplementary Benefits Commission. This assumption of responsibility by social workers entailed a loss of rights for clients. There is no right of appeal, either against refusal of a payment by a social worker, or against the amount paid (and many payments are very small) ... Above all the client does not have the protection of publicly known rules, and may be required to submit to subsequent supervision for an unspecified period."[13]

Jordan and many other welfare rights workers point out that whereas social security regulations provide for a system of appeal, and operate within a set of published rules which provide redress to those who feel they have been treated unfairly, no such provision applies to the system of discretionary benefits provided by the local authority. This may increase the public's distrust of social service departments. It can thus be argued that those working in the family court should not be associated with a system which operates by welfare discretion rather than legal principle. The Finer Committee have pointed out that such arguments would make it very difficult "for the Local Authority to provide the impartial and independent standards which the Family Court Welfare Service must not only possess, but be manifestly seen to possess if it is to achieve its purpose."

(ii) The court itself would be largely unable to control the quality of the social work service that it received from the local authority. Social workers appearing in the court would be accountable to the local authority and not to the court. As we have seen, the Finer Committee considered "there were strong attractions in equipping a new court with a new welfare service specially adapted and responsive to the court's own needs."

Like the probation service the local authority has many other duties and responsibilities which would make it difficult for it to concentrate sufficient resources and energies on the family court. Local authority social services have to be responsive to the policies of the D.H.S.S., a ministry which has no responsibility for judicial services. Since it is likely, and indeed desirable, that local family courts would form part of an overall unified system of family law, which would include the Family Division of the High Court, the Lord Chancellor's Office would have to have governmental responsibility for their administration. It would consequently be anomalous and administratively confusing to have the welfare services of the court accountable to another branch of government working within a different economy and to a quite separate social policy. At a local level it would not be realistic to expect local authority committees to have any direct experience or understanding of the court's needs.

Local authorities are likely to be fully stretched in trying to fulfil their existing statutory obligations. Many areas are chronically short of trained staff, and the turnover and wastage rate is higher than, for example, in the probation service. This research exposed a fair amount of consumer dissatisfaction with the inexperience and youthfulness of many local authority workers, including some with full professional qualifications. Given the continuing restrictions on local authority expenditure there is no real prospect of a major and rapid improvement in the quality even of their existing services. Many local authorities have been forced to suspend long-term family support services even in cases where they have children under statutory supervision. In such circumstances it is hard to see the local authority providing any new family court with more than a moderate service.

(iii) The gist of the arguments of those in favour of the local authority service are based on what would best serve the professional and administrative interests of social workers rather than their clients or the court. In this respect it is significant that the Gingerbread Group, a consumer rather than professional organisation, in their evidence to the Finer Committee was strongly against local authority involvement in the family court.

(iv) This research has shown that in the eyes of many divorcing parents social service departments are seen as the agency that works with the poor, non-coping claimant class. The inevitable, but arbitrary, exercise of discretion under section I of the Children's and Young Persons Act 1963 in providing material benefits has meant that the local authority, like the Supplementary Benefit Commission, has become associated with the culture of poverty. It is strange that while the Finer Committee was so perceptive about the stigmatic effects of the legacy of the Poor Law in the case of the Supplementary Benefit Commission, they should have failed to have recognised the local authorities' share in that inheritance. Had they appreciated the reason for the far greater acceptability of doctors, health visitors and lawyers – namely that because of their universality an approach to them does not involve loss of face or the tacit acceptance of a stigmatic role – the Committee might have realised that if the local authority is associated with the welfare service of the family court, the court itself risks being tainted with this stigma.

(v) The major weakness of both the probation service and the local authority social services is that they are strongly committed to a paternalistic, preventive child-saving approach to welfare. Both services are now primarily agencies of benign social control. This makes them advocate a wide measure of professional discretion, even if it is at the expense of the citizens' rights to manage their own family relationships comparatively free of bureaucratic and state interference. This tends to weaken the very bonds and sinews of family life which the two services seek to support. Welfare bossiness is almost bound to be counter productive, making people either feeble or cross. These research findings suggest that a paternalistic social control approach is emphatically not what the majority of divorcing parents consider desirable.

The case for a specialist welfare service

The important points may be listed as follows:

(i) If the family court, or the new structure that I have proposed, is to have a welfare service specially adapted and responsive to its needs, as the Finer Committee suggested, it follows that the court should be able to control its activities through a clear and direct system of accountability.

(ii) Welfare staff should be able to commit themselves wholeheartedly to the court. Because of their diverse responsibilities chief probation officers or directors of social services would be unable to give undivided attention to the requirements of new court machinery. If they and their committees delegated responsibility they would risk the usual delays and dilution of effort that results from extended and circuitous chains of command, especially when the accountability structure is unclear.

(iii) The existence of a compact welfare and conciliation service with a clear primary task (namely assisting families to reach settlement of disputes and providing reports for the court when settlement cannot be reached) means that expensive administrative bureaucracy could be minimised. In most respects the welfare staff could share the same administrative structure as the other ancillary services of the court, thus avoiding the complications of fragmenting administration between three different organisations, probation, the local authority and the Lord Chancellor's Office.

(iv) A new specialist service would be able to make a more effective claim on resources:

a) *Finance.* A new service backed by the judiciary could well have a more effectively orchestrated voice to argue for money than chief probation officers and probation committees, or directors of social services and their committees, who are likely to be constantly constrained by the financial considerations of their other responsibilities. Neither the Home Office nor the D.H.S.S. is likely to want to divert resources or attention to family litigation, given the existing shortages of resources to maintain an adequate level of other services for which they are responsible.

b) *Staff*. Provided standard conditions of service for social workers could be ensured, there would be no problem of recruitment to a new specialist service. Its nucleus would no doubt be formed from probation staff with a particular interest and experience of family law work. The service would also attract some local authority social workers with an interest in social work within a legal setting. As the family court will in any event require service by the social work profession, the new service would lead to a more efficient deployment of social work resources. The non-stigmatic character of family court work might well attract new recruits to social work, especially married women with experience of parenthood who might otherwise not come into the profession at all. Moreover, as Judge Jean Graham Hall suggested, there should be an opportunity for part-time welfare officers to be attached to the court. Indeed it might be a very good thing if the new service were set up right from the start on the assumption that part-timers would be employed. Increasing numbers of trained married women social workers with families of school age might very well welcome the opportunity to return to work of this kind.[14] As the Finer Committee comments: "their experience with children, as well as their training, would be an advantage."[15] This research has shown that the great majority of divorcing parents seem to find it easier to accept the intervention of social workers who are themselves parents.

(v) The critics of the specialist service claim that it would duplicate the work of other social work agencies. This need not be so, provided the court has clearly defined welfare responsibilities. Instead it would bring to the court the advantages of a tailor-made specialist service, and by providing liaison between the court and other agencies would facilitate their more effective use.

(vi) Only a social work service within the exclusive control of the judiciary can expect to share its impartiality. This is essential if social investigation for the court is to appear unbiased. In his address to the Law Society's National Conference in 1977 the President of the Family Division drew attention to an increase in wardship cases, remarking that this was "due to parents and custodians challenging the decisions of local authorities.... I believe what people want is a completely impartial decision by a properly constituted court with a judge."[16]

(vii) It has become a feature of social work in the 1970s that the larger social work organisations – possibly justifiable on administrative grounds – have led to an increased sense of alienation between field work staff and those with senior managerial responsibility and to a belief that the bureaucracy is out of touch with the needs of clients. There are those who consider that this has much to do with the malaise of modern social work, and has contributed to the high staff turnover, especially in the local authority field.[17] Many older probation officers hanker after the days when their organisation was smaller and more personal, and when the individual probation officer was easily recognised in the courts he served. Many magistrates and judges too regret the passing of this era. There is evidence to suggest that when the close relationship between individual probation officers and the court is replaced by a more institutionalised relationship, the lawyers' traditional suspicion of officialdom comes into play, confidence in the social work service is weakened, and it is used less.[18] On the other hand, some would argue that an elongated management structure has improved the quality of supervision, increased promotion prospects and afforded probation officers and local authority social workers more opportunity for in-service post-professional training and development. Yet rapid promotion to administrative positions means we have too many chiefs and not enough indians to the detriment of those who are the clients. The specialist service could probably provide its staff with good working conditions, despite its smaller size. Since many staff of the new service would already be experienced and well-trained, a consultative model for professional development would in any case be more appropriate than internal supervision.[19] The control aspects of supervision as a means of checking individual discretion would be compensated for by a direct system of accountability to the court, by the provision of legal representation and by open procedures to facilitate accountability to the families comprising the court's clientele.

(viii) Perhaps the most powerful argument for a new service is that many divorcing parents themselves recognise the need for one. The evidence for this is detailed in Chapter 10. The arguments that parents put forward for a new service may be summarised as follows:

a) Probation, local authority social services, and marriage guidance are all unacceptable because they have stigmatic associations of one kind or another. In the parents' view a new service should be as universally acceptable as G.P.s, health visitors or lawyers.

b) The new service must be seen to be as neutral as the court itself in relation to family disputes. The court therefore becomes the natural place in which to house the welfare officer. Close geographical association would also reinforce the qualities of judicial authority and fairness that both court and welfare officers are expected to possess.

c) The economic, social, emotional and legal complexity of marriage breakdown, divorce and remarriage, and their effects on family structure, require specialist knowledge and experience. Many divorcing parents valued the intervention of experienced "family-minded" court welfare officers who appeared to have a special understanding of these matters. By comparison the intervention of "girls from the welfare" or "young student types" – well meaning though they may be – were often viewed derisively if not seen as "downright insulting."

What are the chances of a specialist court welfare service being established? Everything hinges on the outcome of the debate about family courts which in 1979 was largely in a stagnant state (see Chapter 18, *post*). The chief probation officers, as one might expect, have reacted against the idea of an entirely new service which would take over their existing responsibilities in the civil courts. Their report acknowledged the validity of many of the arguments that I have just outlined, but concluded that the appropriate way forward was for the probation service to establish a special "Family Court

Committee" under the aegis of the local probation committee. This would appoint specialist officers who would be directly accountable to the family court and who would be "free to concentrate their attentions upon family court matters exclusively. They would operate under a clear and separate title – for example the Family Court Conciliation and Welfare Service – from separate offices or the Family Court itself."

The report further remarked:

> "It would be prudent to allow separate funding arrangements and to relieve the Home Office of any direct responsibility."[20]

In October 1977 the Chief Probation Officers Conference passed a resolution that the probation service should continue to act as the social work agency of the civil courts and keep under review the possibility of developing a special family court service.[21] Nevertheless, in my opinion the danger remains that the probation service's involvement in a reorganised system of family law will be half-hearted for reasons I have already given.

NOTES

1. In this chapter when I refer to a family court I mean the general judicial machinery to administer family law whether it be as proposed by Finer or along the lines as mentioned in the previous chapter.
2. Finer Committee Report, Vol. 1, p. 191.
3. D. Haxby, *Probation: Changing Service* (Constable, 1978), Table 3, p. 51.
4. J. Birks, *The Role of the Divorce Court Welfare Service* (Unpublished M.Sc. thesis, University of Bristol, 1978).
5. HMSO Probation Statistics, 1973 (Home Office), pp. 12 and 17.
6. Haxby, *op. cit.*
7. First Report from the Expenditure Committee (1971–72) Probation and After-care, H.C. Deb., Vol. 47 (HMSO, 1971).
8. Finer Committee Report, para. 4.324.
9. *Johns* v. *Jones* [1978] 3 W.L.R. 792.
10. The case of *Re P. Supreme Court Taxing Master*, May 15, 1979, J.S.W.L., p. 361, Sept. 1979, shows that recognition is now being

given to the practice of solicitors obtaining reports from independent social workers in child care disputes. This case establishes the precedent for such reports being paid for by the Legal Aid fund.

11. Joel Handler, *The Coercive Children's Officer* (Macmillan, 1973).
12. B. Jordan, *Freedom and the Welfare State* (Routledge and Kegan Paul, 1976), p. 176.
13. *Ibid.*, p. 161.
14. A. and P. Hall, *Part-time Social work* (Unpublished report to D.H.S.S., University of Bristol, January 1978).
15. *Finer Committee Report*, p. 191.
16. Sir George Baker, O.B.E., President of the Family Division of the Supreme Court, *Some Results of Reform*. Public address reported in *Law Guardian and Gazette*, Vol. 34, No. 37, Oct. 26, 1977.
17. Report of the Butterworth Enquiry into the Work and Pay of Probation Officers and Social Workers, Cmnd. 5076, para. 196 (HMSO, 1972).
18. See Roger Hood, *Sentencing in Magistrates Courts* (Stevens, 1962).
19. See G. Caplan, *The Theory and Practice of Mental Health Consultation* (Tavistock) – in which it is argued that effective consultation cannot be provided where consultant and consultee work within the same administrative boundaries. Consultation is being used successfully in the Bristol courts family conciliation service.
20. Chief Probation Officers Conference: Report of the Family Law Sub-committee.
21. See letter of the Secretary of the Chief Probation Officers Conference published in the *Justice of the Peace*, December 17, 1977, p. 751.

18 Conclusion

I have been examining complicated questions of legal and social policy. Any change in the system looks on the face of it difficult to achieve. Reorganising well established social institutions is never easy. Yet what is required of a new system is simple to state. Mostyn has put it in a nutshell:

> "Those who wish to end their marriage should be enabled to do so with the minimum of fuss and formality, having made proper provision for the care of their children, support of the wife (or, where appropriate, the husband) and family and worked out a fair division of the matrimonial assets, assisted, or, if necessary, required in each case to do so. . . ."[1]

The scheme that I propose would, I believe, enable this to happen. It would encourage the pursuit of fair and acceptable settlement and provide the services of family conciliators in that process. Where dispute proved unavoidable it should be regulated by the law. In disputes about children, or where for any other reason the position of children gave rise to concern, the court welfare officer should investigate their circumstances. But the rights of the parents to know what is going on and why, should be safeguarded by a clear code of practice.

Once the system has been set up it might be appropriate to develop within it an ancillary family advisory facility so that people could go to a single place to find out about their legal and welfare entitlements. It might then be possible "for all matters concerning family, children, finance, property and marriage whether the latter be broken, in trouble, or in temporary difficulties only, to be handled under one roof."[2]

I suggest we need a family conciliation and advice office in the family court building. The office might be manned by a rota of local solicitors on the lines of some well established "duty solicitor" schemes, or neighbourhood law centres. It would relieve court administrative staff of their present burden of giving informal advice across the counter.

None of this will happen unless all the participants in the system are agreed about the general principles and objectives. The research I have conducted suggests that the basis of that agreement probably exists at least as far as the majority of divorcing parents are concerned. The available evidence also suggests that many lawyers and welfare officers think likewise.

Whether the new scheme I propose would improve on the old by being more efficient, economic and adaptable might be verified by detailed planning, discussion and feasibility testing. A pilot scheme for a few years in a number of places, monitored by central government would tell us much. As I see it the scheme has the following merits:

(1) It is a development rather than a revolution. It merely seeks to reassemble in more coherent form those parts of the existing structure which, according to consumer research, divorcing parents in general seem to consider meet their families' needs best.

(2) It seeks to clarify tasks and roles, acknowledging formally many of the worthwhile informal practices which have developed in recent years. It would underwrite and facilitate these practices. By so doing it would allow the system to reorder its priorities to accord more appropriately to changing social values and ways of understanding the nature of marriage breakdown, divorce and remarriage and their effect on families.

(3) It would acknowledge and give practical expression to the essential interdependence between the divorcing family and the machinery of the law. The shared search for settlement would tend to reduce rather than exacerbate conflict.

(4) It would provide a structure which would make less incompatible some of the deep conflicts of interest and philosophy between lawyers and welfare officers which lie beneath the surface of the existing structures. The proposed system would provide for a more appropriate and balanced expression of these interests.

(5) The proposal might well arouse less anxiety and opposition than other more radical reforms because it would not fundamentally change the nature of the components of the system but would merely restructure them more appropriately,

thereby allowing them to redefine themselves in relation to each other. Lawyers, welfare officers, judicial officers and administrators all have a part to play in a modern system of family law. The scheme should allow them to agree on common objectives and principles which most of the families who take their concerns to law would share. The structure would be committed to the positive promotion of family wellbeing which would follow from procedures and practices which treated all family members fairly and openly and respected their rights as equal citizens before the law.

Finally it should not be forgotten that it is one thing to plan and establish a new structure, quite another to ensure that it remains sufficiently adaptable and responsive to the requirements of families and to changing social values and needs. Thus we must also think about the most appropriate way both of preparing staff to operate a new system and keeping them up to date with new knowledge and developments in legal practice and in the field of family studies, particularly in relation to divorce, adoption and child care. The new system therefore should have built into it from the very beginning the capacity to monitor and periodically evaluate the effectiveness of its procedures and decisions. This suggests some kind of research programme, perhaps linked to the Lord Chancellor's Conference on Legal Services as Michael Zander has suggested.[3] As the Finer Committee put it:

> "The doing of justice requires knowledge of the results of its own procedures. Legislators, judges, administrators, critics and citizens must have the knowledge of the social consequences of legal actions without which a democratic society cannot keep its institutions under constant and open scrutiny."[4]

Recently the Royal Commission on Legal Services has also strongly argued the case for a co-ordinated research programme carried out under the aegis of a proposed council for legal services.[5] Another way to encourage this might be to set up a college of family and legal studies, perhaps along the lines of the Australian Institute of Family Studies. Its function would be to provide short post-professional legal and behavioural science courses for those who work within the system: lawyers, judges and welfare officers. It would be the focal point for greater collaboration about the practices and policies of family law between such bodies as the Law Commission, the Lord Chancellor's Office, the judges, universities and research sponsoring organisations. The college might also promote and co-ordinate research which should be aimed at building up a reliable body of empirical knowledge about marriage, divorce, family processes generally and such matters as adoption and child care. A number of university departments and researchers could be affiliated to the college so that a federation of centres devoted to family studies might be developed. In this way the effectiveness of the legal machinery and its associated welfare services could be monitored nationally, obsolete and expensive practices identified and changes of legal and social policy anticipated. The college would provide a multi-disciplinary, neutral forum where practitioners, policy makers, academics and not least of all ordinary members of the public could meet to exchange ideas, to discuss the results of research, and generally examine the main issues arising from the interaction of law and family life. In this way all might better understand that a system of family law which emphasised welfare principles should at the same time offer the maximum protection to the rights of citizens be they adults or children. After all, no acceptable system of welfare can be achieved unless its policies and practices are seen to be fair and just.

NOTES

1. F. E. Mostyn, *Marriage and the Law* (Oyez, 1976), p. 75.
2. Ibid.
3. Michael Zander, *Legal Services for the Community* (Temple Smith, 1978), p. 343.
4. Finer Committee, para. 4.417.
5. Royal Commission on Legal Services, para. 4.38.

Appendix: Social Characteristics of Families Studied

This appendix sets out to bring together background information from a variety of sources to highlight some of the more important characteristics of the two groups of families who comprised the interview samples for this study. In particular comparison will be made between several studies of the divorcing population made in different parts of the country at about the same time, namely between 1973 and 1975. The first of these is that of Maidment who made a detailed analysis of court records concerning 95 divorce cases drawn representatively from a North Midlands divorce registry in 1973.[1] The second is the study of 855 court records drawn representatively from 10 divorce courts made by the Centre for Socio-legal Studies at Oxford in 1974.[2] The third is a study of 405 divorce petitions filed in the district registries in Northumbria in 1975 made by the Northumbrian Probation and After-care Service.[3]

From these sources it is possible to identify some characteristics of families where parents divorce, which are not revealed in official social statistics. It is also possible to determine some of the circumstances of those cases in which courts order welfare reports, and to discover whether the particular families with which divorce court welfare officers have dealings differ significantly from the generality of divorcing families.

The basis for divorce

The first set of comparative data concerns the basis for the divorce, using as a yardstick the national figures for 1974.[4] All figures are percentages.

Several points should be noted: In comparison with the other data those from the Bristol research seem to underrepresent petitions relying on the unreasonable behaviour clause. This difference may well be due to a reluctance on the part of

Table A1

The Basis for Divorce

Facts relied on	*National Figures*	*Court Sample*	*Bristol Research Petitioner Sample*	*DCWO*	*Oxford Study*	*North Midland Study*
		n = 763	*n = 102*	*n = 41*	*n = 855*	*n = 95*
	%	%	%	%	%	%
Adultery	27.4	34.6	38.2	61.0	30.1	28.0
Unreasonable behaviour	28.4	13.8	13.7	19.5	30.0	26.0
2 years desertion	5.1	11.0	14.7	–	4.8	7.0
2 years separation	23.0	23.2	23.5	14.6	21.0	21.0
5 years separation	12.6	15.3	7.8	2.4	8.9	14.0
Petition proceedings on combined basis	2.0	2.0	2.0	2.4	4.8	3.0

solicitors in the Western region at that time to recommend that clients should use this basis for their petitions if there was sufficient evidence for an alternative. The adultery and separation clauses were generally easier to prove and spared petitioners the necessity of disclosure in a public court of their partners' conduct. All these samples were taken before April 1977 when the special procedure for undefended divorce was extended to all cases with the consequence that undefended petitions were thereafter dealt with by the registrar on the basis of affidavit evidence alone. Since this research was conducted petitions using the behaviour clause have increased at a proportionately faster rate than those using other clauses of the Matrimonial Causes Act 1973.

The greater use of the adultery clause in the Bristol court welfare sample should be noted. This reflects the fact that proportionately more of the cases in this sample involved situations where the *mothers* had left the home to live with somebody else. Thus this sample also reveals a greater than average tendency for the father to be the petitioner. This is shown in Table A2 below.

Since the introduction in 1971 of the Divorce Reform Act 1969 which sought to abolish the notion of the matrimonial offence and the fault principle upon which it was based, the proportion of women petitioning for divorce has greatly increased. In this respect the Oxford study suggests respondent husbands are more likely to initially indicate an intention to defend when behaviour is alleged than in other cases, even

Table A2

Sex of Petitioner

	National Figures 1973*	*Court Sample*	*Bristol Research Petitioner Sample*	*DCWO*	*Oxford Study*
	%	%	%	%	%
Wife petitioner	66	64	69.6	46.4	72.7
Husband petitioner	34	36	30.3	53.6	27.3

*O.P.C.S. Marriage and Divorce Statistics 1975, Table 4.8.

though most eventually withdraw their defence.[5] This may indicate that the use of the behaviour clause is interpreted by many respondent husbands as implying blameworthy conduct on their part. This might limit the degree of potential co-operation between the parties, protract litigation and add to the cost.

The Length of Marriage

The duration of marriage is an important variable in studying the divorcing population. Official statistics measure this only in terms of legal status from marriage to the point of divorce, rather than to the point of separation. Since the war, data from the Registrar General's annual statistical reviews indicate a slight movement towards earlier divorce as can be seen in the table below:

Table A3

Proportion of Divorce Decrees made Absolute by Duration of Marriage England Wales 1957–73

Duration of marriage (completed years)	*1957*	*1961*	*1969*	*1973*
	%	%	%	%
0– 4	11	11	13	16
5– 9	31	31	33	29
10–14	21	23	21	19
15–19	16	14	13	13
20 and over	21	21	20	23

Source: Social Trends, 1975, Table 1.15.

In the three samples studied by the Bristol divorce project the duration of marriage was sub-divided into the period from marriage to *de facto* separation, and from separation to divorce as can be seen from the following two tables; in the first of which data concerning childless couples arising in the court observation sample are distinguished.

Table A4

Length of Time from Marriage to Separation

	Court Sample n = 583 %	*Childless Couples* n = 137[6] %	*Petitioners Interviewed* n = 102 %	*DCWO Sample* n = 41 %
0– 4	32.4	62.5	31.3	7.2
5– 9	26.3	26.6	35.3	36.6
10–14	16.9	4.4	11.7	39.1
15–19	10.1	5.8	15.7	9.8
20 and over	14.2	4.4	5.9	7.3

When the two interview samples are compared with each other it will be seen that the relationships of those from the court welfare sample lasted on average longer than those from the other group. Thus although welfare officers encounter more cases in which parents are in dispute about their children, it would be wrong to assume that they are more likely to be involved with broken marriages that are less stable, at least in terms of their duration. The reverse seems to be the case.

Table A5

Time between Separation and Divorce

	Petitioner Sample n = 102 %	*DCWO Sample* n = 41 %
Less than 6 months	6.9	22.0
6 months –	15.7	17.1
1 year –	18.6	22.0
2 years –	17.6	24.4
3 years –	12.7	4.9
4 years –	11.8	–
5 or more	16.7	4.9
Not known	–	4.9

The data taken from the representative petitioner sample indicate the extent to which the period of cohabitation (marriage to separation) is extended to make up the total duration of marriage. Many factors influence how quickly people obtain divorce after separation, including the section of the Act that they choose to use. The data in the court welfare sample show that the average length of time between separation and divorce for this group is shorter when compared with the representative sample. This is in part due to the fact that more people in this sample chose to obtain their divorce by the speedier routes – namely through the adultery and behaviour clauses. In many instances they were planning to remarry.

Divorce and Social Class

Until 1945 divorce was largely a middle-class institution. Before that time most working-class couples if they went to law at all sought partial relief from their marital problems in the magistrates courts. From the 1950s onwards social studies investigated the distribution of divorce amongst different social groups the most rigorous being that of Rowntree and Carrier in 1958.[7] For a number of years Colin Gibson of the Legal Research Unit at Bedford College, London, has been continuing this line of enquiry to see how closely the divorcing population and the continuing married population resemble one another in terms of the husband's occupation. In view of the data arising from this work and the opportunity it afforded for comparison, the Bristol investigation also sought to study the social class distribution of the fathers from both interview samples. These data are given in Table A6 below. The three columns on the left reproduce data from Gibson's Bedford College study.[8] The comparative data from our own enquiry is presented in the two right-hand columns. Both studies use the Registrar General's standard classification of occupations. Gibson's material was drawn from a study of 723 divorce petitions filed in 1961 and the data in the second column in Table 4 concerns 598 of these cases in which it was possible to code the husband's occupation with the standard classification.

Table A6

Social Class Distribution by Father's Occupation at Time of Divorce

	Data from Gibson Article					*Data from the 1972–74 Bristol Samples*			
	a) 1961 Continuing Married		*a) 1961 Divorcing*		*b) 1966 Divorcing Registrar General's 1967 Stat. Review*	*Petitioner Sample*		*DCWO Sample*	
	n = 10,967,060 %		*n = 598* %		%	*n = 81** %		*n = 39** %	
Professional (I)	4	21	3	17	12	3.7	19.8	–	17.9
Intermediate II	17		14			16.1		17.9	
Skilled Non-manual (III NM)	13	51	19	56	55	13.6	59.3	15.4	56.4
Skilled manual (III M)	38		37			45.7		41.0	
Partly skilled (IV)	20	28	16	27	33	2.5	21.0	12.8	25.6
Unskilled (V)	8		11			18.5		12.8	

* Not included in these calculations were 8 fathers (six and two) who had been unemployed for a considerable time prior to interview who were classified as economically inactive, and a further 15 fathers from the petitioner sample (all respondents) for whom we had unreliable information.

The data from the two Bristol samples is broadly comparable to the data from Gibson's study. It shows that the distribution of the divorcing population does not differ markedly in terms of the husband's occupation from that of the still married population. If anything the two Bristol samples indicate that social classes I, II and III are somewhat overrepresented in comparison with the Registrar General's 1966 figures, and social classes IV and V under-represented. This variation may be due entirely to the comparatively small size of the samples and therefore might not be representative of the divorcing population as a whole. Gibson's article suggests that while the 1961 national figures showed close similarities between the continuing married and divorcing populations, the Registrar General's 1966 data suggests a slightly greater propensity for divorce amongst social classes IV and V. Gibson suggests that early marriage with its increased risk of later divorce is predominantly associated with manually employed husbands. Since the 1960s and early 1970s were associated with a trend towards earlier marriage, particularly amongst manual workers' brides, there is likelihood that an increasing proportion of the divorcing population will be formed by working class broken marriages.

Family Composition

Table A7

Family Size

	Court Study	*Bristol Sample Petitioner*	*DCWO*	*Oxford Sample*	*North Midlands (Maidment)*	*Northumbrian Petitioners*
	n = 452	*n* = 102	*n* = 41	*n* = 652	*n* = 95	*n* = 405
	%	%	%	%	%	%
1 Child	36.5	27.5	19.5	33	44	40.5
2 Children	41.1	40.2	31.7	40	26	37.8
4 Children	16.5	18.6	19.5	27	15	15.1
5 or more	5.9	13.7	29.3		15	6.7

The distribution in the overall court and petitioner samples from which it was drawn reveals close similarity with both the Oxford and Northumbrian study. The average family size for both these Bristol samples combined is 1.9 children per family in comparison with the national figure of 1.7 for the year 1973.[9] The difference may be accounted for by regional influences as is suggested by the Oxford study.[10]

A significant difference is revealed when the court welfare sample is compared with these other samples; this sample contains proportionately more families with four or more children and fewer single child families. One reason for this disparity may be that the average length of marriage in this sample is greater and the average age of the youngest child is higher. In this sample there were proportionately more children of school age. This suggests that more mothers in this particular sample had completed child bearing. These findings together suggest that the families in the court welfare sample on average may be at a more advanced stage in the family life-cycle than is the case for families affected by divorce as a whole. As might be expected these findings also confirm the evidence from the Oxford study that the larger the number of children in a family the greater the likelihood of courts asking for a welfare report.[11]

Dependent Children

(a) National totals. The Office of Population Census and Surveys has recently published data concerning children with divorcing parents which I reproduce to act as a backcloth against which the data from the Bristol research might be considered. Apart from anything else these data indicate the comparatively large numbers of dependent children who are now the subject of the welfare provisions of divorce law.

Table A8

Children per Divorcing Couple 1970, 1973, 1975
(Figures given to the nearest 1000)

	Number of couples divorced (decree absolute)	*No. of cases where there are no children*	*Children over 16*	*Children under 16*
1970	58,000	15,000	22,000	71,000
1973	106,000	26,000	53,000	127,000
1975	121,000	31,000	57,000	145,000

Source: O.P.C.S. Marriage and Divorce Statistics, 1975 (HMSO, 1978), Table 4.5.

Table A9

Age of Children – Proportion per 1000 children (under 16)
Actual totals to nearest 1000 given in brackets on left

		0–4		*5–10*		*11–15*	*Absolute Total*
1970	(19,000)	264	(35,000)	491	(17,000)	245	71,000
1973	(30,000)	235	(62,000)	485	(35,000)	280	127,000
1975	(33,000)	230	(69,000)	473	(43,000)	297	145,000

(b) Bristol study – Age of the youngest child at separation and divorce.

Table A10

Age of the Youngest Child in the Family
(a) at separation
(b) at divorce

	(a) Separation		*(b) Divorce*	
	Petitioner Sample n = 241	*DCWO Sample n = 111*	*Petitioner Sample*	*DCWO Sample*
	%	%	%	%
Under 5 years old	55.7	41.5	32.5	21.9
5 and over	12.7	14.6	24.5	21.9
7 and over	8.8	31.2	12.7	22.0
9 and over	9.8	12.6	17.6	29.3
12 to 15	2.9	2.4	12.8	4.9

The significant finding is that the court welfare sample was comprised of proportionately more cases in which the youngest child was of school age. In view of the higher proportion of cases in which custody or access is disputed and of cases in which the father has care of the children in this sample, it would seem not surprisingly that the older children become the greater the likelihood of fathers wishing to be in some way actively involved with them after divorce even though this may be contrary to the mother's wishes.

Where children are living

What happens to the care of children when parents separate and divorce? Court records give some indication where children are living at the time petitions are filed or when there is some dispute about care, maintenance or access. The following table gives these data from the Bristol study making comparison with the Oxford and North Midlands studies. It should be noted these data are not strictly comparable since these two studies recorded the position at the time the petition was filed whereas the Bristol research recorded the position at the time parents were first interviewed, in the case of the representative petitioner sample four to six weeks after the petition was heard. Even so the Oxford study suggests that in only 20 per cent. of their sample did the residential status quo differ after proceedings were concluded from that when the petition was filed.[12]

The Oxford study also analysed the position of children in 45 cases where custody was in dispute. We present these findings alongside our own court welfare sample, 29 out of 41 of which were contested cases. These two sets of data are given in the two right-hand columns of the following table.

Table A11

Where Children were Living at Time of Petition

With whom resident	*Bristol Petitioners* *n = 102*	*Oxford Study* *n = 652*	*North Midlands* *n = 95*	*Bristol DCWO* *n = 41*	*Oxford Contested* *n = 45*
	%	%	%	%	%
Mother	76.5	73.3	80	36.5	37.7
Father	12.8	10.3	11	31.7	26.7
Split between parents	5.9	3.7	6	17.1	13.3
In care	2.0	1.2	–	4.9	–
Other – with relatives etc.	3.0	4.8	3	9.7	4.4
Both parents living together	–	6.6	–	–	17.7

The findings of the three representative samples presented on the left are similar. In each approximately 75 per cent. of mothers and 11 per cent. of fathers have care of the children. By comparison the samples on the right, which mostly contain contested custody cases, indicate a very much higher proportion of cases in which fathers have care or in which children are split between parents. The Bristol data also suggests that even when parents are not in dispute judges may be more likely to seek a welfare report when fathers have care of children. Although this finding is not substantiated by the Oxford study, they did find a greater readiness for judges to adjourn cases for affidavit evidence about children where children were living with the father.[13] That study also found that in undefended divorces, when it was proposed that the husband was to have custody, the judge declared himself not satisfied in 18 per cent. of the cases whereas the corresponding figure when custody for the wife was proposed was only 7 per cent.

Most published data only give the position of the children at the time the divorce petition was filed. This is inadequate since it gives little indication how much change or upheaval in circumstances children may have had to face as a result of their parents' separation. By the time divorce occurs the family will usually have established a new arrangement for the children's care which the court may well be reluctant to interfere with. Preliminary field work in the Bristol research suggested that the most critical time in which families are working out arrangements for children, sometimes through a painful process of trial and error, is in the months immediately before and after separation. As suggested in the main text, this could be a more appropriate time for welfare officers to work with families, either at the request of parents themselves or at the instigation of the court. Before we could evaluate whether or not this was the case it was necessary to discover quite how much change in circumstances children can be expected to face on their parents' separation. The following table therefore establishes first, what the position of children was at the time of separation; second, what changes occurred in the children's living arrangements between separation and divorce; and third, how the arrangements for the children's care were arrived at.

Table A12

Where Children were Living at Separation Compared with Divorce

With whom resident	*Petitioner Sample n = 102*		*DCWO Sample n = 41*	
	(a) Separation %	*(b) Divorce* %	*(a) Separation* %	*(b) Divorce* %
Mother	73.5	76.5	39.0	36.5
Father	14.7	12.8	34.1	31.7
Split between parents	2.0	5.9	12.2	17.1
In care	3.9	2.0	4.8	4.9
Other – relatives etc.	6.9	3.0	14.6	9.7

These figures suggest that there is some change in the parent having care if comparison is made both at the point of separation and of divorce. In both samples the proportion of fathers having care decreases slightly, the number of cases in which the care of children is split between parents increases a little. Also the number of instances in which third parties and relatives have care of children as one might expect declines a little. These figures confirm general trends observed in the Oxford study of court records, namely that fathers (7 per cent.) tended to lose care over this period more than mothers (1.5 per cent.).[14] The Bristol figures may well be more accurate since between 15 per cent. and 32 per cent. of the Oxford records did not contain this information.

Even so a comparison between the positions at the time of separation and that at divorce is still an inadequate indicator of the degrees of change that children may have faced in the intervening period. Therefore in the Bristol study all parents were asked how many changes in the accommodation and in the person having care of them their children had experienced in this period. The following table classifies the replies.

Table A13

Changes in Children's Living Arrangements between Parental Separation and Divorce

	Petitioner Sample n = 102 %	*DCWO Sample n = 41* %
No change	34.0	31.1
One change in accommodation – no change in parent	18.6	19.5
Two changes in accommodation – no change in parent	15.7	4.9
Three or more changes in accommodation no change in parent	5.9	7.3
One change in accommodation – change also in parent with care	9.8	17.1
Two changes in accommodation – change also in parent with care	3.9	7.3
Three changes in accommodation – change also in parent with care	5.9	7.3
Other than parents having care	5.9	9.7

These findings are very important. They indicate much more mobility in families than might be deduced from a mere analysis of the children's position at the two points of separation and divorce. In the representative petitioner sample approximately 20 per cent. of children had experienced change also in the parent having care of them. This confirms the suggestion in the Oxford report that it may be that children remain with one parent in about 80 per cent. of cases.[15]

As one might expect, in the court welfare sample where there were usually disputes about the care of children the proportion of cases in which the person having care of the children had changed since separation was as high as 31 per cent.

The amount of change in accommodation is even more remarkable than the degree of change between parents having care. In over 65 per cent. of cases in both samples the children had changed home, and 12 per cent. had experienced three or more moves. In a number of instances the changes have involved children changing school and having to adapt to a quite new living environment.

All parents in each interview sample were asked how they had decided which of the parents should have care of the children. The following table classifies the replies.

Table A14

Whether there was Agreement between Parents about Future Care of Children

	Petitioner Sample *n = 102* %	*DCWO Sample* *n = 41* %
Discussed and agreed	27.5	34.1
Tacit agreement – no discussion	28.5	7.3
No agreement – but the only thing possible	28.5	29.3
No agreement – custody/care of all children disputed	7.8	22.0
No agreement – custody/care of some children disputed	3.9	4.9
No agreement – but DCWO suggested acceptable solution	1.0	2.4
No information	3.0	–

The curious finding is that in the court welfare sample there are proportionately more cases in which there was both specific agreement as well as disagreement about the children. This evidence again supports the view that in this sample where the children were on average older, the fathers tended to have more established relationships with them and to adopt a more positive stance towards them, sometimes with the approval of the other parent, sometimes not. By contrast most of the cases in the petitioner sample where there was tacit agreement involved cases with very young children in which the father had "faded from the picture."

NOTES

1. S. Maidment, "A Study in Child Custody" (1976) 6 *Family Law*, Nos. 7, 8, p. 200.
2. J. Eekelaar, E. Clive, K. Clarke and S. Raikes, *Custody After Divorce* (Centre for Socio-legal Studies, Oxford, 1977).
3. Northumbrian Probation and After-care Service (Unpublished report, 1976).
4. Judicial Statistics 1976, Cmnd. 687. (HMSO, 1977), Table C.13(L).
5. Eekelaar, Clive, Clarke and Raikes, *op. cit.*
6. This figure corresponds closely with the national figures which show that in 1973 24.8 per cent. of divorcing couples were childless.
7. Griselda Rowntree and Norman Carrier, "The Resort to Divorce in England and Wales 1857–1957" *Population Studies*, Vol. II, 1958.
8. Colin Gibson, "Divorce and Social Class in England and Wales" (1974) 25 *British Journal of Sociology* No. 1, p. 79.
9. Social Trends, Table 1.15.
10. *Ibid.* para. 2.11.
11. *Ibid.*
12. *Ibid.* para. 4.7(i).
13. *Ibid.* para. 4.7(v).
14. *Ibid.* Table 10.
15. The form which petitioners have to complete when filing their petition showing the arrangements they propose for children does not ask them to inform the court whether the children have experienced change in the person having care of them since parental separation.

Index